TEACHER DEVELOPMENT

Companion Volumes

The companion volumes in this series are:
Understanding Learning: Influences and outcomes
Edited by: Janet Collins and Deidre Cook
Developing Pedagogy: Researching practice
Edited by Janet Collins, Kim Insley and Janet Soler

All of these readers are part of a course: *Developing Practice in Primary Education*, that is itself part of the Open University MA programme.

The Open University MA in Education

The Open University MA in Education is now firmly established as the most popular postgraduate degree for education professionals in Europe, with over 3,500 students registering each year. The MA in Education is designed particularly for those with experience of teaching, the advisory service, educational administration or allied fields.

Structure of the MA

The MA is a modular degree, and students are therefore free to select from a range of options the programme which best fits in with their interests and professional goals. Specialist lines in management and primary education and lifelong learning are also available. Study in the Open University's Advanced Diploma can also be counted towards the MA, and successful study in the MA programme entitles students to apply for entry into the Open University Doctorate in Education programme.

OU Supported Open Learning

The MA in Education programme provides great flexibility. Students study at their own pace, in their own time, anywhere in the European Union. They receive specially prepared study materials, supported by tutorials, thus offering the chance to work with other students.

The Doctorate in Education

The Doctorate in Education is a new part-time doctoral degree, combining taught courses, research methods and a dissertation designed to meet the needs of professionals in education and related areas who are seeking to extend and deepen their knowledge and understanding of contemporary educational issues. It should help them to:

- develop appropriate skills in educational research and enquiry

- carry out research in order to contribute to professional knowledge and practice.

The Doctorate in Education builds upon successful study within the Open University MA in Education programme.

How to apply

If you would like to register for this programme, or simply to find out more information about available courses, please write for the *Professional Development in Education* prospectus to the Course Reservations Centre, PO Box 724, The Open University, Walton Hall, Milton Keynes, MK7 6ZW, UK (Telephone 0 (0 44) 1908 653231). Details can also be viewed on our web page http://www.open.ac.uk.

TEACHER DEVELOPMENT

Exploring our own practice

edited by

Janet Soler, Anna Craft and Hilary Burgess

P·C·P

Paul Chapman
Publishing Ltd

in association with

Compilation, original and editorial material
© Copyright The Open University 2001
First published in 2001

 Paul Chapman Publishing Ltd
A SAGE Publications Company
6 Bonhill Street
London EC2A 4PU

SAGE Publications Inc.
2455 Teller Road
Thousand Oaks, California 91320

SAGE Publications India Pvt Ltd
32, M-Block Market
Greater Kailash - I
New Delhi 110 048

British Cataloguing in Publication Data
A catalogue record for this book is available from the British Library

ISBN 0 7619 6930 6
ISBN 0 7619 6931 4 (pbk)

Library of Congress catalog record available

Typeset by Dorwyn Ltd, Rowlands Castle, Hants
Printed in Great Britain by Athenaeum Press Ltd, Gateshead, Tyne & Wear

Contents

Acknowledgements

The editors and publishers wish to thank the following for permission to use copyright material:

Robin J. Alexander for 'Pedagogy and culture: a perspective in search of a method', adapted from R. J. Alexander (1999), 'Culture in pedagogy, pedagogy across cultures' in R. J. Alexander, P. Broadfoot, D. Phillips, eds, *Learning from Comparing: new directions in comparative education research, Vol. 1*, pp. 149–180, Oxford Symposium Books; and 'Basics, cores and choices', adapted from R. J. Alexander (1998) 'Basics, cores and choices: towards a new primary curriculum', *Education 3–13*, 26:2, pp. 60–69, paper originally given at the SCAA conference on the review of the National Curriculum, June 1997;

British Journal of Inservice Education for M. Dadds (1997) 'Continuing professional development: nurturing the expert within', *British Journal of Inservice Education*, 1, pp. 31–7; S. Higgins and D. Leat (1997) 'Horses for courses or courses for horses: What is effective teacher development?', *British Journal of Inservice Education*, 23:3, pp. 303–14; and R. Hancock (1997) 'Why are class teachers reluctant to become researchers?', *British Journal of Inservice Education*, 23:1, pp. 85-99;

Taylor & Francis for material from A. Convery (1998) 'A teacher's response to "Reflective-inaction" ', *Cambridge Journal of Education*, 28:2, pp. 197–211; P. Clements (1999) 'Autobiographical research and the emergence of the fictive voice', *Cambridge Journal of Education*, 29:1, pp. 197–205; M. Maclure, 'Arguing for your self: identity as an organizing principle in teachers' jobs and lives', *British Educational Research Journal*, 19:4, pp. 311–22; M. Huberman (1995) 'Networks that alter teaching: conceptualizations, exchanges and experiments', *Teachers & Teaching*, 1, pp. 193–211; Brian Simon (1994) 'Primary practice in historical context' in Jill Bourne, ed, *Thinking Through Primary Practice*, Routledge/Open University, pp. 7–15; P. J. Sikes, I. Measor and P. Woods (1985) *Teacher Careers Crisis and Continuities*, Falmer Press, pp. 57–69; T. Russell and S. Bullock (1999) 'Discovering our professional knowledge as teachers: critical strategies and learning from experience' in J. Loughran, ed. (1999) *Researching Teaching: Methodologies and Practices for Understanding Pedagogy*, Falmer Press, pp. 132–52; and K. M. Zeichner and B. R. Tabachnick (1991) 'Reflections on reflective teaching' in K. M. Zeichner and B. R. Tabachnick, eds., (1991) *Issues and Practices in Inquiry Orientated Teacher Education*, Falmer Press, pp. 1–11.

Introduction to Section 1: Contexts for Professional Practice

All activities are influenced by the wider context in which they take place. In this first part of the book, the readings provide a range of ways into exploring some of the dominant histories and traditions, cultural and political, that underpin the professional development of practitioners in primary and early years education.

The chapters in this section investigate the histories and traditions of professional development. Here we are talking of some of the powerful underpinning values and attitudes in early years education and primary education. Values and attitudes come from a variety of aspects of the education profession and wider society as well as from personal life and have shaped the ways in which primary and early years practitioners are trained and continue to develop as professionals. They include ideas about how children learn, how their achievements should be measured and documented, policies about what counts as the curriculum, what pedagogical approaches are most appropriate and how these should be resourced. The dominant ideologies on all of these issues at different points in time (and in different cultures) influence how teachers are prepared for their role and what forms of professional development are considered to be valid and appropriate. Over time, the dominant ideas and the statutory arrangements for primary and early years education have undergone shifts in focus, reflecting, and at times attempting to influence, wider value changes in society at large.

In addition, although the world is fast becoming more globalised in terms of values, there still remain differences in values between cultures, which in turn influence the continuing professional development of teachers. A related and direct influence on what 'counts' as professional development for early years and primary practitioners is national policy for initial and in-service training. At the time of putting together this collection of readings, there were increasingly centralised controls on the professional development of teachers, from pre-service to in-service training, in England and Wales – a pattern reflecting moves in other countries.

These readings explore a number of themes:

- some of the dominant histories and traditions of professional development;
- cultural and political perspectives on teaching and learning;

1

- notions of professional autonomy;
- changing approaches to curriculum selection, organisation and development and their interface with professional development.

In Chapter 1, Robin Alexander demonstrates how pedagogy may offer a 'window' on the wider culture. He presents a comparative perspective drawing on his recent international research project, *Primary Education in Five Cultures*, which investigated classrooms in England, France, Russia, India and the USA. He sets his discussion of the findings in the context of what he calls 'time past' (in terms of histories and traditions of primary education) as well as 'time present'. One of the imperatives which impelled him to undertake the project was the wish to problematise the tendency, since the 1960s, to polarise the 'progressive' and 'traditional' traditions within public debate on standards of education. He also raises issues about the methodology for investigating pedagogical practices.

In Chapter 2, also from Robin Alexander, the focus is on the importance of historical understanding for contextualising current curriculum and pedagogy and also on the need for radical reconceptualising of both. This time embedding his analysis in the national context for England, he argues for an approach to curriculum development which attempts to look seriously at the skills and understandings demanded by society and which are therefore necessary for children to develop in the twenty-first century. He also notes the impoverished place accorded to analysts such as himself by Her Majesty's Chief Inspector of Schools and by sectors of the press. This chapter documents much of the policy and values background to teachers' work in England at the turn of the century.

In Chapter 3, Brian Simon outlines the complex historical contexts within which primary school teachers' practice developed from the 1860s to the early 1990s. In the first part of the chapter attention is drawn to the ways in which classroom pedagogy and teachers' professional lives were influenced by 'traditional' and 'progressive' approaches to teaching in the years leading up to and beyond the First World War. His account discusses the system of 'payment by results', and the emphasis on defined classroom procedures and didactic teaching; all of which have once again become professional development issues for primary teachers. He argues that the rise of progressivism in this period was a result of liberal approaches being developed for middle-class children in the newly established nurseries and kindergartens. The inspiration for these developments came from the work of Froebel, Pestalozzi and Dewey. Later, in the 1920s, the establishment of the New Education Fellowship aided changes in attitudes towards education and institutionalised the progressive movement.

In the second part of his chapter, Simon argues that despite the rise of progressivism, primary schools remained rigid, precise and whole-class orientated in the two decades following the Second World War. A powerful shift away from more traditionally orientated practices and procedures became possible when comprehensive secondary education developed and the 11-plus examination was abandoned. The recommendation to un-stream classes, proposed by the Plowden Report in 1967, also had a profound effect on primary education. The chapter concludes by describing the impact of the introduction of the National Curriculum in the late 1980s and 1990s and raises the need to address the problems for developing new approaches to practice and pedagogy.

In Chapter 4, the focus shifts to approaches to professional development, and ways in which these are informed by the wider framework of which they are part. In this chapter, Marion Dadds argues against the currently dominant technicist model of pedagogy presented in policy for teacher development. She puts forward, by contrast, an approach to teacher development which values the practitioner's active involvement in self-study, suggesting that this is a far more appropriate way to develop the profession as a whole. She presents the two models as part of a continuum of professional development. This is based on 'delivery models' at one end, and the cultivation of self-understanding by the active engagement of the practitioner in their own self-study, in ways which articulate their experience and knowledge, at the other. Her chapter contains case study insights from teachers whose self-study is leading to deep changes in understanding of their own professional practice.

In Chapter 5, the final one of this part of the book, Steven Higgins and David Leat build on the discussion of some of the trends in teacher education introduced by earlier authors. For example:

- the existence of competing and radically different models of so-called appropriate and effective teacher development;
- the move towards competence-based initial teacher education and, increasingly, towards this model in continuing professional development;
- the squeezing out of approaches which involve critical scrutiny of such fundamental questions as the purposes of education or pedagogy.

They attempt to map out these conceptualisations diagrammatically to include a number of dimensions: the movement from novice to expert practitioner, the nature of professional knowledge, the nature of knowledge of the domains being taught, the role of reflection, the nature of the personal engagement in enquiry and aspects of professional development which are essentially to do with the social context of teaching and learning. They go on to suggest that not only do different kinds of professional development have strengths and weaknesses for different purposes but also individual teachers have different learning preferences.

1

Pedagogy and Culture: a Perspective in Search of a Method

Robin Alexander

Challenge and Response

In this chapter, I argue that the central educational activity which we call pedagogy – the purposive mix of educational values and principles in action, of planning, content, strategy and technique, of learning and assessment, and of relationships both instrumental and affective – is a window on the culture of which it is a part, and on that culture's underlying tensions and contradictions as well as its publicly declared educational policies and purposes. I contend that one of the best ways to illuminate the relationship between culture and pedagogy is to adopt a comparative perspective and that such a perspective is an important and necessary part of the quest to understand and improve the science, art or craft of teaching. However, having a perspective is one thing: finding methods which do justice to that perspective is rather less straightforward.

The chapter's context is primary education, and the larger project to which it relates is one of a sequence which has aimed to understand and explain the character of primary education, especially primary education in England, in order to play some part in improving it. During this journey I have ranged over the English system of primary education as a whole from national policy to LEA mediation, school-level provision and the transactions of individual teachers and pupils. I have undertaken conceptual analysis and critique of the ideas and ideologies by which, ostensibly at least, the practices of English primary education are sustained, guided and justified. I have examined the complex relationship between those ideas and how teaching is actually conducted. Using methodologies as different as survey and case study, systematic non-participant observation and anthropological fieldnotes, computerised analysis of classroom discourse and teacher biography, I have sought to gain a purchase on that practice empirically, and I have sought to use the resulting data to construct explanatory and predictive theories about primary teachers and primary teaching (Alexander, 1984, 1988, 1995, 1997; Alexander, Willcocks and Kinder, 1989).

As this work has evolved I have found it increasingly important to keep in view the influence of two contexts: the context of *time present* – the system as a whole, the complexity of the contemporary web of policy and culture within which classrooms are embedded; and the context of *time past* – the powerful continuities of educational history, especially the continuing resonance in late twentieth-century English primary education of the structures and assumptions of the nineteenth-century elementary system.

As I proceeded with this agenda the arguments for a stronger international perspective on primary teaching revolved round three imperatives: *political, conceptual* and *methodological.* None of them was novel: all had exercised others besides myself for a long time But their frustrating longevity was precisely the point. Short of violent revolution, going international seemed the most promising way to make progress.

The *political* imperative was to loosen the rhetorical stranglehold of the traditional/progressive polarisation into which the public debate about standards and quality in primary education has been routinely corralled since the 1960s. On this matter the prognosis is no more encouraging now than it was then. The debate may well have gone international but the flurry of educational cherry-picking which attends each newly published international league table of educational performance has so far been of a kind which supports rather than challenges the quintessentially English traditional v. progressive polarity. Consider the current advocacy of homework, textbooks and whole-class teaching, for example, and the way the OFSTED *Worlds Apart* report of Reynolds and Farrell (1996) was used to buttress yet another 'back-to-basics-and-common-sense-teaching' campaign.

The *conceptual* imperative was successfully to confront the continuing historical dominance of a particular view of the purposes and content of primary education which has informed and reinforced the political polarisation to which I have just referred. In this, the sharp divide between what I have called 'Curriculum I' (the so-called 'basics' of literacy and numeracy) and 'Curriculum II' (everything else) is open neither to discussion nor to negotiation (Alexander, 1984) The model, rooted in the nineteenth-century elementary system (which had its counterparts in several other countries), was reasserted in the core/non-core hierarchy of the National Curriculum, as implemented from 1988 onwards, and has been given a further shot in the arm by the current obsession with literacy and numeracy targets and by the presumption that educational 'standards' and 'effectiveness' are defined at the primary stage by these alone. The dominant values informing this view of primary education – the 1990s as in the 1870s – are economic instrumentalism, cultural reproduction and social control.

The *methodological* imperative was to find ways of addressing six familiar but stubborn problems of classroom research.

The first is a sense that if the concepts and practices of primary education are historically and politically constrained, so perhaps are the available methods for researching them. Arguably, the educational division between Curriculum I and II has its methodological counterpart in the polarisation of so-called 'hard' and 'soft' educational research – quantitative and qualitative, psychometric and ethnographic, pre-ordinate and responsive, which in turn testifies to the pervasive power in Western (and especially

English) thought of dualism, positivism, and the 'two cultures' divide between maths and science on the one hand, arts and humanities on the other. It is therefore necessary to ask whether understanding teaching really turns on a choice between so-called 'quantitative' and 'qualitative' techniques.

Secondly, it seems important to ask whether 'generalisability' – that cardinal criterion for judging the claim of educational research to provide evidence which is usable in the context of policy – should continue to be defined as an exclusively *numerical* construct. By the rules of this canon, any research can claim to offer *insight* in respect of particular schools, classrooms, teachers or children, but if that research fails to meet the statistical criteria of conventional sampling procedures it is deemed to have a limited evidential basis for claims about the wider educational system of which the particular people and phenomena studied are a part. How far are this insistence, and this arithmetical monopoly, justified, not least in the politically charged context of 'evidence-based' and 'evidence-informed' practice (Sebba, 1999)?

Thirdly, in the particular field of classroom research there is the problem of the parts and the whole. Somehow, we have become adept at dissecting teaching but poor at reconstructing it: good at isolating factors in 'effective' classroom practice such as opportunity to learn, time on task, cognitively challenging questioning, informative feedback and so on (e.g. Sammons, Hillman and Mortimore, 1995), but less able to demonstrate how these and other elements are reconstituted by teachers and children as coherent and successful learning encounters with a beginning, a middle and an end. Moreover, the factorisation of pedagogy has proved a boon to policy-makers and quangos caught up in the rhetoric of 'standards', for such research provides ready legitimation both for shopping lists of teacher training competencies and school inspection criteria and for disembodied nostrums like 'interactive whole-class teaching'. The concern here, then, is to find a way of complementing the increasing *atomisation* of teaching with a convincing kind of *holism*.

Fourthly, I wanted to develop ways of capturing the sights and sounds of the classroom which would take me forwards from deconstructed behaviours derived from coded observation schedules and 'thick description' based on fieldnotes both of which I had used before. I wanted to develop a methodology for accessing much more of this than I had been able to capture in previous projects. Moreover, experience as a classroom observer in different contexts had taught me that while it is possible to reach a general conclusion about a lesson's direction, character and impact within that lesson's time-frame, it is rather more difficult within this temporal constraint to apprehend the lesson's deeper layers of meaning. That is what makes researching teaching so very different from inspecting it. It was therefore important to come away from a lesson with as much of it intact as possible, permit both extended analysis and writing up in a form which those who created the lesson – teachers and children – would recognise.

Fifthly, there was the familiar macro–micro problem of how to unpack that elusive relationship between society, culture and policy on the one hand, school and classroom practice on the other.

Finally, coming full circle and tying together the methodological and conceptual concerns indicated in this chapter's title, I wanted to say something useful about *pedagogy*, about how we conceive of teaching itself. As an extension of the teaching-as-art-or-science debate to which my catalogue of methodological problems relates, I was particularly exercised by the question of whether there is an irreducible core of elements in teaching which are universal in the sense that in some form they are replicated in any and every context and can therefore form the basis for legitimate extrapolation from one context to another.

Such musings led to the project *Primary Education in Five Cultures* which ran from 1994 to 1998 and will feature in an international study of primary education to be published shortly (Alexander, 2000). The five countries – England, France, Russia, India, USA – were chosen to provide both contrast and comparison. The contrasts – of scale, geography, history and culture – are obvious. Apart from the specific comparisons I discuss below, the most striking promise of comparison lay in discovering how educational policies and practices reflect five rather different versions of democracy.

The data were gathered at two 'levels' in order to gain purchase on the macro–micro question. Level 2, the school, provides a combination of interview and observational data, the latter including fieldnotes, completed classroom observation schedules, videotapes, lesson transcripts, documents, photographs and end-of-day journals. The classroom data, the core of all this material, relates to two age-groups – six- and nine-year-olds – and therefore both permits cross-cultural comparison of the educational experiences of children of these ages (deliberately chosen as being at the mid-point of Key Stages 1 and 2 in the England/Wales system) and gives purchase on development and progression. The other commonality is that about half the lessons observed were language and literacy, thus allowing, again, a cross-cultural commentary on this most universal and basic of basics. The overriding comparative theme, it will by now be clear, was pedagogy.

Two researchers were present at each lesson: one (myself) to interview the teacher, to complete the observation schedule and write fieldnotes, the other to videotape and take photographs. In the Russian and Indian classrooms there was also an interpreter present who gave a *sotto voce* running commentary and translated for me as necessary, enabling me to obtain a basic grasp of the meanings being exchanged during the lesson, which I could then insert in the fieldnotes for matching against the video-recordings and transcripts. Also present in some of the Russian classrooms, it has to be said – and those who have researched in Russian schools will recognise the scenario – were various significant others, watching, checking, commenting and sometimes even attempting to intervene.

The Level 1 interviews with policy-makers and officials, both national and local, punctuated the Level 2 work in schools and enabled me to explore what some (e.g. Archer, 1979; Broadfoot, 1996) see as a key variable in national education systems, the extent, form and impact of centralisation/decentralisation and the balance of power and influence as between government, regional or local administration and the school, and within the school between its head and its teachers. They also provided a useful context for a face-validity check on how far the characteristics of the schools and classrooms observed were typical of the region, state or country, and for testing at one level issues and hypotheses arising at the other.

The lesson videotapes and interview audiotapes were later transcribed and (where the medium was French, Hindi or Russian) translated. Complete translation of the interviews also allowed me to check the interview questions as posed and the answers as offered against the interpreter's versions and to examine how far the act of interpretation mixes mere translation (if such a notion is admissible) with cultural or political intervention.

This range of data-gathering techniques enabled me to address two of the concerns mentioned above: the need for classroom data which though at one step removed from the events themselves retain much of their immediacy and permit revisiting (especially important when access to schools has taken two years to negotiate and is unlikely to be repeated); and the search for holistic ways of analysing teaching. Holism is an easily enunciated and overused word but an extremely complex concept. In teaching it has both spatial and temporal dimensions. That is to say, to capture a 'whole' lesson one needs not just to record the entire sequence from beginning to end (the temporal dimension) but also to capture as much as possible of the depth and diversity of what is happening at any one moment in time (the spatial dimension). Having said that, it is clear that while holism implies a bounded entity, the paradoxical reality is that the whole, at least where teaching is concerned, is infinite. You can no more see, hear, record or analyse everything that happens in classrooms than you can apprehend the universe, for not only are the dynamics of thirty individuals in interaction immensely complex but what is arguably the most important part of the action goes on inside those individuals' heads.

However, for all their necessary selectivity, the combination of lesson videotapes, photographs, lesson fieldnotes, documents, lesson transcripts, interview transcripts, and end-of-day journal entries adds up to a rich dataset. No less important, each lesson can be revisited to allow deeper or alternative analysis.

Generalisability: Statistical or Cultural?

When we consider this kind of material, what can be said about the second of my six methodological problems, that of representativeness and generalisability? How far can what I derive from individual schools claim to address the condition of primary education anywhere beyond those schools themselves?

It is important to note that this problem is not confined to qualitative research, for when one considers the size and cultural diversity of India, Russia and the USA, and for that matter France and England, it would take a project of considerable size and astronomical cost to satisfy conventional sampling criteria, and almost certainly one would end up with data which sacrificed depth to quantity. To have some sense of the scale of the problem, we should bear in mind that there are 20,000 primary schools in England, but 80,000 in the USA and 530,000 in India. However, the obsession with numbers is part of the problem, and I would argue that if we are prepared to detach them from their usual numerical connotations, 'typicality' and 'generalisability' can be entirely legitimate aspirations of qualitative research. The extent to which this claim can be supported, however, rests on two conditions, one conceptual and the other methodological.

The conceptual condition is that one must accept that the culture in which the schools in a country, state or region are located, and which teachers and pupils share, is as powerful a determinant of the character of school and classroom life as are the unique institutional dynamics and local circumstances which make one school different from another. For culture is not extraneous to the school, nor is it merely one of a battery of variables available for correlational analysis in process–product research. Culture both drives and is everywhere manifested in what goes on in classrooms, from what you see on the walls to what you cannot see going on inside children's heads.

Thus, any one school or classroom can tell us a great deal about the country and education system of which it is a part, but only if – and here I come to my second condition – the research methods used are sufficiently searching and sensitive to probe beyond the observable moves and counter-moves of pedagogy to the values these embody. On this basis, a close-grained ethnographic study of one school in Japan, another in China and a third in the USA can be generalisable culturally if not statistically, as the study by Tobin, Wu and Davidson (1989) triumphantly demonstrates. Conversely, a national study which sacrifices intensity of analysis to sample size is unlikely to be representative in its own terms nor will it offer much by way of insight.

From Parts to Whole: Identifying Elements of Pedagogy

I turn now to the question of how one makes sense of classroom data of the kind generated in the Five Cultures project. The basic unit of analysis was the lesson. For each lesson we had verbatim fieldnotes, same-day preliminary accounts and summaries, together with approximations of the range and frequency of teachers' and pupils' actions and interactions, videotapes, transcripts, photographs and interviews. The first stage of analysis was to pilot a procedure for categorising, quantifying and describing the elements in a lesson. We then took ten lessons, two from each country, five involving six-year-olds, and five involving nine-year-olds, and applied the resulting two-part framework.

The first part of the framework, which was grounded in the full range of data for the lesson, concentrated on the organisational and behavioural aspects of pedagogy: lesson *aims*; learning *tasks*; lesson *structure*; lesson *stages and sequence*; lesson *elements* (teaching group, task focus, pupil generic activities, pupil differentiation, teacher time, pupil time); and start-to-finish *narrative*.

The second part of the framework was grounded in the tapes and transcripts alone and concentrated on the lesson discourse: the *form* of each interaction 'stanza' (participants, length, focus, characteristics and functions); *key words and phrases* (relating to subject matter, management, behaviour and other values); and *messages and meanings* (again relating to subject-matter, management, behaviour and other values).

In each case there was a conspicuous attempt from the start to deploy analytical categories which – as argued for earlier – balanced the parts and the whole, the form and the meaning.

This kind of analysis has generated some useful findings and hypotheses relating to themes which have been prominent in my own classroom research and more generally in the several English lines of pedagogic research which include the work of Bennett *et al.* (1984), Galton and Simon (1980), Galton *et al.* (1999), Mortimore *et al.* (1988), Tizard *et al.* (1988), Pollard (1985), Pollard *et al.* (1994), Woods and Jeffrey (1996), and Edwards and Mercer (1987). In particular, I can now press much further my earlier analysis of seven major elements of teaching:

- the use made of classroom *space and resources*;
- forms of *pupil organisation and grouping*;
- the nature and demand levels of the *learning tasks* which pupils are required to undertake;
- the range and balance of the classroom *activities* through which these tasks are pursued;
- the way *time* is used during lessons, by both teachers and pupils;
- the character of teacher–pupil and pupil–pupil *interaction and discourse;*
- the spectrum of classroom judgements, especially *differentiation* and *assessment.*

Mapping Pedagogy Across Cultures

The next stage was to find a way to relate the resulting categorisations and accounts within lessons, across lessons, and across countries. What the preliminary analysis allowed was the setting out of a number of *dimensions* of pedagogy, some grounded in the earlier UK research, some arising from this project's international data, whereby we could chart on continua the similarities and differences between lessons and examine the possibilities and limitations of broader country–country comparisons. The idea is informed by the proposition that education, like social structure, law, kinship, technology, communication and so on, is a cultural universal or invariant while pedagogy is its core cultural variable.

The development of what I call *cross-cultural pedagogic continua* can be illustrated by taking what in English primary schools is called 'display', but – since that word is so evidently charged with peculiarly English meanings – it is more proper to refer, cumbersomely but neutrally, to 'wall-mounted teaching materials'. Taking the lessons analysed, the relevant continuum for this dimension of pedagogy extends from the use of such materials as 'rules and reminders' through 'work-in-progress' to 'showcase'. Having located each classroom on the continuum, we can then examine within-country and between-country differences by noting the way that the lessons cluster (see Figure 1.1).

WALL-MOUNTED MATERIALS	Rules and reminders	Work-in-progress	Showcase
England			---
France		---	
India	-------------------------------------		
Russia	-------------------------------------		
USA	-----------	---	

Figure 1.1   *Use of wall-mounted teaching materials*

Thus, for example, in all the Russian classrooms the wall material consisted mostly of permanent rules, injunctions and reminders, in relation to matters like posture and handwriting. In the Indian classrooms these permanent messages were moral rather than procedural. In most of the English classrooms the walls were used very much as a semi-permanent showcase for children's (and teachers') work, and in this matter the word 'display' is used by English teachers exactly fits the function since high priority was attached to the quality of presentation. In France, however, we found a wider range: from rules and reminders to the much more transitory collections of 'work-in-progress' where words, problems, information, drawings and so on were pinned up temporarily, referred to over the next day or so, added to and then taken down and replaced by others. Here the classroom was less a showroom or gallery than a workshop or studio. In the USA we tended to find an eclectic mix of all three – children's finished work on display, work-in-progress exhortations and pocket homilies, usually relating to attitudes and relationships, and, in every classroom, the Stars and Stripes and the Pledge, focus for an unvarying daily ritual.

It will be noted that such a procedure gives a somewhat flat picture: it is, by definition, one-dimensional. Thus, even in so apparently mundane an example as wall-mounted materials, brief description hints, at additional, cross-cutting dimensions: 'transient–permanent', for example, and 'moral–procedural'. The continuum, then, is a staging post in the analysis, not its terminal point.

Nevertheless, even with this very basic example we can see that the cross-cultural continuum serves two functions. The first is to identify, on a given dimension of pedagogy, the range of practices across all five countries and all the classrooms observed in those countries, together with – assuming that together the classrooms provide a fair diversity of educational thinking and practice – a range of possibilities to inform our larger debate about pedagogy *per se*. The second function is to help in our attempts to tease out *cultural specifies* and *universals* or *invariants* in teaching from the cultural *variables*. The fact that on this particular dimension there were both similarities within each of the five cultures, and striking differences between them, is helpful in the context of comparative study. From such comparisons we can venture hypotheses about how the classrooms are perceived in relation to teaching and learning in each of the countries, and how these perceptions relate to prevailing policies, theories of pedagogy, professional roles and so on. Had there been no country-specific clustering the dimensions would still have supported the first, 'universal', pedagogic analysis.

From this simple application of the cross-cultural continuum procedure, we can see how it can be used in the context of some of the other dimensions uncovered and/or used in the fieldwork. We can construct continua – that is to say, representations of significant between-lesson variation – in respect of aspects of teaching as diverse as lesson length (see Figure 1.2), how lessons are structured (Figures 1.3 and 1.4), the balance of oral and written work (Figure 1.5), the character of the pedagogical language and of teachers' questions (Figures 1.6 and 1.7), the breadth of a lesson's focus (Figure 1.8), the relative emphasis on subject-matter and affective/behavioural issues (Figure 1.9), the range and manner of delivery of the lesson's messages (Figure 1.10), and the view of knowledge which pervades the whole (Figure 1.11).

LESSON LENGTH: MINUTES	20	30	40	50	60	70	80	90
England			-----	-----	-----	-----	-----	-----
France		-----	-----	-----	-----			
India		---						
Russia			---					
USA			-----	-----	-----	-----	-----	-----

Figure 1.2   *Length of lessons*

LESSON STRUCTURE A	Formulaic, fixed	Developmental, flexible
England		————————————————
France	————————————	
India	———————	
Russia	———————	
USA		————————————————

Figure 1.3   *Structure of lessons (A)*

LESSON STRUCTURE B	Short, regular episodes	Irregular, mixed length episodes
England		————————————————
France	————————————————	
India	———————————	
Russia	—————————	
USA		————————————————

Figure 1.4   *Structure of lessons (B)*

BALANCE OF ORAL/WRITTEN	Mostly oral	Oral/writing/reading balance	Mostly reading/writing
England		————————————————	
France		—————————————	
India	———————————		
Russia	—————————		
USA		—————————————	

Figure 1.5   *Balance of oral and written work in lessons*

PEDAGOGIC LANGUAGE	Precise, formal, technical	Imprecise, conversational, vernacular
England		————————————————
France	—————————————	
India	———————	
Russia	—————————	
USA		————————————————

Figure 1.6   *Pedagogical language*

TEACHERS' QUESTIONS	Mainly closed	Mixture of closed/open	Mainly open
England		————————————————	
France		—————————————	
India	———————		
Russia	—————————		
USA		————————————————	

Figure 1.7   *Teachers' questions*

LEARNING TASK FOCUS	Narrow	Broad/diffuse
England		--
France	------------------------------	
India	--------	
Russia	-------------------	
USA		---

Figure 1.8   *Learning task: breadth and diffuseness of focus*

TEACHING EMPHASIS	Subject-matter emphasis	Affective/behavioural emphasis
England		---
France	----------------------------------	
India	-----------------------------	
Russia	----------------------------------	
USA		---

Figure 1.9   *Balance of emphasis in lessons on subject-matter and affective/behavioural issues*

TEACHING MESSAGES	Linear, cumulative	Multiple, complex, simultaneous
England		--
France	---------------------------------------	
India	-----------------	
Russia	------------------------	
USA		---

Figure 1.10   *Manner in which teaching messages are conveyed*

VIEW OF KNOWLEDGE	Codified, rule-bound, received	Uncodified, negotiable, reflexive
England		--
France	---------------------------------------	
India	------------------------------	
Russia	------------------------------	
USA		--

Figure 1.11   *View of knowledge informing lessons*

By moving on to the next stage and taking dimensions such as these together, we begin to see teaching in the round and open up some of its tensions and dilemmas, including those tensions in matters of value which reflect the wider culture. We also find that particular combinations of positioning on the dimensions recur, and from these we can construct pedagogic paradigms. The paradigms are descriptive rather than normative, and provide a useful simple way of pointing up essential contrasts in teaching which go well beyond the one-dimensional polarities to which we are daily treated by politicians and the press.

Here are two examples which will take this out of the realms of the abstract. We have a number of lessons which despite their different contexts and content share the following combinations of characteristics, or placings on the continua:

Paradigm A
- short and unvarying lesson length (30–45 minutes) (Figure 1.2)
- clear and formulaic structure (Figure 1.3)
- clearly demarcated and relatively brief stages or episodes, bounded by introduction and recapitulation (Figure 1.4)
- a succession of prescribed and clearly bounded learning tasks, each broken down into small steps (relates to Figures 1.4 and 1.8)
- a clear sense of pace, imposed by the teacher and sustained throughout
- unambiguous and unvarying routines and rules of procedure which are both followed and rarely referred to
- a limited range of messages conveyed, and most of these directly related to the lesson's subject-matter (Figures 1.8 and 1.10)
- simple physical organisation
- a mixture of oral and written work, both of them structured and proceduralised, with use of appropriate technical terminology (Figures 1.5 and 1.6. touching on 1.7)
- limited variation in learning outcomes.

We have another group of lessons which, again in very different contexts, share the following:

Paradigm B
- extended lesson length (1–1½ hours) (Figure 1.2)
- discernible but loose structure (Figure 1.3)
- longer sub-stages, with ragged boundaries between them (Figure 1.4)
- routines and rules of procedure which are frequently mentioned, often renegotiated and sometimes contested (touches on Figures 1.9 and 1.11)
- one or two broad learning tasks which are each treated as unitary, rather than broken down into small steps (Figures 1.4 and 1.8)
- little sense of pace: the speed of teaching and learning are shaped by events as they happen rather than by the teacher's advance planning
- complex physical organisation
- a wide spectrum of messages conveyed, ranging from content and classroom procedure to personal and interpersonal values (Figures 1.8 and 1.10)
- a predominance of written work, with oral encounters conversational rather than structured (Figures 1.5 and 1.6, touching on 1.7)
- wide variation in pupil outcomes.

If this were a study of school and classroom effectiveness one might expect a pre-test–post-test programme of such teaching tracked over a year or two to show that the second group of lessons was less effective than the first, for they appear to fall short on several of the more familiar effectiveness indicators. Indeed, the first group is closely aligned to Rosenshine's classic (1987) model of effective direct instruction. However, my purpose in presenting them in this form is to make some rather different points. First, these are extremes: in between are lessons which combine elements from both ends of the various continua. Second, in only two of the five countries, India and Russia, was there a high degree of consistency and predictability in the way the various continua combined.

The first list is in fact characteristically Russian or indeed continental: we observed this formula in nearly all of the Russian classrooms, in both Moscow and southern Russia, and Level 1 interviewees in Moscow – at the Ministry of Education and the Russian Academy of Education – confirmed its national prevalence. Indeed, in her interview with me the Russian Federation's Director of Primary Education was happy to trace its pedigree back in an unbroken line through the vicissitudes of perestroika, the Soviet system and Tsarist autocracy to Jan Kornensky (the seventeenth-century Czech educational reformer we know as Comenius): history is indeed a necessary adjunct of comparativism. The second list, however, though derived from several Michigan classrooms, can be contrasted with other very different combinations from the same three school districts in that state. Similarly, lessons observed and recorded in Michigan, northern England and southern France tended to combine between-lesson consistency on some continua with inconsistency on others, less so in France than in England and Michigan, but with much greater pedagogical variation in France than is implied by that overused image of the Minister of Education with his stopwatch. By and large, the further west we travelled, the greater the variation in pedagogy. The variation says as much about values as about effectiveness, and it is to this matter that I shall turn shortly. First, however, to another of my initial problems, that of the parts and the whole.

The Parts and the Whole

Taking the lesson as the basic unit of analysis, preparing narrative accounts and attending to matters like lesson structure, alongside specific pedagogic elements like planning, task-related behaviour, organisation, time on task and discourse, will take us some way to achieving that balance of dissection and reconstruction for which I argued earlier. However, the more I revisit the Five Cultures lesson tapes and transcripts the more I find that in my quest to make sense of the totality of what I have observed and recorded on each occasion I need analogies and metaphors of a kind which the social sciences simply cannot provide.

Eliot Eisner (1985) has long argued the value of artistic, especially visual, modes of analysis and evaluation in educational settings, and some ethnographers apply the techniques and conventions of literary criticism, of different literary genres and of devices like metaphor and metonymy (Atkinson, 1990).

The language of the classroom is an obvious candidate for scrutiny within a literary–critical paradigm, as an alternative to computer word-counts on the one hand and ethnomethodological analysis on the other. However, in my search for ways of understanding the whole, as opposed to the parts, I find a different art-form, that of music, even more persuasive.

Teaching, like music, is *performance.* That performance can be preceded by *composition* (lesson planning) and in execution is thus an *interpretation,* or it can be partly or completely *improvisatory.* The performance of teaching can be in planning *orchestrated* and in execution *conducted* – with varying degrees of competence and persuasiveness, with participants staying together or losing their way, and with consequences which may move, excite, bore or alienate. In both its planning and execution, teaching is bounded and constrained, as is music, by *time*, which far from being a one-dimensional measure as implied by that familiar variable 'time on task' is in fact many-faceted. Time in teaching comprises *time-intended* and *actual time spent*, and in each of these we have *pulse, tempo* or speed and *rhythm.* The critical temporal variable in teaching is, I would suggest, not the current official preoccupation (in respect of literacy and numeracy, for example) with overall *time intended* and *spent*, but the *internal time* of a lesson, its *tempo* or *pace*, or its ratio of time taken to content encountered, allied to lesson *dynamics*, that subtle admixture which generates (or destroys) the energy and commitment which children give to the task in hand.

Similarly, a lesson can be dominated by one or more clearly discernible *themes, melodic lines* or indeed *leitmotifs*, and these can be *harmonically* sustained or they can be woven together in a *contrapuntal* relationship; or the lesson can descend into cacophony. The whole is bounded by *form* – and in teaching, as in music, there are many forms, from the single, loose programmatic movement, to the formal episodic structure of the classic central European lesson plan, framed by *introduction* and *recapitulation* and punctuated by *rondo-form* recalls of the main theme. Beyond form in this sense are the larger musical structures and genres, and we have in our data exemplifications of lessons orchestrated and conducted as *operatic* episodes (in a Russian village school) and lessons bearing a strong resemblance in their reiterative, ritualistic and antiphonal character, and their priest–acolyte relationship (as in many of the Indian classrooms), to sacred music or religious ritual. Indeed, my Bombay colleague Denzil Saldanha, having viewed some of the Indian tapes, sees this as a definite cultural continuity from religious to secular India rather than merely a convenient analogy.

If this were merely an exercise in analogy it would be interesting but little else. However, having worked hard to understand teaching over many years I find the perspective a genuinely useful one in tackling the problem of relating the parts and the whole as I have outlined it. Especially, I find

that this approach to the concept of *form* illuminates the relationship between the structure and organisation of teaching and its meaning; that
tempo takes us beyond the familiar process variables of 'time for learning',
'opportunity to learn' and 'pupil time on task'; while *melody*, harmony,
polyphony and *counterpoint* help me to unravel the way the messages of
teaching – whether explicit or implicit, congruent or incongruent – are
developed and relate to each other over the course of a single lesson. For
this, the musical metaphor is a useful adjunct to the more commonly evoked dramatic distinction between *text* and *subtext* (in the same way my use
of musical form can usefully be set a against visual–spatial principles like
proportion, *balance* and *perspective*).

Together, these concepts also help me to unpack some of the differences
between the lessons I have observed and recorded in the five countries. Thus,
to gloss Figures 1.3 and 1.4, for example, there is a clear contrast in the data
between, on the one hand, those lessons whose themes will vary from one
lesson to the next but whose length, tempo and form remain predictably and
reliably the same, and, on the other hand, those lessons which pursue the
more ambitious but risky strategy of multiple and even conflicting themes
within a many-layered structure and a rambling time-frame, sometimes suc-
ceeding because of the skilful way they are orchestrated and conducted,
sometimes losing pace, coherence and the attention of the pupils.

Again, risking comparison across the five cultures, the form of the
lessons we observed became more variable and complex as we moved west.
Moreover, the increased complexity was at two distinct levels: *organisation*
and *message* or *meaning* (the theme initiated in Figures 1.9–1.11).

Let me elaborate this notion of layered complexity. In no lesson that I
have ever observed was there not a powerful subtext of values relating, for
example, to: the extent to which knowledge is open or bounded, provisio-
nal or uncontestable; how ideas should be handled; the kinds of authority
the teacher and the curriculum embody; how individuals and groups should
relate to each other; and what counts as success in learning. However, we
found four sharp contrasts across classrooms and cultures in respect of such
message systems. First and most obviously and predictably, in their substance: knowledge, the teacher's authority and successful learning were
defined differently in different cultural contexts. Second (Figure 1.9), in the
relative emphasis given to subject-matter and affective and behavioural
issues. Third, in the extent to which such messages were either secure and
therefore implicit, or less secure and therefore perforce explicit and frequently reiterated. Fourth, in the manner in which the messages were
conveyed (Figure 1.10). In respect of the last two, the sharpest contrasts, as
in so much else, were between most of the Russian lessons and many of the
Michigan ones. In the one context the substantive messages about the
nature of knowledge, teaching and learning and about behavioural norms
and expectations were unambiguous yet also largely tacit; in the other
context they were the subject of frequent reminders by the teacher and
often intense encounters ranging from negotiation to confrontation.

In this one may wish to detect the contrast between lately abandoned totalitarianism and the confusions of the world's most self-conscious democracy. However, the Michigan classrooms also exhibited the greatest organisational complexity. Here we had a combination of organisational complexity and a contrapuntal and sometimes cacophonous message system, with classroom exchanges veering back and forth between negotiation over the learning task and negotiation over behaviour, and some marked inconsistencies between each. It was not – as usually argued – the organisational structure *per se* which led to the general lack of pace in learning and the high levels of pupil distraction that we observed in some of the Michigan lessons, but the high level of negotiation to which the teachers were committed, and the consequently problematic and confusing nature of the messages which were sometimes conveyed. The organisational complexity simply exacerbated this.

Holistic analysis of this kind offers not just the academic luxury of another way of characterising teaching but, for those of us also concerned with the quality and improvement of education, new ways to understand how and why some lessons and some teachers are more effective than others. I do not dispute the importance to the improvement of teaching of isolating variables like 'high expectations', 'clarity of presentation', 'advance cognitive organisers' and 'ability grouping' (Creemers, 1997), but I do feel that an equally strong case can be made for assaying alternative, more integrative paradigms.

The Macro–Micro Relationship

The other imperative in comparative classroom research that I identified was that of finding a way to relate events in the classroom to the society of which it is a part. The normal formulation of this imperative as the 'macro–micro problem' can be misleading if it is taken to imply that schooling and society are separate social systems. The reality, whether we are interested in the formal relationship between national policies and school administration, the less predictable relationship between educational policies and lessons as planned and presented, or the complex and subtle ways in which cultural values are manifested in pedagogy, is that culture must be understood and researched as intrinsic and pervasive rather than, as it tends to be in school effectiveness research, extraneous.

We can proceed on the basis of social theory, grand or grounded. We can enlist Gramsci (1971), Bourdieu and Passeron (1977) or Apple (1990) to provide one kind of explanatory framework through theories of hegemony, cultural capital and cultural reproduction. This will situate what we observe in classrooms in a very specific way as part of an irresistible historical and political tide in which the individual teacher or child is relatively powerless. Or we can use the postmodernist preoccupation with fragmentation, pluralism and individualism to set the classroom and the state in a much less certain relationship (Giroux, 1992). Or again, as economic globalisation induces governments like that of the UK to define the function of state education in ever more instrumental terms, we should perhaps provide the corrective of a more reflective and critical analysis of the relationship between education and the economy (Levin and Kelly, 1997; Brown *et al.*, 1997; Robinson, 1999).

However, theories of hegemony and cultural reproduction begin to crumble when one studies pedagogy within countries undergoing substantial change or losing their collective sense of direction. I can exemplify this, once again, in the contrasting contexts of Russia and the USA.

In many Russian classrooms I observed, and both teachers and officials confirmed in interview, a continuity and stability in pedagogic values and practices from Soviet days which contrasted markedly with post-Soviet policies and rhetoric and with the economic and social dislocation of the world outside the school. There was a strong emphasis on rules, deference to the teacher, and individual striving for the collective good. There was a sense of pride in the school and a sense of occasion about each lesson.

In Michigan, I found teachers explicitly working to counter a range of what they saw as undesirable values and tendencies prevalent in the community and wider society, especially rampant individualism, materialism, intolerance, violence and economic instrumentalism. The pursuit of this objective introduced considerable and usually unresolved tensions into their teaching as, on the one hand, their discourse and classroom rituals and routines were heavy with the rhetoric of caring and sharing while their moral posture of tolerance meant that much of the pedagogic content of their teaching, especially in the area of children's writing, was dominated by the contrary language and mores of mass television – from O. J. Simpson to the Simpsons.

These contexts were very different, but neither of them was readily amenable to the simple hegemonic concept of pedagogy. In the Russian schools there was a formal commitment to post-Soviet values, certainly as far as the 'humanised' curriculum was concerned. Yet with this commitment was combined evident continuity in pedagogy, which though ostensibly now more 'democratic' remained in the main firmly locked into the habitual transactions and underlying values of Soviet and indeed pre-Soviet times. In both cases, the wider societal context was one of dislocation and value-dissensus. Parents of the Moscow and Kursk children were trying to survive acute financial hardship and the degeneration of civic infrastructures. The Michigan parents and teachers were anxious about the collapse of traditional values and their children's personal safety (a concern shared by many of the Russian teachers). The schools' responses to this shared problem, however, were very different. In enacting continuity of educational practices and their underlying values from Soviet days, the Russian classrooms provided a context of stability to which pupils responded positively and which parents appeared to endorse. In contrast, by appearing simultaneously to oppose and condone the prevailing cultural values some of the Michigan teachers created only moral confusion. And out of that moral confusion came procedural and behavioural problems, loss of classroom control and a diminution of the teacher's ability to promote learning.

These examples test the explanatory value of theories of hegemony and cultural reproduction, and point up just how problematic it can be to explicate the macro–micro relationship in the context of school and classroom research. The postmodernist option in the two contexts exemplified looks decidedly tempting, though I could also provide contrasting examples, especially from India, France and England, which would clearly exemplify Giroux's claim (1992) that pedagogy is a 'technology of language, power and practice that produces and legitimates forms of moral and political regulation that construct and offer human beings particular views of themselves and the world'.

The examples should also remind those who define pedagogy in terms of technique alone not only that the value context is important and powerful, but that value-congruence and value-dissonance are undoubtedly significant contributory elements in effective or – dare we now say? – harmonious teaching.

Conclusion

In this chapter I have emphasised the importance of building up rich datasets which include video and photography and maximise the opportunity for revisiting teaching as it happens. I showed how one might attempt to balance atomistic and holistic data and data analysis. I suggested that the idea of the 'cross-cultural continuum' could counter the current 'best buy' approach to international comparison while also helping to tease out further the cultural invariants and variables in teaching. I voted teacher–pupil discourse as the pedagogic 'text' most in need of detailed study. I argued that we should try to find additional metaphors, analogies and constructs for making better sense of the overall structure, form and meaning of teaching, and to this end I tentatively invoked the constructs of music, another kind of composition and another kind of performance, but in many respects, closer to teaching than we may realise. And I illustrated the problematic nature of the macro–micro relationship, once one moves beyond the familiar comparativists' preoccupation with systems and structures and begins to study teaching at the level of values.

I end with two general observations about the policy context of comparative classroom research in this country, as it now stands.

Comparative research is currently being used to buttress the laudable and necessary commitment to raising standards in education, and especially primary education. Comparative *classroom* research can identify important preconditions for effective teaching. But it can and should be used far less selectively and uncritically than it has been so far. Taken in the round, comparative research not only offers pointers for raising educational standards; it also challenges some of very assumptions on which the current drive for standards are based. For example:

- The assumption that the relationship between pedagogy, attainment in literacy and national economic competitiveness is direct, linear and causal (attainment and economic performance being multi-factorial, the reality is much more complex).
- The assumption that whole-class teaching, internationally, is a correlate only of educational success (as I show in Alexander (1996), its international ubiquity means that it is associated with all levels of educational and economic attainment and therefore correlates with none).
- The assumption that a concern with children's development and ways of learning is an ideological aberration, and a peculiarly English one at that (it is not – it is of increasing concern to policy-makers, as well as educators, in countries as diverse as France, Russia and India, and for that matter, Japan and China).
- The assumption that the key temporal variable in pedagogy is *time on task* (my project indicates that *pace* and *episodic structure* deserve equal attention) and the linked argument that increasing time on task will therefore raise standards (it may, but not without attention to the way time is used).
- The assumption that the way to raise standards in literacy and numeracy is to downgrade the rest of the curriculum (international curriculum and assessment data of the kind in the QCA database compiled by O'Donnell and Le Métais – as well as the lessons of our own educational history – should puncture that one).
- The assumption that reading and writing can be detached from talk and should constitute the exclusive focus for the development of literacy. (Our data show, especially in France and Russia, a considerable counterbalancing commitment to *oracy*, and the development of spoken language as an adjunct, not merely an alternative, to writing. Because half of our lessons are language/literacy lessons, we shall have quite a lot to say about this important aspect of primary education at a later stage in the analysis.)
- The assumption that the pedagogic power of classroom interaction resides chiefly in teacher-initiated question and answer sessions, or so-called 'interactive whole-class teaching' (my video and transcript material uncovers a much more extensive spectrum of discourse, and indicates a much broader concept of effective interaction).

The other point I want to make concerns 'effectiveness', since May 1997 the official adjunct to 'standards'.[1]

While it is clear that the monopoly by one kind of research of a concept as important as school effectiveness is neither tenable nor helpful, I am not one of those who dismisses the dominant school effectiveness paradigm, as represented most prominently in the work of David Reynold and his colleagues (Reynolds *et al.*, 1994; Reynolds, 1999; Creemers, 1997) as being of no value. However, it is time that we confronted some of the paradigm's more fundamental weaknesses, the more urgently because of the way it appears to have seduced the inhabitants of Sanctuary Buildings.

First, the school effectiveness enterprise as currently conducted manages to defy both logic and common sense by making culture peripheral to cross-cultural analysis.

Second, for inherent methodological reasons this kind of research is unable to engage with the purposes, meanings and messages which elevate pedagogy from mindless technique to considered educational act. However, though I count this a weakness, and a serious one, others count it a strength, because they can use it to justify devising a uniform, all-purpose, context-free and content-neutral model of effective teaching and imposing it on England's 20,000 primary schools and 182,000 primary teachers.

Third, in as far as what comes out of such research depends in an exact way upon what you put in, there is considerable arbitrariness in the list of variables which the dominant school effectiveness paradigm includes and excludes (see, for example, the frequently cited model of Creemers, 1997). This is aggravated by the self-referenced and therefore tautologous character of much of the school effectiveness literature.

Fourth, the claim that this particular branch of educational research is a discipline in its own right is surely premature. It has as yet little of the internal dialectic of conflicting theories and methodologies which give a discipline the hard edge of scepticism which is essential to its vitality, and it displays scant interest in the debatable lands between one discipline and another which expose the strengths, limitations and potential of each. Moreover, it is validated less by the usual disciplinary mechanism of rigorous internal critique than by the patronage which it happens to enjoy among those seeking academic legitimation for their policy agenda.

In a climate which is more than usually hostile to educational research and to the theory and speculation which are its proper and essential companions, gaining acceptance for a richer spectrum of pedagogic analysis is bound to be difficult. Yet in this chapter I hope that I have shown how it is possible to strengthen and extend our understanding of teaching by invoking radically different ways of studying and defining it. The more centralised, controlled and uniform our education system becomes, the more vital it is to use international comparison to remind us of the alternatives.

Note

The UK Labour Government elected in May 1997 appointed a Standards Minister and a Standards Task Force, and established a Standards and Effectiveness Unit within the Department for Education and Employment.

References

Alexander, R. J. (1984) *Primary Teaching.* London: Cassell.
Alexander, R. J. (1988) Garden or jungle: teacher development and informal

primary education, in W. A. L. Blyth (ed.) *Informal Primary Education Today: Essays and Studies*. London: Falmer Press, pp. 148–88.

Alexander, R. J. (1995) *Versions of Primary Education*. London: Routledge.

Alexander, R. J. (1996) *Other Primary Schools and Ours: Hazards of International Comparison*. Warwick: University of Warwick Centre for Research in Elementary and Primary Education.

Alexander' R. J. (1997) *Policy and Practice in Primary Education: Local Initiative, National Agenda*. London: Routledge.

Alexander, R. J. (2000) *Culture, Pedagogy and Power: an International Study of Primary Education*. Oxford: Blackwell.

Alexander, R. J., Willcocks, J. and Kinder, K. (1989) *Changing Primary Practice*. London: Falmer Press.

Apple, M. (1990) *Ideology and the Curriculum*. London: Routledge.

Archer, M. (1979) *The Social Origins of Educational Systems*. London: Sage.

Atkinson, P. (1990) *The Ethnographic Imagination: Textual Constructions of Reality*. London: Routledge.

Bennett, S. N., Desforges, C., Cockburn, A. and Wilkinson, B. (1984) *The Quality of Pupil Learning Experiences*. Hove: Lawrence Erlbaum.

Bourdieu, P. and Passeron, J-C. (1977) *Reproduction*. London: Sage.

Broadfoot, P. (1996) *Education, Assessment and Society: a Sociological Analysis*. Buckingham: Open University Press.

Brown, P., Halsey, A. H., Lauder, H. and Wells, A. S. (1997) The transformation of education and society, in A. H. Halsey, H. Lauder, P. Brown and A. S. Wells (eds) *Education: Culture, Economy and Society*. Oxford: Oxford University Press, pp. 1–44.

Creemers, B. P. M. (1997) *Effective Schools and Effective Teachers: an International Perspective*. Warwick: University of Warwick Centre for Research in Elementary and Primary Education.

Edwards, D. and Mercer, N. (1987) *Common Knowledge: the Development of Understanding in the Classroom*. London: Methuen.

Eisner, E. W (1985) *The Art of Educational Evaluation*. Lewes: Falmer Press.

Galton, M. and Simon, B. (1980) *Progress and Performance in the Primary Classroom*. London: Routledge.

Galton, M., Hargreaves, L., Comber, C., Wall, D. and Pell, A. (1999) *Inside the Primary Classroom: 20 Years On*. London: Routledge.

Giroux, H. (1992) *Border Crossings: Cultural Workers and the Politics of Education*: London: Routledge.

Gramsci, A. (1971) *Selections from the Prison Notebooks,* edited by Q. Hoare and G. Nowell-Smith. New York: International Publishers.

Levin H. M. and Kelly, C. (1997) Can education do it alone? in A. H. Halsey, H. Lauder, P. Brown and A. S. Wells (eds) *Education: Culture, Economy and Society*. Oxford: Oxford University Press, pp. 240–52.

Mortimore, P., Sammons, P., Stoll, L., Lewis, D. and Ecob, R. (1988) *School Matters: the Junior Years*. London: Open Books.

O'Donnell, S., Le Métais, J., Boyd, S. and Tabber, R. (1998) *INCA: the International Review of Curriculum and Assessment Frameworks Archive* (CD-ROM). London: QCA.

Pollard, A. (1985) *The Social World of the Primary School*. London: Routledge.

Pollard, A., Broadfoot, P., Croll, P., Osborn, M. and Abbott, D. (1994) *Changing English Primary Schools: the Impact of the Education Reform Act at Key Stage One*. London: Cassell.

Reynolds, D. (1999) Creating a new methodology for comparative educational research: the contribution of the International School Effectiveness Research Project, in R. J. Alexander, P. Broadfoot and D. Phillips (eds) *Learning from Comparing: New Directions in Comparative Educational Research, Volume I*. Oxford: Symposium Books, pp. 135–48.

Reynolds, D., Creemers, B. P. M., Nesselrodt, P. S., Schaffer, E. C., Stringfield, S. and Teddlie, C. (1994) *Advances in School Effectiveness Research and Practice.* Oxford: Pergamon.

Reynolds, D. and Farrell, S. (1996) *Worlds Apart? A Review of International Surveys of Educational Achievement Involving England.* London: OFSTED.

Robinson, P. (1999) The tyranny of league tables: international comparisons of educational attainment and economic performance, in R. J. Alexander, P. Broadfoot and D. Phillips (eds) *Learning from Comparing: New Directions in Comparative Educational Research, Volume 1.* Oxford: Symposium Books, pp. 217–36.

Rosenshine, B. (1987) Direct instruction, in M. J. Dunkin (ed.) *The International Encyclopaedia of Teaching and Teacher Education.* Oxford: Pergamon.

Sammons, P., Hillman, J. and Mortimore, P. (1995) *Key Characteristics of Effective Schools: a Review of School Effectiveness Research.* London: OFSTED

Sebba, J. (1999) Developing evidence-informed policy and practice in education. Paper presented to the 1999 conference of the British Educational Research Association.

Tizard, B., Blatchford, P., Burke J., Farquhar, C. and Plewis, I. (1988) *Young Children at School in the Inner City.* London: Lawrence Erlbaum.

Tobin, J. J., Wu, D. Y. and Davidson, D. H. (1989) *Preschool in Three Cultures. Japan, China and the United States.* New Haven: Yale University Press.

Woods, P. and Jeffrey, B. (1996) *Teachable Moments: the Art of Teaching in Primary Schools.* Buckingham: Open University Press.

2

Basics, Cores and Choices: Modernising the Primary Curriculum

Robin Alexander

Introduction

The primary curriculum is on the move – or is it? This chapter could be viewed as being of historical interest only but for the fact that history teaches us that when the dust of curriculum reformist rhetoric subsides we usually find that change has been far outweighed by continuity, the things which most needed to change have not, and the lessons of the past have been ignored. The chapter originated as a contribution to the review which led to the introduction of a revised National Curriculum from September 2000 (DfEE and QCA, 1999). This review was initiated by the School Curriculum and Assessment Authority (SCAA) and taken over by its successor, the Qualifications and Curriculum Authority (QCA). This chapter was one of a number of papers which SCAA commissioned for a national conference on prospects for the primary curriculum. It took place shortly after New Labour's May 1997 landslide election victory on the slogan 'education, education, education'. The new government honoured its predecessors' commitment to national curriculum review, but reduced the review's options by placing the key areas of literacy and numeracy under direct ministerial control. These were made the subject of separate strategies which prescribed in considerable detail not only content but also time allocations, lesson structure and teaching methods (DfEE 1998a, 1998b). This was the first time in recent history that national government had sought to control 'pedagogy as well as curriculum. This, in bare outline, is the background. The paper follows pretty well as it was first presented, though I have added a brief postscript on how matters stand three years on.

Prospects for Curriculum Reform

With the arrival of a government committed to 'education, education and education', the review of the National Curriculum will be either an event of the profoundest importance for the future of this country or a damp squib, a mere tinkering at the margins of the apparatus of orders, key stages, programmes of study, levels and assessment, which leaves their fundamentals intact and vital questions about the proper purposes of state education unanswered, and indeed unasked.

What clues as to the likely outcome of the review do we have so far? First, in its proper and necessary pursuit of higher standards of literacy and numeracy the government appears to be signalling not only that these are pre-eminent but also that they are all that matter. So, for 'education, education, education' it seems that we must read, at the primary stage anyway, 'basics, basics, basics'.[1] Second, the curriculum review *Framework* document suggests a certain ambivalence about the scope of the proposed review, offering on its first page a commitment to 'fundamental thinking and . . . debate about the nature and structure of the school curriculum while on its last page diffidently toning this down to 'a possible revision of the National Curriculum . . . should this be felt to be necessary' (SCAA, 1997).

This shift, incidentally, reasserts the reductionism of the period since 1988. ERA started with a concept of curriculum in which the National Curriculum was the innermost of three circles; beyond it were a 'basic' curriculum and, beyond that, a 'whole' curriculum. Since then, 'national' and 'whole' have become synonymous (and this was underscored in the change of name from a National Curriculum Council to a School Curriculum and Assessment Authority). The cross-curricular themes, skills and dimensions of the 1988–9 National Curriculum Mark 1 disappeared without trace in Dearing's 1993 National Curriculum Mark 2, implemented in 1995; while the 1996 values consultation paper from SCAA and the National Values Forum (National Forum, 1996), which was widely commended as a reinstatement of social morality in the face of that notorious Thatcherite *fiat* 'there is no such thing as society', was ousted from the agenda, like so many other educational initiatives of real worth, by the more dependable appeal of 'standards' and 'basics'.

To express the problem thus is not to imply that the course plotted since 1988 is fixed for all time. Rather, my concern in beginning in this vein is to direct attention to the gravity – and excitement – of the choice we confront. We have an opportunity to match the millennial rhetoric with genuinely millennial decisions. Whether we seize this opportunity depends on those who participate in this review and, above all, on the government. My own position is clear. The review must be a radical one, and it must be allowed freely to consider versions of the primary curriculum for the twenty-first century which are markedly different from the one imposed on the country in 1988.

I want to rehearse three essential perspectives on the five 'key areas' nominated in the review *Framework* document, before commenting on some of the areas themselves. The perspectives set the post-1988 English model of the curriculum in the contexts of time, space and pedagogy. In such a brief chapter they cannot do more than start the ball rolling.

The Context of Time: Lessons of History

There are two main lessons of history in the present context. The first is that we are unable to break free of it. The second, which is certainly not a paradox, is that people of power and influence tend to act as though history has nothing to teach them.

Thus, in its scope and balance (or imbalance) the 1988/1995 National Curriculum bore a striking resemblance to all of its primary and elementary predecessors, so much so that Dearing's 1993 assertion that 'The principal task of the teacher at Key Stage 1 is to ensure that pupils master the basic skills of reading, writing and number' (Dearing, 1993) was uncannily close to the 1861 Newcastle Commission's assertion that 'The duty of a state in public education is to ensure the greatest possible quantity of reading, writing and arithmetic for the greatest number'. The other echo, explicitly admitted by Kenneth Baker in 1987–8, was the public/grammar school emphasis, again reaching back into the nineteenth century, on a canon of bounded subjects including alongside the 'basics' the 'humanising' claims of, history, geography and art, and – *mens sana*, etc. – PE (Alexander, 1995).

Thus it was that an Act of Parliament bearing the proud label 'reforms' could prescribe for our primary schools, regardless of all those debates about the curriculum in the 1970s and early 1980s (including the important HMI framework document *The Curriculum from 5 to 16*, DES, 1985), the familiar combination of elementary (3Rs), grammar (non-core foundation) and Butler compromise (RE as compulsory yet separate). Thus it was that for all its radicalism on the social and physical context of primary education, the 1967 Plowden Report grounded its discussion of curriculum in the same far-from progressive subject labels that had framed curriculum discourse in this country for most of the previous century (CACE, 1967). Thus it was that we were misled into presuming that the concerns about 'breadth' and 'balance' which exercised Dearing might yield, as they implied, discussion about what a broad and balanced curriculum ought to entail: instead, they were merely a shorthand for the logistical challenge of 'manageability' – how to fit an unquestioned model of curriculum more effectively into the time available. Thus it was that the pre-Dearing cross-curricular themes, skills and dimensions could not permeate the established curriculum in the way asserted but had to be bolted on to it – the more readily to be unbolted a couple of years later. And thus it is that nearly every other official or quasi-official statement on how the curriculum should attend to this country's future has responded to its brief by repeating or at best marginally updating the curriculum of the country's past.

The formula from which we seem so incapable of escaping is the one I characterised in a book published in 1984 (Alexander, 1984) as comprising a high priority, protected, and heavily assessed 'Curriculum I' (justified by reference to utilitarian values like economic need), sharply differentiated from a low priority, vulnerable, unassessed 'Curriculum II' (justified by reference to vague notions of 'rounded' or 'balanced' education).

Given that this is 2000, not 1870, the historical questions are as simple as they are necessary. Should 'core' and 'basics' be treated as synonymous? Should core and non-core be so sharply differentiated? Even if a notion of 'basics' is as essential at the primary' stage in the twenty-first century as it was in the nineteenth, should these 'basics' be defined in pretty well the same terms as they were when the task of elementary schools was to provide a minimal education for the urban poor with a view to ensuring social conformity and well-run factories?

The other lesson of history I identified was late twentieth-century arrogance about its significance. A striking feature of many educational pronouncements during the interventionist 1980s and 1990s is the failure to acknowledge and build on past thinking and practice. In academic writing the condition is mani-fested by those who cite no research earlier than, say, 1990 and thus rather than break new ground by building systematically on the work of their pre-decessors at best replicate it, at worst achieve not even that. The principle of 'cumulation', so important in the physical sciences, seems to be poorly under-stood in education. Similarly, in the policy arena, the 'new' curriculum models and agendas, as we have seen, are in fact dispiritingly old, and the so-called debate on pedagogy is actually going backwards.

Why is this? The charitable explanation is laziness, or perhaps amnesia induced by policy overload. Where academics and politicians are con-cerned, however – for they can make no such excuse – a rather more venal motive may be at work: that of knowingly ignoring or misrepresenting past ideas and achievements in order to buttress present claims to originality, radicalism and authority. 1997, for the Blair government, was 'year zero', the start of a 'modernising' crusade which would explicitly belittle or ignore the achievements and lessons of previous decades, and marginalise alterna-tive viewpoints as 'the forces of conservatism'.

The Context of Space: Lessons of International Comparison

We are by now familiar with the exercise of international comparisons in education. Hard on the heels of the IEA, IAEP, OECD, TIMSS and other league table exposures of the country's poor educational performance (as judged, inevitably, in terms of 'Curriculum I' outcomes only), have come the solutions: homework, textbooks and 'interactive' whole-class teaching, as used in Switzerland, Germany and Taiwan (see, for example, Reynolds and Farrell, 1996; Luxton and Last, 1997; Prais, 1997; DfEE Numeracy Task Force, 1998). Informing these prescriptions are two questionable assumptions: first, that there is a direct, linear and causal relationship between pupils' test scores in reading, number or science and a country's economic performance,[2] second, that there is a similar relationship between these test scores and the presence or absence of whole-class teaching. Ergo, we are told, a régime of interactive whole-class teaching will reverse the years of national decline and propel Britain up the league tables of educational and economic performance.

International comparison is both essential and instructive, as those of us who are engaged in it have discovered, but it is genuinely instructive – in the sense of offering insight rather than soundbite – if applied comprehensively and with due regard for the conventions of empirical research, rather than selectively. The current cause-effect analysis, for example, is an exercise in less than rigorous correlation which conveniently ignores those countries with high test scores in the basics but problematic economies; and those with poor test scores but booming economies. And it ignores the fact that being almost a universal feature of primary education, whole-class teaching can be shown to correlate, world-wide, with every level of educational and economic performance which we may care to identify – high, low, middling and all points in between. Apart from that, the advocates of this solution to our problems display a pretty poor understanding of the research evidence on whole-class teaching itself, as Maurice Galton has argued (Galton, 1998). For that necessary understanding, prefixing 'interactive' is no substitute.[3]

The current vogue for international comparison ignores other lessons too, and these bear pressingly on the review of the school curriculum. In contrast, as is shown in the QCA-sponsored NFER comparison of curriculum and assessment in sixteen countries, the universal dominance of the 3Rs at the primary stage, like the near-universal dominance of whole-class teaching, is only part of the story. Thus, if we take the sixteen countries featured in the NFER analysis (Le Métais and Tabberer, 1997), we find that at the primary stage:

- the national language and mathematics are compulsory in all sixteen countries;
- science, art, PE and societal/civic education are compulsory in all but two of them;
- a modern foreign language, technology, history, geography and music are compulsory in something over half of them;
- religious education, environmental studies, moral education, domestic science and lifeskills are compulsory only in a small minority of them.

Put another way, England at the primary stage goes against the international trend (a) in excluding societal/civic education; (b) in excluding a modern foreign language; (c) in making religious education compulsory. And in common with several other countries it relegates, at least as far as the official curriculum is concerned, areas like environmental studies, health, moral education and lifeskills to the status of options.

Further, if we examine in greater detail the curricula of specific European countries with demographic and economic circumstances not unlike our own, we find that the critical point of variation is not my 'Curriculum I' (the three/four subject core) but 'Curriculum II' (the non-core foundation and beyond), and especially the extent to which children in their primary schools engage with the question of what it means to be a social being, whether as a member of a family or local community, or as a citizen in a democratic society, or as user, inheritor and custodian of finite global resources, or as part of an interdependent community of nations. It seems to me to be not insignificant that these are precisely the areas which feature most prominently in the National Forum for Values in Education framework to which I referred earlier. On the basis both of international comparison and national consensus, then, there are pointers here for curriculum review which we cannot afford to ignore.

Alongside these comparisons we might place others. Leaving aside for a moment the very different distribution of power between national government, local/regional government and schools in many other countries, or the sharp contrast between coercive/punitive and supportive/facilitative models of inspection, there is the matter of the balance in the curriculum of mandatory and optional, and of national requirement and local variant. Thus, to take Switzerland, one of the countries whose teaching methods our primary schools are being urged to copy, there is considerable local discretion and variation beyond the nationally prescribed subjects of mother tongue, mathematics and a foreign language, so much so that it might invite even the most naive of international comparers to ask whether a centrally prescribed curriculum really is one of the keys to raising educational standards. Certainly, many other countries have decided that reform is best served by loosening the grip of national government on curriculum and pedagogy and in this respect are heading in the opposite direction from England.

Finally, we might note that high standards in the 3Rs are not incompatible with a broad and balanced curriculum. On the contrary, the international evidence shows that the countries which outperform Britain in literacy and/or numeracy do so from a curriculum base which is often as broad as ours. Even the English inspection evidence confirms this (DES, 1978; OFSTED/DfEE, 1997), though governments prefer to ignore the finding. 'Basics' wins votes; 'breadth and balance' does not.[4]

To reduce the richness of what is suggested by the international research evidence on curriculum and pedagogy to the shibboleths of phonics and whole-class teaching is to reveal the mountain which has to be climbed before we in this country can have a proper debate about education in the twenty-first century.

The Context of Pedagogy: Lessons of Research on Learning and Teaching

If pedagogy is defined as the 'how' of education and curriculum as the 'what', then this section may seem irrelevant to questions about the purposes, structure and content of the primary curriculum. However, properly conceived, pedagogy is both the how and the what, for decisions about how to teach are, or ought to be, shaped in part by the character of the knowledge and understanding we wish children to acquire; and decisions about both of these are, or ought to be, inseparable from questions about how children develop and learn.

There is an immediate corollary for curriculum review. During the past decade or so, the argument that children's development and learning are essential ingredients of professional understanding and decision-making has in some quarters been rejected or ridiculed as tantamount to raising the (red) flag of 1960s progressivism. This nonsense – as unhelpful to the cause of improving educational standards as was the earlier tendency to argue that a concern for curriculum was incompatible with a concern for children, or that because young children do not see the world in terms of subjects then subjects have no place in the curriculum – can now be replaced by a saner and more comprehensive pedagogy which unites subject-matter, development, learning and teaching.

If we endorse this shift, we are bound to address two kinds of question. The first is about the nature of the primary curriculum as a whole. Is the proper model for the next century one which pushes down into Key Stage 1 knowledge structures which originate in the thinking and practices of those working at Key Stages 3 and 4, and indeed beyond? Can the evolved form of a subject, as Jerome Bruner argued nearly forty years ago, really be translated into a form which enables it to be taught 'effectively in some intellectually honest form to any child at any stage of development' (Bruner, 1963, p. 33)? Or should the foundations for later learning be laid in a different way, by mapping out two quite distinct kinds of knowledge and understanding: (i) those necessary to provide a foundation for KS3/4 subject learning; and (ii) those necessary in the here and now of early childhood and KS1? These objectives are not, as some tend to insist, mutually exclusive, but complementary. A complete education can attend to children's present as well as to their future, just as it can attend to personal fulfilment as well as to societal and economic need.

The second kind of question is more straightforward, and arises once the first has been answered. Having mapped out a curriculum structure which is both developmentally apposite and, in terms of subsequent stages of education, epistemologically coherent, how should the components of that structure, whether we call them subjects or something else, be translated into an appropriate and viable sequence or programme of learning tasks? What kind of 'scaffolding', to use an important Vygotskian term which is now in danger of becoming as bowdlerised as was 'discovery' in the 1960s, is needed to bridge what children know and what we want them to know?

To ask these questions is to risk incurring the response that we cannot afford to go back to the days when there were endless questions about the primary curriculum but no answers, a frustrating situation to which the then government's summary imposition of a nine/ten-subject national curriculum might seem in retrospect to have been a fair or inevitable response. ('If you people don't sort out a way of defining the primary curriculum,' Eric Bolton, one of the current HMCI's predecessors, presciently warned me in 1985, 'then the government will impose its own definition.') But in the primary world of the early 2000s there seems to be a clearer understanding than in the early 1980s of curriculum matters in general and epistemological matters in particular, and a greater willingness to acknowledge their importance. For this improved understanding the exercise of implementing the National Curriculum can take some of the credit. The climate for asking my two questions, fundamental though they are, is therefore as right now as it is ever likely to be.

So much for the first bout of ground-clearing. For the second we can go to the 'key areas for consideration' set out in the 1997 curriculum review *Framework* document. They included questions – on each of which I shall now reflect, – about the purposes of education, the relationship of curriculum to lifelong learning and the world of work, and about curriculum flexibility and structure.

The Purposes of Education

The current arrangements provide some point of purchase on the all-important question of what a primary education is actually for, and it is good that in its 1997 review document SCAA was prepared to put this question first. For example, the sentiments in ERA's first chapter ('a broad and balanced curriculum which (a) promotes the spiritual, moral, cultural, mental and physical development of pupils at the school and of society; and (b) prepares such pupils for the opportunities, responsibilities and experiences of adult life')[5] have been shown to be pretty meaningless. The National Curriculum is broad and balanced only in so far as it manifests the equilibrium of tautology: every child is entitled to a broad and balanced curriculum; the National Curriculum is every child's statutory entitlement; therefore the National Curriculum is a broad and balanced curriculum. In practice, it is clear that of the various purposes which a state education could properly pursue, utilitarian, and more specifically economic, imperatives have been paramount. In relation to all the other imperatives arising from a complex, pluralist society such as ours, and from the needs of individuals trying to make their way in that society, the National Curriculum may be fairly broad but it is not balanced: and balance rather than breadth is the real issue here (Kelly, 1990; Alexander, 1995).

I stress – because in the context of this country's dichotomous way of looking at education I probably need to – that I strongly endorse the attention given to economic/workplace-directed purposes in our education system. However, a review of the National Curriculum must also recall and debate – for there was no debate the first time round – the other purposes with which these might or should be balanced. The new debate, therefore, will need to address some pretty searching questions about where the existing primary curriculum has attended, and where the new primary curriculum will attend, to:

- economic and workplace needs in the context of change, globalisation and uncertainty;
- individual development, freedom and fulfilment;
- personal and collective morality;
- social justice, cohesion and inclusion;
- culture, broadly and pluralistically conceived;
- the needs and obligations of the citizen in a democratic society.

In these matters, as I suggested earlier, we can learn from international comparisons. The educational purposes distilled from considering these six themes are fundamental rather than peripheral: in curriculum terms they must be intrinsic rather than bolted on.

Lifelong Learning and the World of Work

The essential truths to grasp in assessing how a primary curriculum can prepare for lifelong learning and the world of work are these. First, on the basis of current medical and demographic projections, there are children entering primary education now who will live not just well into the twenty-first century but also into the twenty-second. Second, the scale and unpredictability of change in the economic and occupational structure of this country are likely to be at least as great during the next century as they have been in the present one. Third, though 'the world of work' will impinge on everyone, individuals will be part of that world for but a proportion of their lives, and the imperative of lifelong learning is therefore both powerful and urgent.

The usual response to the mind-boggling implications of these truths is to talk vaguely about a curriculum for 'adaptability' and 'flexibility'. Admirable and necessary though these principles are, they generate two further problems. First, they cast the individual very much in the passive role of victim or recipient rather than active agent of social change (which takes us back to the issue of citizenship). Second, they carry no clue about implementation.

The curriculum for Key Stages 1 and 2, therefore, must be above all an *empowering* one. Literacy (which must include IT and media literacy) provides one – in our world undoubtedly the most critical – kind of empowerment; numeracy another. But for the first and arguably most important stage of education these, *pace* Dearing, are not enough, and we need to identify alongside literacy and numeracy the other kinds of knowledge, understanding and skill which individuals will need in order actively to shape their lives rather than passively to get by. To those habituated by history into viewing state primary education as a means of ensuring subservience and conformity, this requirement will seem not – as it should seem – basic and obvious, but dangerously radical.

Flexibility

We no longer bother to ask what happened to Dearing's twenty per cent. The school curriculum and the National Curriculum are, to all intents and purposes, one. The invitation to consider the issue of flexibility is therefore welcome and important. National evidence indicates that the weight of current requirements for curriculum and assessment, even after Dearing's ministrations, allows little room for manoevre within, let alone beyond, the National Curriculum. International evidence, on the other hand, shows some at least of our successful economic competitors providing a primary curriculum in which national requirements are contained so as to allow considerable scope for both the wider curriculum and local variation. The combination of both kinds of evidence suggests that in this country the current balance of statutory and discretionary is probably wrong.

The Structure of the National Curriculum

When this question is framed in terms of programmes of study, attainment targets and so on, it begs, or possibly pre-empts, two others. First, is the sharp division of a national curriculum into a high-priority, narrowly conceived core and a lower-priority array of 'other foundation subjects' appropriate? Second, what subjects (using the word neutrally, simply to indicate discernible components of a curriculum, rather than, necessarily, the traditional subjects with which we are familiar) should our particular national curriculum contain?

In this brief commentary I do not want to get into the business of PoSs and ATs. Rather, I'd hope that we can focus our attention on the need to challenge the current notion of core/non-core, certainly at Key Stage 1, and probably at Key Stage 2 also. I have indicated my unease about the way the nineteenth-century Curriculum I/II divide has fossilised into structures for social and educational circumstances which are manifestly different from those for which it was designed. Adding science and IT to the core was sensible enough, but no more than tinkering, and adding citizenship and a foreign language to these could make matters more difficult.

If we can become clearer about the purposes of the primary stage of education, and if we are prepared to accept – as invited above – a more generously conceived balance of the economic, occupational, personal, cultural, moral, social and civic, then the inappropriateness of the current curriculum model will be understood. We need, almost certainly, a core curriculum of some kind; but it must include a much wider spectrum of knowledge, understanding and skill than the current idea of core subjects allows. Indeed, the great mistake in 1987/8 was to treat core *curriculum* and core *subjects* as synonymous.

In case this seems too radical, there is actually a fairly easy way of tackling it, at least for feasibility purposes. First, examine the existing Orders and ask not which of the nine KS1/2 subjects (and RE) should be in the core and which outside it, but which *aspects of every subject* are essential to a complete education – for it is what lies beneath the subject labels, rather than the labels themselves, which matters most. Doing this counters the 'winner takes all' consequences of the current approach, whereby because one aspect of a subject (numeracy in mathematics, for example) is essential, every other aspect of that subject is given ring-fenced 'core' status and is treated as *de facto* more important than those aspects of the non-core subjects which by any reasonable definition are of greater significance. In the alternative dispensation, the curricular equivalent of proportional representation, we would almost certainly find that the core should contain aspects of those subjects currently relegated to the margins of 'other foundation'.

This exercise would reorder priorities within the existing ten-plus-one canon of subjects and would seem to represent a minimal definition of what curriculum review should entail, though judged against the historical persistence of the 'basics plus' model it would represent a considerable change because it would give key aspects of the arts and humanities the protection from erosion which they have rarely enjoyed.

The exercise as presented here has the virtue of manageability within current constraints and time-scales, and of not requiring a programme of teacher retraining. The more radical variant, however, is to stop treating the existing subject canon as sacrosanct. On this basis, the sequence would be: (i) identify the purposes of primary education as invited; (ii) identify and map out those fields of knowledge, understanding and skill which, properly fostered, will achieve these purposes (these could well include some of the existing subjects alongside other fields hitherto relegated to the status of options and cross-curricular themes, as well as areas like a foreign language, citizenship and social education to which I referred earlier); (iii) identify, in respect of every field thus mapped out, those kinds of knowledge, understanding and skill which are essential at KS1 and 2 (no longer treating 'primary' as monolithic); (iv) define these as the core.

This new core – a core curriculum rather than core subjects – would not need a second tier of lower-priority 'other foundation' subjects to meet the statutory requirements of breadth and balance, for it would be in itself considerably broader and more balanced than the current triumvirate. Beyond the new core curriculum, therefore, would be a combination of discretionary elements and options which would also include wider aspects of some subjects in the core.

Once this fundamental task is addressed, the second order questions about programmes of study, attainment targets and levels can be considered.

Conclusion

The debate now is about values first, structures and content second. In this context we might note that *Values in Education and the Community*, timely and well-conceived though it was, failed to engage as completely as it might with the existing curriculum. The document proposed an audit of the curriculum to discover where the proposed four key values and thirty principles could be located, but it failed to examine the values which the curriculum *already* reflects and manifests, for all aspects of the curriculum, of any curriculum, are suffused with values of some kind. To take one example, the pluralist thrust of the National Values Forum document could well be at odds with the cultural exclusivity (not to mention nationalism) which has driven some of the more prominent contributions to the debate about English, history and RE in recent years.

Even if the basic structure of the curriculum remains the same after the review, it is essential to examine the value messages which it delivers about what matters most – and least – in the learning and life of individuals and in the culture and progress of society. There is little point in proposing a grand statement of educational purposes for the next century if the curriculum as prescribed and transacted does not reflect them.

We have a clear choice, as I have noted, between a fundamental re-think and adjustment at the margins. I want the former, which is all the more necessary now for having been avoided in 1987–8 and 1993–4. I do not for one moment deny the gains made at the primary stage since the muddle and inconsistency of pre-ERA laissez-faire were replaced by something altogether more coherent and purposeful. However, the case against allowing what in 1987–8 was an unexamined ideologically loaded and backward-looking model of curriculum to serve, by default, as the basis for state education in the next century seems pretty powerful too, for a curriculum is validated by its purposes, not merely by being purposeful; and though pragmatic and logistical criteria for decisions about what and how to teach are important, they should be subsidiary to philosophical and ethical ones.

Nervousness about radical reform is understandable. The teaching profession is dispirited by over a decade of change piled upon change, and policy-makers want their agenda to be pursued and delivered without distractions. For this and other reasons we may well end up with no more than Son of Dearing, or the Bakerlite Curriculum Mark 3. Yet at least let us consider the alternatives. Among those floated in this chapter, I would hope that we might look particularly at the case for five radical shifts:

- from values as optional extras to values as intrinsic;
- from the old 3Rs concept of 'basics' to one which reflects a fresh contemporary analysis of what is essential for both individual empowerment and social progress in the twenty-first century;
- from a small number of *core subjects* to a more broadly conceived *core curriculum* which draws on a wider and more diverse spectrum of knowledge, understanding and skill;
- from a concept of KS1/2 conceived mainly as preparation for KS3/4 to one which also addresses the imperatives and needs of early and middle childhood;
- from a view of state education still enslaved by the elementary/grammar legacy of the nineteenth century to one which is attentive to the very different needs and circumstances of the twenty-first.

Postscript

That was what I said in 1997. What, since then, has been the balance of change and continuity?

In 1997 I anticipated that in arguing that we should start questioning the Victorian Curriculum I/II structure I might be regarded as dangerously radical, and so it turned out. Bang on cue government 'standards' tsar Michael Barber attacked me for being excessively pessimistic about the likely impact on the wider curriculum of the government's standards agenda. HMCI Chris Woodhead went considerably further, and accused me of proposing a model of 'empowerment' in which children do not learn to read (Woodhead, 1998). Readers of this chapter can of course judge how preposterous this accusation was, though the press had a field day and I, Ted Wragg and John Macbeath (the other two academics singled out by Woodhead) were pilloried by the *Daily Mail* as 'the trio of academics failing our schools . . . at the real heart of darkness over falling pupil performance' (Halpin, 1998). As the debate developed during 1998 and 1999, a clear split emerged between proponents of the traditional 'basics plus' version of the primary curriculum and those who wanted genuine modernisation. The latter included a broad and substantial coalition of opinion from industry, business, the arts and religion, as well as from education.

For its part, QCA demonstrated genuine concern to keep options open, though it was somewhat boxed in by the government's 'standards' rhetoric. The review, then, was not the radical reappraisal I had argued for. In 1999, citizenship, whose absence I had noted from international comparison as one of the more glaring curriculum anomalies, appeared at last in National Curriculum Mark 3 – tentatively though, since at the primary stage it was to be non-statutory. Alongside it, but again non-statutory, were the National Values Forum statement and suggestions for modern foreign languages at Key Stage 2, both of which I had also commended. Meanwhile the IT/ICT revolution proceeded apace and the government pressed for Europe-wide school internet access to keep Britain and the European Union competitive with the United States. Here, at least, there were to be major changes.

Yet though there was less overt talk of 'core' and 'other foundation' subjects, the statutory range and hierarchy of the National Curriculum remained firmly within the long-established boundaries of Curriculum I and II. Government insisted that in order to guarantee its literacy and numeracy targets for the year 2002, as little of the curriculum should be altered as possible. For their part, teachers began to report that the Curriculum I/II divide was being exacerbated on a day-to-day basis by the pressures of the literacy and numeracy hour, and that history, geography, art, music and physical education were now vulnerable as never before. Even science, one of the true success stories of the decade after ERA (as demonstrated in English pupils' TIMSS performance), began to feel the pressure. At the same time, though citizenship and an updated concept of personal and social education had appeared on the official scene, they were prevented from disturbing the historical status quo by being classified as optional.

Notes

1. These words anticipated by seven months the Secretary of State's announcement of January 1998 that from September 1998 primary schools need not teach the previous-prescribed programmes of study in design and technology, history, art, music and PE.

2. For an extended critique of this assumption, see Robinson (1999).

3. For a critical analysis of the uses and abuses of international comparisons in primary education, see Alexander (1996). For a detailed comparative study of primary education in five countries, which covers the entire gamut from national policy to the classroom interactions of teachers and children, see Alexander (2000).

4. When the Commons Education Committee was enquiring into the work of OFSTED during 1998–9, I drew attention to the discrepancy between OFSTED's published evidence and its public pronouncements on the question of the relationship between curriculum breadth and balance and standards in the basics. The Committee endorsed my concern (House of Commons Education and Employment Committee, 1999).

5. Education Reform Act 1988, chapter 1; Education Act 1996, chapter 1.

References

Alexander, R. J. (1984) *Primary Teaching*, Chapter 3. London: Cassell.

Alexander, R. J. (1995) *Versions of Primary Education*, Chapter 6. London and New York: Routledge.

Alexander, R. J. (1996) *Other Primary Schools and Ours: Hazards of International Comparison.* Warwick: Centre for Research in Elementary and Primary Education.

Alexander, R. J. (2000) *Culture and Pedagogy: an International Comparative Study of Primary Education.* Oxford: Blackwell.

Bruner, J. S. (1963) *The Process of Education.* New York: Random House.

Central Advisory Council for Education (England) (1967) *Children and Their Primary Schools.* London: HMSO.

Dearing, R. (1993) *The National Curriculum and its Assessment: Interim Report.* York and London: NCC/SEAC.

Department of Education and Science (1978) *Primary Education in England: a Survey by HM Inspectors of Schools.* London HMSO.

Department of Education and Science (1985) *The Curriculum from 5 to 16: Curriculum Matters 2.* London: HMSO.

DfEE (1998a) *The National Literacy Strategy: Framework for Teaching.* London: DfEE.

DfEE (1998b) *The Implementation of the National Numeracy Strategy: the Final Report of the Task Force.* London: DfEE.

DfEE and QCA (1999) *The National Curriculum: Handbook for Primary Teachers in England.* London: DfEE/QCA.

DfEE Numeracy Task Force (1998) *Mathematics Matters.* London: DfEE.

Galton, M. (1998) *Reliving the ORACLE Experience: Back to the Basics or Back to the Future?* Warwick: Centre for Research in Elementary and Primary Education.

Halpin, T. (1998) The trio of academics failing our schools, by Woodhead. *Daily Mail,* 26 February.

Kelly, A. V. (1990) *The National Curriculum: a Critical Review.* London: Paul Chapman.

Le Métais J. and Tabberer, R. (1997) *International Review of Curriculum and Assessment Frameworks: Comparative Tables.* Slough: NFER.

House of Commons Education and Employment Committee (1999) *Fourth Report of the Education and Employment Committee, Session 1998–9: the Work of OFSTED.* Volume I, paras 220–1, and Volume III, pp. 153–5.

Luxton, R. and Last, G. (1997) *Underachievement and Pedagogy.* London: National Institute for Economic and Social Research.

National Forum for Values in Education and the Community (1996) *Consultation on Values in Education and the Community.* London: SCAA.

OFSTED/DfEE (1997) *National Curriculum Assessment Results and the Wider Curriculum at Key Stage 2: Some Evidence from the OFSTED Database.* London: OFSTED/DfEE.

Prais, S. J. (1997) *School Readiness: Whole Class Teaching and Pupils' Mathematical Achievement.* London: National Institute for Economic and Social Research.

Reynolds, D. and Farrell, S. (1996) *Worlds Apart? A Review of International Surveys of Educational Achievement Involving England.* London: OFSTED.

Robinson, P. (1999) The tyranny of league tables: international comparisons of educational attainment and economic performance, in R. J. Alexander, P. Broadfoot and D. Phillips (eds) *Learning from Comparing: New Directions in Comparative Educational Research, Volume I.* Oxford: Symposium Books, pp. 217–36

School Curriculum and Assessment Authority (1997) *Developing the School Curriculum: a Framework.* London: SCAA.

Woodhead, C. (1998) Blood on the tracks: lessons from the history of educational reform. RSA Annual Lecture, 24 February.

3

Primary Practice in Historical Context

Brian Simon

The nature of primary teaching has become a highly charged political issue over the last few years. This has been marked by a strong, indeed almost unceasing, attack on 'modern' (sometimes called 'progressive') methods in the primary school by powerful sections of the media (especially the tabloid press), supported, on occasion, by government spokespersons (for instance, Kenneth Clarke, when Secretary of State for Education and Science, 1991–92). These have focused on a call for the return to streaming, whole-class teaching, and of course for more 'rigorous' assessment and testing. There has also been a call for a return to subject teaching (language, maths, science, technology, history, geography, and so on), fuelled by the imposition of the National Curriculum (defined on a subject basis) in place of topic and project work involving integrated (or cross-curriculur) approaches. The report of the so-called 'Three Wise Men', commissioned by the government and published early in 1992, raised all these, and other related issues (Alexander, Rose and Woodhead, 1992). A widespread discussion is taking place about the nature and purpose of primary education among teachers and more widely among the public as a whole.

There is a tendency, in this discussion, to present 'traditional' and 'progressive' approaches as stark alternatives, and to see the issue as one of struggle between these, as if each was, in practice, the opposite of the other, and as if all schools fell into one or other of these categories. But, as I hope to show, this is not an accurate representation of the position. The situation, both in the schools themselves and in thinking about primary education, is a great deal more complex than this reduction to a struggle between opposites appears to indicate. In order to understand something of this complexity, it is worth looking briefly at the way primary education has developed historically, and tease out some of the influences which have formed its procedures in terms of both school organisation and classroom teaching.

The first thing to get clear is that primary schooling has a long history, and that it came into being in specific circumstances that determined its nature – in the early days at least. Elementary education for Britain's then enormous working class was imposed as compulsory during the 1870s, but was first established, in its 'modern' form, earlier – at the beginning of the nineteenth century. That the workers should be educated (or schooled, rather), was very widely seen as a *political* (and economic) necessity by

41

about 1870. This perception was closely related to the extension of the franchise (in 1867) and to a growing awareness of the strength of foreign competition fuelled by more advanced systems of education on the Continent. However, in the closing decades of the nineteenth and early twentieth centuries, the determination to educate the workers led to overcrowded schools with huge classes (between 50 and 100 was common), while fully trained teachers formed only a small minority of those coping with them. In order to get by, the strictest discipline was imposed; very precise classroom procedures were devised while the teaching itself was (indeed, had to be) exclusively didactic, involving drill methods, much class repetition, and so on.

There was very little scope for creativity in these schools – informal relations between pupils and teachers were impossible. Considerable reliance was placed on corporal and other forms of punishment. The system of 'payment by results', brought in during the 1860s and remaining in force until the late 1890s, linked the individual teacher's salary with the number of passes pupils achieved in annual exams in 'the basics' conducted by HMIs. As a direct result of all these influences a highly mechanised system of teaching was fastened on the schools, their teachers and pupils, and it was this system that flourished up to and beyond the First World War and that provided the soil from which present practices grew. Of course, this system was outwardly successful – in the sense that the imposition of schooling in this form did result in the production of a literate population in terms of both language (reading and writing) and numeracy (facility with the manipulation of figures in simple sums). The system also, of course, brought the entire child population within the area of organised and institutionalised schooling and so, in a sense, promoted their disciplining as 'citizens'.

However, while this huge system was being built up (with extraordinary rapidity), certain developments were taking place which began to call such procedures into question. Quite outside the now publicly provided system (under the control of the School Boards, as they were called), new, and certainly more liberal, approaches were being developed in the nurseries and 'kindergartens' being set up for middle-class children, especially in London and the North (particularly Manchester and Leeds, where German immigrants, often successful industrialists, were prominent). These took their inspiration from the work of the German (Prussian) educator Friedrich Froebel. Influenced by the innovative Swiss teacher and educator, Pestalozzi, Froebel's activities had, in the 1860s, come under the political ban in Prussia as a clear reaction to his liberal outlook.

Here, the approach to education and teaching took a very different route from that of the mass elementary schools just described. Classes were, of course, small, while Froebelian philosophy emphasised the child's inner development, and provided scope for, and encouraged, his or her spontaneous activity. Froebel held that each child was born with certain inner qualities, or propensities, and that it was the job of the educator, during the child's early years, to 'make the inner outer', as he put it. Didactic teaching, at this stage, was inappropriate, even deadly. What was needed was the provision of a rich environment giving scope for children's many-sided activity, the satisfaction of their curiosity and so on. The teacher's job was primarily to facilitate this development – to provide the conditions for the child's growth.

This view of education, already making a considerable impact in the period 1860 to 1900, was reinforced by the influence of the American philosopher and educationist John Dewey, by that of the Italian Maria Montessori, and in England by the influence of another remarkable woman, Margaret McMillan, the real founder of the nursery school movement in Britain. Indeed, the whole issue exploded in 1911 when Edmond Holmes, the ex-Senior Chief Inspector of Schools (a very prestigious post), wrote, after retirement, a striking book entitled *What Is and What Might Be*. This contained a searing critique of the over-didactic and anti-humanist nature of mass elementary education, as well as a passionate description of an (actually existing) country school utilising modern methods, based on an amalgam of the teaching of the educationists just mentioned. Holmes in fact proposed that our entire system should be transformed along the 'progressive' lines implemented by his Egeria – the head of the (anonymous) school he described in his book. Coming from such a source, this book was widely influential; indeed, the whole movement favouring 'progressive' forms of education was soon to be institutionalised through the establishment of the New Education Fellowship in the early 1920s. Although centred on private schools, this movement (for the 'New Education') carried all before it from an ideological point of view during the 1920s and 1930s – greatly assisted by a shift in the general mood relating to education as a result of the horrifying experience of the First World War. By 1939, a leading historian has concluded, a watered-down progressivism had become the 'intellectual orthodoxy' amongst most leading educationalists (Selleck, 1972, p. 156), even if practice in the elementary schools remained primarily didactic (classes remained large in those days, so the scope for informality and 'progressive' approaches was necessarily limited).

But there was one area where the new approaches could effect a significant entry to the heart of the state system: within the few nursery schools now brought into being and also, by extension, within the infant schools. These latter have a long history of enlightened practice, going right back to the early years of the nineteenth century when Robert Owen established his famous infant school (for children aged 2 and upwards) at his model factory at New Lanark. This tradition was fractured, but, almost by chance, the 1870 Act made school entry at the age of 5 compulsory – earlier than every other European country – while infant schools (or departments) for children aged 5 to 7 were established as separate entities within elementary schools. These achieved a certain independence, even in the late nineteenth century. It was here that Froebelian influences were concentrated,

some School Boards, for instance, attempting to bring in somewhat mechanised versions of Froebelian methods and approaches. When, in the 1960s,
there took place what some have called the 'break-out' in primary education, it was practice as developed independently in the infant schools which
now spread upwards into the junior school range (7 to 11). This needs to be
borne in mind.

As already mentioned, in spite of the hegemony (or primacy) of 'progressive' approaches intellectually (as it were) in the inter-war period, the
actual conditions within the schools acted as a powerful force preventing
any transformation of the system at that time. However, during this period,
the seeds of change were planted through structural reorganisation, and
this slowly began to create a new situation. These changes were signalled
by three influential reports from the Consultative Committee to the Board
of Education – an official advisory body which no longer exists. This consisted of educationists – teachers, administrators and others – but having
considerable prestige at that time, and given the responsibility of charting
the way forward. The first of these, the Hadow Report of 1926, proposed
what became finally the break at age 11 – and so the establishment of
separate primary schools catering for children aged 5 or 7 to 11. Earlier
these had been lumped in with older children in all-age elementary schools
taking children from 5 to 14. The Hadow reorganisation on these lines was
accepted as official government policy in 1928. By the outbreak of the
Second World War, in 1939, roughly half the children aged 5 to 11 were in
separate primary (or infant and junior) schools or departments, half remaining in the old-type 'all-age' elementary schools.

Now, for the first time, it was possible to consider the needs of children
of primary school age as an entity, and in 1931 and 1933 the Consultative
Committee produced two more important reports, one on the primary
school (Hadow, 1931), the other on infant and nursery schools (Hadow,
1933). Both these reports, which also received official support, were highly
influential in the development of thinking about primary education; both
fundamentally accepted, and propagated, a 'progressive', 'child-centred'
approach. Both included the same key phrase identifying the nature of a
true education as the Committee saw it: 'The curriculum of the primary
school,' the reports affirmed, 'is to be thought of in terms of activity and
experience, rather than of knowledge to be acquired and facts to be stored.'
This emphasis on 'activity and experience' marked a fundamental change
in thinking about the main thrust of education at the primary stage, and
was to prove highly influential when conditions improved within primary
schools in the late 1950s and 1960s.

Following the Second World War, the opportunity for any serious break-
out from the didacticism of the past (inherited from the nineteenth
century) was lost; primary education now went through a critical phase
and, in a sense, one marked by increasing frustration which lasted some 20
years (1945 to 1965). The immediate cause of this had more to do with
secondary than primary education. The 1944 Education Act, as is well

known, introduced 'secondary education for all' – indeed, that was its great achievement. But although this Act did not lay down how this secondary education should be organised (it had to be provided to meet 'the different ages, abilities and aptitudes' of the children), in practice governments in the post-war period, both Labour (1945–51) and Conservative (1951–64), imposed the 'tripartite' system of parallel grammar, technical and modern schools. Of these the grammar schools monopolised the road to opportunity (professions, universities, and so on), so that competition to enter these escalated rapidly, the decision as to whether a particular child should gain entry being determined by performance at the 11-plus examination. By definition, only about 25 per cent, on average, were or could be successful; the rest were relegated to the modern school (technical schools only took about 3 per cent of the age group). To do the best by their pupils, all primary schools that were large enough now adopted the system of streaming, whereby the intake was divided into two, three or more streams according to the pupils' performance at the age of 7 (sometimes earlier) on a juvenile test, usually of 'intelligence'. This system had, in fact, been strongly recommended by the inter-war report on the primary school (Hadow, 1931), on the advice of the leading educational psychologist at that time, Cyril Burt.

Two circumstances emerging at this time increased the pressure on primary schools to adopt this method of inner-school organisation. The first related to enhanced parental aspirations for their children which emerged as a significant factor following the Second World War. Only those selected for 'A' streams had any serious chance of passing the 11-plus, for which young children were now increasingly prepared while at school. Second, governments now gave priority to completing Hadow 'reorganisation' when building materials at last became available in the 1950s, so that the remaining 50 per cent of children in the old all-age schools were, over a period, now provided for in separate junior or primary schools. This was the condition making streaming possible and, as Brian Jackson (1964) put it, streaming spread 'with barely credible rapidity' throughout the country. Indeed, the late 1950s and early 1960s were the high point of this form of inner-school organisation.

One aspect of streaming is that it permitted the extension of inherited didactic teaching procedures, in theory at least. A streamed class was supposed to contain children of a similar level of 'ability' (or 'intelligence'). It was theoretically (or intellectually) respectable, therefore, to continue to rely on whole-class teaching as the main approach, and this also, of course, allowed a further lease of life to the didacticism which, as we have seen, was endemic within elementary (and so primary) education from the start. In other words, during these 20 post-war years, the situation became crystallised. Primary schools were bound into a rigid and precise structure through this form of organisation, legitimised both by the actual existence of the 11-plus exam, and by the theory and practice of 'intelligence' testing which, with its insistence on the inborn, fixed and unchangeable nature of 'intelligence', seemed to give educational credence to this form of organisation. As everything ground almost to a halt it was difficult to see by what means any serious transformation of the situation could be brought about.

However, just such a transformation was in view, and it came suddenly and with extraordinary rapidity in the late 1960s and early 1970s. Its fundamental causation must be found among the economic and social, and indeed scientific and technological, changes which characterised British society in the post-war period – particularly the growth of new, science-based occupations consequent upon the 'third industrial revolution'. All this certainly led to enhanced aspirations on the part of parents for their children and, with this, a strong shift of opinion against the divided and crystallised system which determined, at so early an age, children's opportunities and so their futures.

This movement of opinion expressed itself educationally in a very strong grass-roots movement, or swing, against the 11-plus and the then existing divided system of secondary education, and as a consequence, in favour of the comprehensive secondary school. Such views spread rapidly throughout the country from the late 1950s and early 1960s, culminating in the issue of Circular 10/65 by the Labour government in July 1965, requesting local authorities to submit plans for comprehensive education. It became a 'roller coaster', in Margaret Thatcher's words, in the early 1970s, so that, by the early 1990s, well over 90 per cent of secondary pupils (in the maintained system) were in comprehensive schools in England, over 95 per cent in Wales, and 100 per cent in Scotland.

At the same time, primary schools, liberated (if that is the right word) from the exigencies of preparing children for the 11-plus, now began to abandon streaming – a deliberate act undertaken by the teachers in individual schools, but one which developed with extraordinary rapidity during the mid to late 1960s and early 1970s. The Plowden Committee, which issued the last report of the Central Advisory Council for Education (England) in 1967, itself proposed the abandonment of streaming, and there is no doubt that this recommendation had a profound effect.

This created a new situation. As schools unstreamed, teachers, who generally by now strongly supported this move, had to work out for themselves how to cope in the new situation. There was little or no official advice. Research studies had not yet penetrated the classroom to any extent; there was, therefore, little information as to what was actually happening. The Plowden Committee, while recommending unstreaming, did not tangle with the issue as to *how* the unstreamed class should be organised and *how* its teaching should be structured, except in the most general way. What took the place of the streamed 'homogeneous' classes for whom didactic, whole-class teaching had been seen as appropriate, was the so-called 'informal' classroom where children worked as individuals or in groups under the aegis of the teacher. New, more flexible, techniques had to be developed. What followed was a period of experiment, of trial and error, by hundreds, indeed thousands, of individual teachers, assisted, for the most part, by local advisers (who were learning from the teachers' experience as much as vice versa).

There was a powerful shift in these years towards creative activities of all kinds, but especially in the field of music, dance, drama, art and crafts, and writing. Many primary schools were transformed as ideas, long current, could actually now be implemented (by now the size of classes had been reduced). There was, however, certainly less emphasis on intellectual, cognitive or concept development as an educational goal, even though much effort was made to bring a new understanding of mathematics into the primary school. There is no doubt also that pupil–teacher relations became easier, more friendly and informal. Researchers have shown, however, that it would be wrong to over-emphasise the significance of the transformation. The great mass of primary schools did not suddenly transform themselves – far from it. Surveys have shown that the old-established emphasis on 'the basics' continued in most schools, that the traditional narrowness that marked elementary education still persisted. The ideal 'Plowden-type' primary schools identified by the Committee in their report formed only a small proportion of all such schools.[1] Nevertheless, there certainly had been an important shift of emphasis.

The Plowden Report (1967) – the most recent and massive examination of primary school procedures and practices – has been criticised for the emphasis given to the uniqueness of each individual child, and therefore for too great a stress on the need to *individualise* the teaching–learning process. If each child has to be treated individually, it is argued, the complexity of classroom organisation becomes overwhelming, while, at the same time, it becomes impossible to develop effective pedagogic means relevant to the needs of children generally. It was criticism of this kind which was to come to the fore in the new circumstances created by the passage of the Education Reform Act of 1988 and subsequent developments.

The Act created a new situation in English (and Welsh) education through its imposition of a National Curriculum defined in terms of nine separate subjects, together with their programmes of study, attainment targets and standard assessment tasks (SATs). Primary schools, while certainly retaining subject teaching in some areas (for instance, English and mathematics), also relied extensively on topic and project work, interdisciplinary in nature, to cover other areas of knowledge and skills. For the latter, group and individual work tended to predominate. The requirements of the National Curriculum, however, clearly challenged classroom procedures which had developed following the 1960s. As mentioned at the start of this chapter, a widespread discussion now took place on primary school practices, led, in part, unusually by the Secretary of State himself, who encouraged a rethink though suggesting a return to the more directly didactic approaches of the past.[2]

The outcome was the appointment of the committee of inquiry into primary education late in 1991, with a brief to report in six weeks. This they achieved. Their report recognised that the imposition of the National Curriculum, together with its attendant assessment requirements, has set quite new problems for schools and their teachers. These problems will certainly require new solutions and the report itself made many suggestions. Some quite radical revision of the National Curriculum was also suggested and, it is generally agreed, this also is necessary. Primary teachers were known to be under excessive pressure in their attempts to carry it through as proposed.

In facing the new situation, thinking based on over-simplified reduction of differences of view to that of the crude dichotomy between 'traditional' and 'progressive' approaches is less than helpful. The primary teacher has enormous responsibilities, involving promoting both the social and the intellectual development of young children. But a great deal more is known about the nature of children's mental development that was the case 50 or more years ago.

The teacher, and her advisers, need now to work out, in the new situation, approaches which are most relevant, and most effective, in promoting learning, and in developing pupils' abilities and skills across a very wide range of activities. What also has to be worked out in the new situation relates to the search for the most effective forms of classroom organisation to achieve these aims.

There is not likely to be any simple answer. Over the years the teaching profession has built up an enormous fund of experience and so of knowledge as to different approaches. This provides a firm base for the future given that there is a readiness to jettison obsolete practices in the light of evidence, and to continue the search for new and more effective ways of promoting growth, intellectual and other, among those most resilient and rewarding of subjects, the primary school pupils.

Notes

1. For an analysis of the Plowden Committee's findings on this question, see Simon (1981).
2. 'Primary Education – a Statement' by Secretary of State for Education and Science Kenneth Clarke, DES 412/91, 3 December 1991.

References

Alexander, R., Rose, J. and Woodhead, C. (1992) *Curriculum Organisation and Classroom Practice in Primary Schools: a Discussion Paper*. London: DES.
Hadow Report (1926) *The Education of the Adolescent*. London: HMSO.
Hadow Report (1931) *The Primary School*. London: HMSO.
Hadow Report (1933) *Infant and Nursery Schools*. London: HMSO.

Jackson, B. (1964) *Streaming: an Education System in Miniature*. London: Rout-
   ledge & Kegan Paul.
Plowden Roport (1967) *Children and their Primary Schools*, 2 vols. London:
   HMSO.
Selleck, R. J. W. (1972) *English Primary Education and the Progressives, 1914–1939*.
   London: Routledge & Kegan Paul.
Simon, B. (1981) The primary school revolution: myth or reality? In B. Simon and J.
   Willcocks (eds) *Research and Practice in the Primary Classroom*. London: Rout-
   ledge & Kegal Paul.

4

Continuing Professional Development: Nurturing the Expert Within

Marion Dadds

The Teacher Training Agency is currently elaborating its framework for continuing professional development (CPD) as part of its national strategy for teacher education. When it is implemented this will be another historic innovation in educational reform.

A good national plan that recognises the continuing needs of teachers as learners in a changing society is to be welcomed. Multiple and complex social change places multiple demands on teachers. A well-educated, flexible, highly competent teaching force is required to handle these changes and to foster practices which are responsive to the educational needs of all children.

Within the Teacher Training Agency framework for CPD outlined to date, however (Millett, 1996), an educative view of professional development has yet to be conceptualised. An educative model is necessary in order to avoid perpetuation of the 'delivery' model of teaching which has characterised the implementation of national curriculum, national testing and school inspection. The teacher-as-technician model associated with the delivery concept of educational reform, in which the teacher is positioned as the uncritical implementer of outside policies, is inappropriate for developing a well-educated teaching force. For several years, many have been worried about the tendency towards these technicist, 'empty vessel' models of educational reform in which the teacher's role is to receive, and deliver, centrally packaged decisions. 'Delivery' or 'empty vessel' models of educational reform are, essentially, crude behaviourist models which assume erroneously that 'good practice' will come about from those outside schools making judgements for, and on, those inside. On their own they are extremely limited because they have little, if anything, to say about the crucial role of teachers' understandings about, and experiences of, children in the development of their work. Nor do they have anything to say about the variety and complexity of processes which teachers undergo as they continue to learn about their professional craft; as they continue to gain new knowledge and understanding; reconstruct their attitudes, beliefs, practices; struggle with the difficulties of the change process. Nor do delivery models fully account for the complexities of curriculum as experienced and 'received' by children, as teachers mediate between standard reforms and the educational needs of unique learners.

Delivery models are also dangerous, for they assume that those who work closest to children should have their thinking about the nature of 'good practice' arranged for them by those outside schools. It cannot be in the best interests of our children to be educated by teachers whose intellect and professionalism are viewed in this way. It is antithetical to democracy and the educative enterprise.

On the other hand, professional development based upon the cultivation of informed understanding, judgement and 'voice' can help to counteract the more obvious failings of the worst delivery models. This style of professionalism may be essential for the best of our national arrangements to be transformed into worthwhile learning experiences for children. Here, the inner knowledge, judgement and wisdom of the professional teacher is seen as one of the greatest resources available to children. As such, they must be nurtured and enriched through CPD courses and other experiences.

Teachers and headteachers do not enter into CPD as empty vessels. They bring existing experiences, practices, perspectives, insights and, most usually, anxieties about the highly complex nature of their work. They usually enter CPD courses brimful of thoughts and feelings; with implicit or explicit beliefs about education and their work with children. They come with differences, disagreements, preconceptions, uncertainties, missions. These are all useful resources which can be drawn upon and studied in CPD processes.

Tragically, however, many come with a convincing feeling that what is inside them is not valid because it is 'only personal' to them. Somewhere along the line, many have learnt to feel that others' visions and experiences are much better than their own. They have learnt to seek the 'expert' outside but deny that there may be a potential 'expert' within. Somewhere, somehow, they have been taught to devalue their inner voice, their own experience, their own hard-earned insights about children and classrooms. The imposition on schools of educational reform from 'multiple structures of outside expertise' (Dadds, 1996) in the shape of the School Curriculum and Assessment Authority, the Office for Standards in Education (OFSTED) and, now, the Teacher Training Agency, may be exacerbating this. Many feel increasingly surrounded by a growing number of organisations and pressure groups claiming to know about their insider work and, what is more, to know better, including government, media, industrialists and, periodically, members of the royal family.

Many teachers and headteachers coming to CPD courses in recent years report being on the brink of bowing out to 'the experts'. 'Let's stop struggling and just give them what they want,' said one primary headteacher to me recently on a course I was running (not an uncommon sentiment), in response to the Chief Inspector, Chris Woodhead's latest exposition about class teaching on the BBC television programme *Panorama* (Woodhead, 1996). These conditions of dominant outside expertise, backed by structures of power, make it more difficult to foster good quality professional development that generates wise judgement and action from the inside, especially when this involves radical insider critique of the outsider, centralist agenda. Yet how unwise it would be to leave uncultivated, unrecognised and unused, the perspectives of those who work closest to children on a daily basis.

In this national 'delivery culture' which has evolved since 1988, many attenders on CPD courses have pinned their hopes on finding someone else's Holy Grail as the ultimate answer to the complexities and dilemmas of their work. They hope that a CPD course will establish what Schön (1971) has called 'the stable state' when all will be manageable, understandable, unproblematic. The 'outside expert' is often elevated to saintly status, a responsibility far beyond the liking of most. Those seeking stable state answers from others may feel disappointed with their formal CPD course, even though they know in their hearts that their expectations are unrealistic. Life, classrooms and schools will never be straightforward and unchallenging. And in these cases, we are reminded again of the dangers of erecting systems totally upon outsider, expert views. No one has simple, tidy solutions to the complex challenges and demands of teaching and management. There are practices, words of advice, tips, debates, theories to share and examine along the way. But at the centre of professional development there has to be the nurturing of inner wisdom and critical judgement about what can be provided for each child in each situation. This is the practitioner's responsibility. This is why the inner voice must be cultivated; personal theories must be evolved; belief in and responsibility for the professional self seen as crucial and indispensable. Outsiders' theories can be drawn upon, used, judged, engaged. But they can only ever be supportive resources in the development of this informed and sensitive inner judgement.

Educational reform initiatives which do not focus on developing these inner resources are not, in the long term, good value for money. Of course, teachers and headteachers rightly expect to draw upon others' expertise and knowledge during a structured professional development course; to meet many new and stimulating ideas and practices; to know something not known before; to extend their repertoire of understanding, attitudes and skills. They hope to meet course tutors and course members who can help to expand their views of what is desirable and possible in classrooms with children. They hope to formulate their thinking a little more coherently than before; to feel empowered to develop practices with more confidence, insight and commitment. Yet even the longest CPD course is short compared to the never-ending learning required of good professional development. This is why the evolution of informed personal theories of practice is crucial. When the formal CPD course has ended, professional judgement in the classroom goes on, often without continuing support. So the learning has to be made personal for it to be used independently.

The following example of powerful professional development reminds us that significant growth can never be based on transmission or delivery of facts and information alone. The teacher's learning was triggered by an African-American grandmother's reaction to her granddaughter's standardised test score report. The teacher told the story to her professional development group. Lessons were drawn about the moral and human nature of assessment systems.

> [The] grandmother brought the point home to me. She took righteous exception to the 'failing marks' I reported for her granddaughter. She said, 'What does this say about my child – that she's a moron, she's stupid and slow? Does it say that I read to her every night? Does it say that her mother's in jail and her daddy died last year? Does it tell you that she's getting her life together, slowly? Does it say that she's learning songs for Sunday School? Does it say she wants to be a doctor? What does this piece of paper say about my baby? I don't want it near her. She needs good things. She's had enough in her life telling her that she's no good. She doesn't need this and I won't have it. If your school can't come up with some better ways to know what my child can really do, then I refuse to sign a piece of paper that says my child is no good.'
>
> (Hollingsworth, 1994, p. 29)

There is so much to admire about the teacher who shared this story with her in-service colleagues. First, she seems to have been brave enough to open her learning to public debate. Second, she seems to have been wise enough to take the shock of this incident as an opportunity for her own growth. She learned something radical and she learned it painfully. Third, she was honest enough to acknowledge the tension between her own beliefs and the school practices within which she operated for she added that 'the grandmother expressed for me the misgivings we have about how we support the children in our schools'. There are lessons here for us all.

Jane's learning was just as powerful. She attended a CPD course on reading which I ran and decided to study a 'difficult' child in her class who was experiencing literacy problems. Jane wanted to understand better the nature of the difficult behaviour and the reading problems. She wanted to develop practices that would help. Her search for understanding of the child turned into a deeper, if more painful, understanding of herself as a teacher. As she probed and reflected, she began to wonder if her own attitudes and behaviour were part of the child's problems. As she explored her feelings for the child and ways of interacting, she saw a somewhat negative and hostile teacher. And she did not like what she saw. So a study which started as a search for understanding of a child turned into one in which the teacher felt it necessary to reconstruct her own sense of 'self'. The child's reading experiences and behaviour were caught up in this complex web.

Stuart's learning was as radical in a different way. He trialled the language experience approach to reading with Michael, an 11-year-old who had made very little progress over the years with other methods and whom previous teachers had, by now, confirmed as a 'non-reader'. This method worked spontaneously to create motivation and interest. With Stuart, Michael produced his own books which he wanted, and was able, to read. The method unlocked energies which had not previously been seen, for

Michael saw himself and his life written into his personal literature. Needless to say, the teachers simultaneously reviewed their image of the child. He was no longer seen as a 'non-reader' but, rather, a child who had not learned to read with the previous less personalised methods. As another teacher said recently, who had a similar experience during this same course, 'I had to stop looking for the problem in the child and start looking at what contribution our methods might be making to the failure.'

The willingness of these teachers to study and question their work closely and in depth is admirable. Such a disposition provides the crucial inner conditions for growth and for professional development which changes the world in small but significant ways for children.

This kind of learning demands open-mindedness to new possibilities. There is also a resolve to ask searching questions of practice and to confront one's existing assumptions. The examined questions which arise for teachers from their daily practices with children, and which often challenge basic assumptions (Abercrombie, 1960), can be central to professional learning (Drummond, 1995). But the intellectual and affective processes set in motion by such questioning are not always comfortable (e.g. Dadds, 1993; Drummond, 1995; Nias, 1987). Fortitude and courage are needed. Receiving facts and information is as nothing in comparison.

Such learning also, usually, needs time and does not come simply as a result of awareness-raising of new content on in-service education and training (INSET) courses (although this can play a part within the complex learning process). The surface moments of insight usually mask deeper stages of maturing thinking which have been incubating over time. Jane's study, for example, took almost a year. No one could have 'poured' the learning into her, ready-made for her to 'deliver'.

Learning is a social experience, so professional growth is usually fostered through exchange, critique, exploration and formulation of new ideas. Language interaction in supportive and challenging collaborative contexts is often indispensable (Candy, Harri-Augstein and Thomas, 1985; Harris, 1983; Dadds, 1990; Nias, Southworth and Campbell, 1992). With the help of sympathetic others, the open-minded teacher-learner can scaffold his or her way to new states of knowing, feeling and acting in the interests of pupils. Talk is often the medium through which this multiple growth takes place, but the talk has to be relevant to the task. Practice seems to develop best, for example, when collaborative talk in the workplace or CPD course focuses upon pupil learning rather than extraneous matters; where 'teachers build up a shared language' (Smyth, 1991, p. 88). This is why outsider frameworks and processes such as those of OFSTED inspection may have little to offer to teachers' learning for they do not engage the insider with the outsider in well-structured, well-focused 'learning conversations' (Candy, Harri-Augstein and Thomas 1985, p. 115). Only when OFSTED inspectors go beyond the summative processes of the formal framework (subvert it, as some inspectors secretly say) and engage in formative feedback dialogue with heads and teachers, do they open up new possibilities for learning. The effectiveness of CPD experiences can, thus, be in great part a consequence of the learning context, be it that of the culture of a CPD course or the learning culture of the school and professional reference group (Dadds 1995). The values, attitudes, interactive practices within the learning context can have as great an influence on the learning teacher as his or her own inner qualities and professional drives. The development of inner expertise cannot be divorced from the nature of the outer context.

Thus, we see no 'empty vessel' professional development in these brief examples of teachers engaged in significant learning. These are glimpses of demanding and, often, dangerous engagement with deep questions about children's learning. They are stories of 'teachers as strangers' (Greene, 1973), working as intellectuals on their own practice, trying to see their teaching through fresh eyes in order to think of it anew.

This looking inwards is not egocentric. It is an essential act of professional responsibility, done in the cause of considering children's educational needs and rights. It is done for the purpose of understanding better how these needs and rights might be met. Others' theories and experiences can help to illuminate a way through these periods of reconstruction but they cannot be poured in ready tailored to do the complete job. Outsiders can help, advise, support, engage dialogically but the learning can only come from the active inner life, motivation and resources of the learner.

These are also teachers who have adopted the courage to 'struggle against unthinking submergence in the social reality that prevails' (Greene, 1973, p. 269), be it that of the school, the national framework or one's own ritualistic actions in the classroom. They have adopted a critical enquiry mode of development. And in confronting their own questions about the mysteries of learning, these teachers have turned to personal experience and insight as their tutors. They have launched themselves on their own learning journeys; have chosen to see through their own eyes (Greene, 1973) rather than those of others' borrowed visions.

These examples also show that professional learning is not simply a matter of 'reading off' others' expert theories and 'reading them in' unproblematically to practice (Hamilton, 1994). The stories show something of the complex relationship between knowing and acting. The journey of professional growth into new and better practices is often unpredictable; often non-linear; often emotional as well as cerebral. It demands the capacity and strength to ask questions; to analyse and interpret feedback; to discipline the emotions generated by self-study; to change established practices in the light of new understanding; to remain interested and professionally curious.

Let us hope, then, that a view of professional development predicated upon the growth of personal understanding, judgement and agency will find its necessary place in our new national plans as the framework is elaborated and translated into CPD practices. Let us hope that the notion of the 'reflective practitioner', scorned in the past by some politicians, will be given serious consideration by the Teacher Training Agency. Thoughtful, enquiring teachers with a sense of inner expertise and responsibility are well equipped to engage in the higher level, and rapid, daily deliberations of classrooms. They are also in an advantageous position to add their informed voice to the many debates we need to have about quality in education and the many critiques needing to be brought to some outsider perspectives as well as some insider practices. We must hope that there will be no more national systems based upon a behaviourist view of teachers, headteachers and curriculum, for if the system treats professionals like empty vessels we may reap the empty rewards sooner than we think. We want the best for our children. And there are more valid, if challenging, models of professional development to be had than the delivery one, for we know that 'it is in wondering and questioning that learning begins' (Greene, 1973, p. 268).

References

Abercrombie, M. L. J. (1960) *The Anatomy of Judgement*. London: Penguin.

Candy, P., Harri-Augstein, S. and Thomas L. (1985) Reflection and the self-organised learner, in D. Boud, R. Keogh and D. Walker (eds) *Reflection: Turning Experience into Learning*. New York: Kogan Page.

Dadds, M. (1990) Teacher appraisal for teacher development, *Cambridge Institute Newsletter*, January.

Dadds, M. (1993) The feeling of thinking in professional self study, *Educational Action Research*, Vol. 1, pp. 287–303.

Dadds, M. (1995) *Passionate Enquiry and School Development: a Story about Teacher Action Research*. London: Falmer Press.

Dadds, M. (1996) Supporting practitioner research: a challenge. Paper presented to conference, Supporting Practitioner Research: a Challenge, University of Cambridge, July

Drummond, M. J. (1995) Teachers asking questions. Paper presented to Association for the Study of Primary Education Annual Conference, September.

Greene, M. (1973) *Teacher as Stranger*. Belmont: Wadsworth.

Hamilton, D. (1994) Clockwork universes and oranges. Paper presented to British Educational Research Association Conference, Oxford, September.

Harris, I. B. (1983) Forms of discourse and their possibilities for guiding practice towards an effective rhetoric, *Journal of Curriculum Studies,* Vol. 15, pp. 27–42.

Hollingsworth, S. (1994) *Teacher Research and Urban Literacy Education*. New York: Teachers College Press.

Millett, A. (1996) *National Standards for Teachers*. London: Teacher Training Agency.

Nias, J. (1987) *Seeing Anew: Teachers' Theories of Action*. Geelong: Deakin University Press.

Nias, J., Southworth, G. and Campbell, P. (1992) *Whole School Curriculum Development in the Primary School.* London: Falmer Press.

Schön, D. (1971) *Beyond the Stable State*. London: Temple Smith.

Smyth, J. (1991) *Teachers as Collaborative Learners*. Buckingham: Open University Press.

Woodhead, C. (1996) BBC *Panorama,* June.

5

Horses for Courses or Courses for Horses: What is Effective Teacher Development?

Steven Higgins and David Leat

Introduction

In this chapter we aim to consider the issue of effective support for developing teachers' practice. It is stimulated by a realisation that there are radically different perspectives on teacher education and by a desire to bring some coherence to these potentially conflicting viewpoints. The first of these perspectives is personal and comes from a university education department where research and experience combine to indicate that trainee teachers are individuals with different responses to a one-year postgraduate teacher training course. In addition, we are mindful that the effect of teacher training institutions upon students may be somewhat less than might be hoped, as courses may influence students very little in their beliefs (Bramald, Hardman and Leat, 1995) and any effects may be 'washed out' in the first year of teaching (Zeichner and Tabachnik, 1981). The second perspective is in the light of current national debates about the training of pre-service teachers which represent teaching predominantly as a competence-based profession. Course requirements (TTA, 1997) for primary teacher training in the UK suggest that getting enough lectures about subject knowledge and effective teaching methods, and then being shown what to do, will meet all the needs of professional learning. The inspection system for Initial Teacher Training (ITT) has been made more rigorous and one institution has been closed after failing to meet required standards. The increasing involvement of the Teacher Training Agency (TTA) in continuing professional development seems likely to strengthen the competence approach to assessing professionalism. The final viewpoint is that of schools where there are a range of factors in play. These may be characterised as a tension between meeting demands for accountability (appraisal, inspection, league tables, etc.), whilst maintaining professional commitment towards developing practice. The dangers in getting this balance wrong is in one direction low morale and feelings of deprofessionalisation and in the other direction lack of public or political confidence in the teaching profession.

Each perspective tends to generate a particular or partial view of professional development. In this article we aim to give an overview of teacher development with these perspectives in mind, and to try to identify the strengths and weaknesses of these apparent perspectives. It is written with an acknowledged bias as we believe that the current climate does not give enough attention to individual development needs. However, the other perspectives have strong claims either through the legitimacy of power (the right of might) or the democratic claims of accountability.

We are, therefore, intending to offer help to those responsible for providing professional development by clarifying means and ends in teacher development which could therefore allow more informed choice of appropriate developmental strategies or approaches. It may also help to clarify some possible outcomes of government reforms in teacher education. The chapter deliberately uses a number of figures and diagrams. The intention of these is to present various aspects of teacher development visually, so that they can be more easily interpreted and related one to another – to provide a bigger picture.

Personal Experience and Perspective

Both authors work with emerging and experienced professionals: students on a one-year pre-service (PGCE) teacher training course, and groups of teachers in their first and second years of teaching as well as experienced teachers in a variety of in-service roles, including higher degree courses, school-based INSET sessions and curriculum development consultancy. In these roles we encounter the differing perspectives described earlier and we try to work with each as the context dictates. Our acquaintance with the literature on teacher development provided a spur to try to resolve contradictions as there are a number of paradigms which compete and overlap. Instead of just working with the perspectives as we encountered them, we felt that we needed to examine the relationships between them so that we could be more deliberate in our response to and our use of these perspectives in practical contexts. To give an extreme example, a struggling PGCE student will have different developmental requirements compared with an articulate Masters student pursuing an action research route.

Further stimulus came from an internal evaluation of an innovative programme of support for newly qualified teachers (Ford, Higgins and Oberski, 1996). The New Teacher in School programme (NTIS) is intended for those entering their first year of teaching and was introduced into the University of Newcastle's Continuing Professional Development (CPD) Programme in the autumn of 1994. The course is innovative in that few higher education establishments involved in postgraduate teacher training offer additional support of this nature. The programme runs over a period of two years. In year 1 there are three conferences complemented by a personal link with university tutors. In year 2 the programme is more intensive and involves regular evening sessions over two terms. As most of the participants came through Newcastle University's PGCE course it was a challenging opportunity to consider the effects of the pre-service training as well as how to work effectively with recently established professionals. This crystallised our perceptions of the competing perspectives on the newly qualified teachers both through their own words and through the words of some of the members of staff responsible for their development, including headteachers. The views held by senior staff tended to mirror those of most of the new teachers in that the needs of newly qualified teachers were seen to revolve around the practical issues of classroom management. However, one senior staff member acknowledged the more 'cerebral' nature of the university's perspective and this exemplified the view expressed by other headteachers that the advantage that the higher education could offer was in terms of providing a wider context in which to place Newly Qualified Teacher (NQT) development. Furthermore, one student valued the discussion about 'broader issues of education' typifying a more personal approach to professional development. A teacher in the second year of the programme indicated that she regarded the programme as a 'signpost which helped me remember where I was trying to get to'. Within this sample, therefore, there were many concerns about basic teaching competences, or the means of teaching, but also some desire to consider the ends.

As teacher education comes increasingly under the spotlight, there is a growing realisation of the need for greater continuity, which might provide an almost seamless progression from initial teacher education, through induction, to continuing professional development. This view is reinforced by the Teacher Training Agency's (TTA) involvement and identification of NQT status as one of the five steps in professional qualifications leading ultimately to headship. The implicit framework for a continuity of provision is to be welcomed. However, as it stands, the competence framework for such development is likely to omit a number of avenues for professional development, especially those which explore the purpose of education or teaching.

Conceptualisations of Teacher Development

A variety of models of teacher development have been offered in the literature. In our initial desire to understand the relationships between them, we attempted a simple mapping exercise, representing particular models as circles. By their relative position and overlap, we hoped to develop our understanding of them as a set (Figure 5.1). We also wondered whether the perspectives outlined in the introduction (personal, governmental and school) would neatly overlay our map. Although the mapping process advanced our thinking, the final picture was unsatisfactory as we could not adequately represent the complexity of relationships between the models in this way. Furthermore, the literature in relation to some of the conceptualisations is far from homogeneous. As Adler (1991) has noted in relation to the reflective paradigm, reflection does not mean the same thing to different authors. Cruikshank (1987), for example, describes a process in which teachers reflect in a journey towards mastering a prescribed set of teaching skills, whilst Zeichner and Tabachnik (1981) regard the process as critical enquiry into the purposes of education.

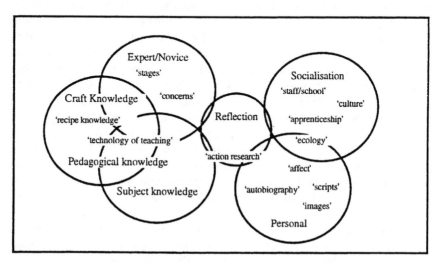

Figure 5.1   *Models of teacher development*

Although the mapping process failed, it reinforced an understanding that the models are not mutually exclusive. We felt strongly that they represent different perspectives, generated by different contexts and insights. Accordingly, we still felt that they could be placed in overarching frameworks which can then be used both to describe and understand the national debates, and clarify some of the confusion in what effective teacher development might be. Through such a framework one can be more conscious, deliberative and metacognitive in the choice of the model or dimension to suit a particular context or person. Each of the models has a number of assumptions, and when these are appreciated the selection can be more informed and deliberate. Without this understanding it is too easy to be hurried down one particular route or approach by dictat or custom without questioning the probable effect. As professionals in teacher education we have to be concerned about the purposes of our work. We are not simply technicians, we must consider means and ends in order to be effective.

Conceptualisations of teacher development can be categorised as to their intent. Some are descriptive and seek only to document the difference between teachers of different expertise (novice to expert models, e.g. Leinhardt,

1988; Livingstone and Borko, 1989). Others are explanatory and attempt to explain why teachers develop as they do as in the literature on images and autobiography (e.g. Knowles, 1992). We tried to add this further dimension to the model to show more appropriately how the different perspectives related to each other. This proved too complex to illustrate easily. Instead, we simplified the questions about the purposes of the models of *what* develops, *how* development happens (descriptive) *why* development occurs (explanatory) and *where* that development occurs (context). Our next step therefore was to try to align models in relation to these central enquiry questions:

- What changes?
- How and why do these changes take place?
- What influence does context have?

The self emerged as the most appropriate centrepiece of this diagram (see Figure 5.2). This diagram was a step forward as it helped to clarify the contribution that different models can make to teacher development. However, the diagram still had some frayed edges. Whilst the question. 'What?' is perhaps an appropriate headline for models relating to craft knowledge and subject or pedagogical knowledge, socialisation literature relates strongly to both the 'Where?' and 'How?' questions, which we have tried to indicate on the diagram. Our intention through the diagram is to encourage all those with a stake in teacher development to ask critical questions in professional development situations such as:

- Who is this person? Who are these people?
- What changes are we seeking?
- What is the significance of the context (school culture, socialisation, locality, etc.)?
- How might changes be effected?
- What are the likely consequences of choosing different approaches?

There are a number of areas of confusion which may appear if the assumptions and limitations of a specific conceptualisation are not made explicit. For example, in the novice to expert transition it is not clear how novices become expert. Rich (1993) clearly illustrates that expertise is not necessarily transferable to new teaching situations. We would further argue that because a novice to expert model is largely descriptive and centres on the question of what distinguishes experts, or what constitutes expertise, it is presumptuous to use it as a strong component in deciding the nature of professional development courses. So, for example, the TTA's proposed primary initial teacher education course requirements (TTA, 1997) demand high levels of input in relation to mathematics and English subject knowledge. These proposals have been reportedly based on reviews of literature on effective teachers in these subject areas. We seem to be proceeding on the assumption that if we deliver enough sessions on subject knowledge, subject application and technical skills, then trainee primary teachers will automatically be better prepared, but it does not *necessarily*

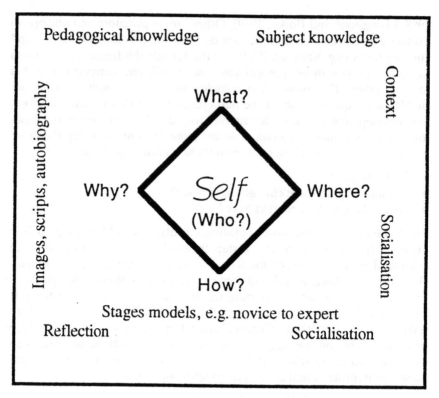

Figure 5.2   *What, why, how and where*

follow that addressing specific technical skills will lead to the desired development. We mean that an over-reliance on this thinking is in danger of ignoring how such expertise is really developed and the influence that context imposes – as through school placements. On the other hand, a reliance on reflective paradigms which use personal histories and images of teaching as raw materials can leave some teachers and student teachers frustrated by a lack of guidance for action (Leat, 1995). In this situation there is the danger that an explanatory theory becomes prescriptive.

It may be noted that these questions are framed as if voiced by an 'other', who could be an inspector, adviser, line manager, headteacher or tutor, which implies that the control of professional development is invested in these people. This, in itself, raises many questions about locus of control which we return to below.

Horses for Courses

As was alluded to earlier, individual teachers differ markedly, which is an unremarkable statement in itself. More significantly, their teaching styles differ (Tobin and Fraser, 1989), their views of teaching and learning differ (Cooper and McIntyre, 1996), their relationships with pupils vary (Wubbels and Levy, 1995) and they have differing effects on achievement. This variance would seem to argue for a differentiated approach to professional development: courses for horses, as our title suggests.

In Figure 5.3 we offer another diagrammatic representation, which elaborates this metaphor 'horses for courses'. Under the heading 'What changes' are listed some of the constructs used to describe teachers and their expertise. The horizontal parallel lines are labelled 'How' and these represent some of the professional development routes that could be offered to a teacher depending on the construct under development and the particular context. The point being made is that a conscious choice can be made in relation both to the construct chosen and the route offered, and this could be different for two teachers in the same school doing similar jobs. We appreciate that such a complex choice would need to be informed by a special insight, but we write with the purpose of building awareness of this understanding.

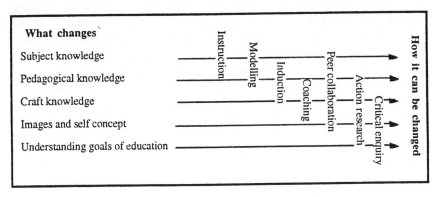

Figure 5.3 *'What' versus 'How'*

Some caveats have to be entered about the diagram. First, the 'routes' (shown vertically) are open to debate and clarification. We would encourage others to amend these terms or insert new ones. Secondly, we imply no preference by arranging them in the order shown. Critical enquiry is not better than instruction, it is different and is probably better suited to certain purposes. Thirdly, a period of professional development could include any combination of these routes; they are not mutually exclusive. Finally, the diagram is just that. If the letters on our routes do not cut a particular line we are not arguing that it is totally inappropriate for that construct.

By instruction we would mean lecture and seminar formats. We use modelling to mean conscious attempts to copy the thinking and actions of other teachers. Induction is used to describe formal and informal processes which communicate the routines, norms and values of an institution. By coaching we would mean professional development support that reaches inside the classroom, and provides both feedback and advice on performance. Peer collaboration represents professional growth achieved through working by choice with others in some joint venture. Action research is that cyclical process whereby teachers investigate their own practice, typically involving data collection, reflection and the reformulation of practice. By critical enquiry we mean a reflective process whereby aspects of the self are one focus of the enquiry, and in the process of development questions of the purpose of education and one's role in it are reviewed.

Our proposition, therefore, is that one approach to teacher development with a set agenda for what needs to be developed is clumsy in the extreme. No one approach is likely to meet the needs of teachers to improve their effectiveness. To consolidate this argument we present some brief examples from research literature on teacher differences.

Student teachers assume basic competence in the skills to make classrooms run smoothly at different rates. For example, Lawes (1987) found that student teachers' ability to judge pupils' comprehension, interest and ability from watching silent videotape of a class was related to the student's teaching effectiveness, as rated by the tutor and supervising teacher. Those who develop this perceptual ability quickly are ready to operate on this information whilst those who are slower will be delayed. With regard to more visible behaviour, Neil (1989) compiled ratings of student teachers from referees and at interview on posture, willingness to meet gaze, calmness of behaviour and gesture characterising enthusiastic speech. These ratings were compared with ratings during the course by supervising teachers and tutors of control, calmness, enthusiasm and progress, showing a positive relationship. He concluded: 'calm, dominant behaviour . . . seem(s) to allow student teachers to maintain control, they can then show their enthusiasm for their subject and thus build up positive relationships with classes'. The teaching skills described here might be characterised as first order. It is difficult to argue that the whole cohort in these two studies have the same developmental needs. The struggling students may benefit from a competence approach, with meticulous instruction, modelling and coaching, but this could constrain and frustrate those for whom such skills are easily developed.

Chandler, Robinson and Moyes (1991) used the construct of the proactive student teacher to correlate against ratings of performance. They described a small minority of students who have high levels of personal commitment and motivation who go beyond the normal expectations of traditional teaching. There is the implication here that we are now dealing with a smaller proportion of teachers who appear to be developing in a markedly different way. These teachers are innovative and willing to try things out, and these least cautious students were rated more highly than their more cautious contemporaries. This is an approach to learning which is not easily subsumed into a competence framework, nor to coaching or modelling; in such circumstances action research and the exploration of personal effectiveness seem better approaches.

Finally, the study by Rich (1993) throws issues of competence into stark relief. He describes an Israeli study in which a number of teachers who were rated by superiors as expert and a number who were not so rated were given instruction to allow them to implement co-operative group work in their classrooms. In the process of implementation all the teachers showed some characteristics of novices, including anxiety, in the classroom. Some experts emerged from the process as proficient in using co-operative groups, but not all. Furthermore, some of the non-expert teachers emerged as proficient in this new style. It would appear that the range of teachers in this study had very different experiences in the implementation process, which would argue for some differentiation in the professional development that they received.

Locus of Control

Who is in control of the development is a crucial issue. Any approach to professional development which ignores this issue is missing a vital component. The main dilemma in this area is about how precisely the outcomes of a programme of development can be specified.

Cole's (1991) idea of a community of learners aims to establish the ecological conditions for development, but this might not be acceptable to those requiring specific determinable outcomes from a programme of development. However, her observations about the pivotal role of the individual cannot be ignored. There are three main possibilities for considering who controls the development. First, there are the individuals themselves. The individual is the key to *any* development. All the subsequent models make the assumption that the individual is a willing and able participant in developmental programmes. Certain approaches such as the reflective paradigm or images and auto-biographical models make this explicit. The second grouping can broadly be described as managerial. Competence models fall into this category as they see development as identifiable and deliverable according to an institutional planning and implementation framework. Approaches using the school development plan would usually fit into this view as would novice to expert models and technical skills approaches. The third option for the locus of control is situational. In this the agent of change is seen from a situational or ecological viewpoint. Those developing or changing are not in complete or direct control, but are affected by the particular and complex context of their school. All of these viewpoints have some validity and they are not mutually exclusive. Development can perhaps be seen as the interplay between the different elements. In practice, change and development can and does occur in each of these areas. In order to promote efficient development it will be necessary to consider all of these aspects to see which is most relevant in order to be effective in particular circumstances. To some extent the particular focus will depend on desired outcomes.

In Figure 5.3 we suggested that a number of related approaches could be set against how development can be effected. In Figure 5.4 the locus of control shifts significantly across the development.

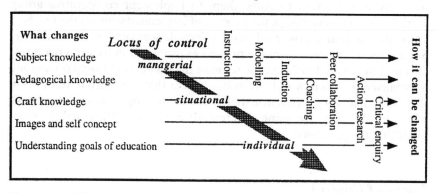

Figure 5.4   *What, how and the locus of control*

It is important to recognise that people are problematic if they think they are being manipulated, hence our concern that a perspective that only concentrates on the 'what' will fail to carry the teachers along with the intended development. The result is likely to be that the process of development will be inefficient and the desired outcome will not be reached as teachers adopt, adapt, and subvert new skills and techniques according to their existing practice, and their existing conceptualisations of teaching and learning.

In this chapter we are suggesting that the locus of control needs to be made explicit on two levels:

1. For those *working with* teachers. This will make deciding upon the means of development more conscious. The 'what' may be broadly agreed, but the process needs to take into account the complexity of individuals and contexts.

2. To raise awareness of *teachers themselves* as to the purpose of development. Studies such as Nolder and Johnson (1995) suggest that a crucial part of the process of professional practice development is making the process explicit to the learner.

Imposed development will clearly have an effect, but the results may not be those intended. Establishing procedures to enforce desired results will also have effects, again probably not those intended. Without consent, imposed development will be reinterpreted, and at best subverted or, more likely, ignored or refused. At worst, it will have unintended consequences that both sides agree are detrimental to pupils' learning. The perceived locus of control is an important part of this equation.

From a more theoretical stance, Ashcroft and Griffiths (1989), in advancing the cause of the reflective paradigm in teacher education in which critical enquiry is fundamental, argue that values related to open-mindedness, responsibility and wholeheartedness need to be developed. They quote Zeichner (1983): 'rather than just accepting existing traditions or curricula and imitating current practice, the effective teacher is seen as one who reflects on the question of what ought to be done.' There is reinforcement here, therefore, for the idea that a critical characteristic is both motivation and adventure: the energy, confidence and commitment to experiment, to try things out and take to risks.

Conclusions

Our conclusion is that the conceptualisations that we have discussed are incomplete and the perspectives that they offer, though valuable, do not encompass the complexity of developmental needs in particular individual circumstances. Our interpretation would be that the assumptions ignore the human complexity of professional or practice development. The choice of appropriate support for professional development needs to be more flexible, more informed and more deliberate if it is to be effective.

References

Adler S. (1991) The reflective practitioner and the curriculum of teacher education, *Journal of Education for Teaching,* Vol. 17, pp. 139–50.

Ashcroft, K. and Griffiths, M. (1989) Reflective teachers and reflective tutors: school' experience in an initial teacher education course, *Journal of Education for Teaching,* Vol. 15, pp. 35–52.

Bramald, R., Hardman, F. and Leat, D. (1995) Initial teacher trainees and their views of teaching and learning, *Teaching and Teacher Education,* Vol. 11 pp. 23–31.

Chandler, P., Robinson, W. P. and Moyes, P. (1991) Is a proactive student teacher a better student teacher? *Research in Education,* Vol. 45, pp. 41–52.

Cole, A. L. (1991) Relationships in the workplace: doing what comes naturally? *Teaching and Teacher Education,* Vol. 7, pp. 415–26.

Cooper, P. and McIntyre, D. (1996) *Effective Teaching and Learning.* Buckingham: Open University Press.

Cruikshank, D. R. (1987) *Reflective Teaching: the Preparation of Students of Teaching.* Reston: Association of Teacher Educators.

Ford, K., Higgins, S. and Oberski, I. (1996) *The New Teacher in School: Year One Evaluation Report.* Newcastle upon Tyne: Department of Education, University of Newcastle.

Knowles, J. G. (1992) Models for understanding pre-service and beginning teachers' biographies: illustrations from case studies, in I. Goodson (ed.) *Studying Teachers' Lives.* London: Routledge.

Lawes, J. S. (1987) Student teachers' awareness of pupils' non-verbal responses, *Journal of Education for Teaching,* Vol. 13, pp. 257–66.

Leat, D. (1995) The costs of reflection in initial teacher education, *Cambridge Journal of Education,* Vol. 25, pp. 161–73.

Leinhardt, G. (1988) Situated knowledge and experiences in teaching, in J. Calderhead (ed.) *Teachers' Professional Learning.* London: Falmer Press.

Livingstone, C. and Borko, H. (1989) Expert–novice differences in teaching: a cognitive analysis and implications for teacher education, *Journal of Teacher Education,* Vol. 40, pp. 36–42

Neil, S. R. St J. (1989) The predictive value of assessments of non-verbal skills of applications to postgraduate teacher training, *Journal of Education for Teaching,* Vol. 15, pp. 149–59.

Nolder, R. and Johnson, D. C. (1995) Professional development: bringing teachers to the centre of the stage, *Mathematics in School,* Vol. 24, pp. 32–46.

Rich, Y. (1993) Stability and change in teacher expertise, *Teaching & Teacher Education,* Vol. 9 pp. 137–46.

Tobin, K. and Fraser, B. J. (1989) Investigations of exemplary practice in high school science and mathematics, *Australian Journal of Education*, Vol. 32, pp. 75–94.

TTA (1997) *Training Curriculum and Standards for New Teachers,* Teacher Training Agency Consultation Document, Portland House. London: TTA.

Wubbels, T. and Levy, J. (1995) *Do You Know What You Look Like? Interpersonal Relationships in Education.* London: Falmer Press.

Zeichner, K. M. (1983) Alternative paradigms of teacher education, *Journal of Teacher Education,* Vol. 34, pp. 3–9.

Zeichner, K. M. and Tabachnik, B. R. (1981) Are the effects of university teacher education washed out by school experience? *Journal of Teacher Education,* Vol. 32, pp. 7–11.

Introduction to Section 2: Facilitating Professional Development

The chapters in this section have in common an approach to the professional development of teachers which moves beyond individual reflection on practice. A proliferation of terms such as 'reflection' 'reflection on practice', 'reflective practitioner', etc. have blurred the meaning of these words for teachers and the course of subsequent action is often indistinct. Almost every teacher education course in the UK over the past twenty years will have utilised at some time the notion of reflection on practice and encouraged trainee teachers to focus upon this as a means of professional development. The methods that have been used to encourage trainee teachers to do this will have been as various as the institutions they attended. The chapters in this section address this problem in a variety of ways, yet in all, the notion of a critical incident or phase alongside reflection is evident. In particular, the following themes are discussed by the authors:

- professional development through critical incidents, biographies, narratives and life history;
- individual versus collaborative professional development;
- reflective practice.

All the readings draw attention to issues associated with practitioners developing their own models of professional development through the exploration of personal issues and incidents in teachers' careers.

The sociological traditions upon which these ideas are based are most succinctly explained by C. Wright Mills (1961) who argued that in order to know how human beings define and create their sense of meaning it is necessary to explore the interrelationship between the individual and society. Mills referred to what he called the 'sociological imagination' which would enable an understanding of the larger historical scene and the relevance this has for the inner life and external career of individuals. He explored through the notion of 'personal troubles/public issues' how individuals are constrained by the institutions in which they work and how they may negotiate or construct meaning in order to make sense of their own lives. This idea has been more recently developed through the work of researchers who have used life history and autobiography in ethnographic

69

research (Burgess, 1984; Walford, 1987). Indeed, educational researchers now often borrow ideas from across disciplines as boundaries become more malleable and the genre blurred. Goodman (1998) describes an approach to educational research which has become known as critical ethnography, that synthesises theory and ethnographic research, as he argues that it is not possible to get away from ideology and biography. Personal lives and professional contexts are a complex and changing mosaic as political, private and public issues impinge upon everything we do.

In Chapter 6 by Kenneth Zeichner and Robert Tabachnick the authors note the diverse interpretations of reflective practice and explore the meanings and purposes that lie behind four different but overlapping traditions that have informed primary teaching and practices. These traditions are: the academic, which stresses the emphasis on subject matter and subsequent translation into knowledge; social efficiency, which emphasises the application of teaching strategies founded in research; developmentalist, which prioritises teaching that is sensitive to student interest; and finally, a social reconstructionist version, which stresses reflection about the social and political context of schooling. They argue that none of these traditions is sufficient to provide good teacher training and development and ask why is it so difficult to provide examples of teachers working in a reflective way? Part of the answer, they argue, is that reflection is regarded as a private activity while teaching is a public activity. The two activities, reflection and teaching, in this model are separate. They go on to explore and develop the issue of reflective teaching as a social issue where 'meanings' are grounded in and confirmed by social relations in a particular social context. The authors conclude that it is through shared experience and perspective that teachers will come to understand the meanings of reflection and the action that is generated.

In Chapter 7 the notion of critical dialogue is explored as a method for transforming teachers' professional knowledge. The authors, Russell and Bullock, who are tutor (Tom) and student (Shawn), read and comment on e-mail accounts of teaching–learning experiences. Shawn, the student teacher, reflects on his experiences of both teaching practice and lectures. Tom reflects on the process of teaching Shawn and his fellow students, as well as commenting on Shawn's thoughts about his teaching practice. Personal learning from experience is their starting point and through a series of headings under themes such as journal of experience, metacognition, and pedagogical sounding board, they explore the process of teaching. While the examples come from teaching secondary school science, the way in which Tom and Shawn share experiences and learn from each other has relevance for all teachers in primary and secondary schools. Through working collaboratively, this tutor and student teacher are able to reflect on their personal accounts of teaching in order to further their professional knowledge. It provides an example of collaborative professional development based on reflection on practice.

In Chapter 8, Patricia Sikes, Lynda Measor and Peter Woods explore critical phases and incidents in teacher careers. This is a classic piece which, although written in the mid-1980s, discusses issues which have relevance for teachers today. The term 'critical incident' has been used widely in the research literature on classroom teachers and indeed has a long tradition in ethnographies of other cultures. In many readings it is synonymous with periods of strain; beginnings and endings of a teacher's career; turning points which are brought about by surprise or shock. The authors identify three types of critical phases: extrinsic; intrinsic; and personal. Following the initial critical incident there is usually a counter incident which is successfully managed by the teacher. They argue that the critical incident does not necessarily introduce anything new into the practices of the teacher but acts to crystallise ideas, attitudes and beliefs which are already being formed. However, the counter incident is particularly significant for teachers. While the critical incident or phase creates the turning point, it is the counter incident which signals and confirms the direction.

The chapters in this section of the book are based on the premise that descriptions of pedagogy and reflections upon past personal and professional lives can enable teachers to project into their future professional development. Formative influences, which can occur either during training or at different times in a teaching career, encourage teachers to develop a personal view of teaching based upon shared experience in a common social context.

References

Burgess, R. G. (ed.) (1984) *The Research Process in Educational Settings: Ten Case Studies*. Lewes: Falmer Press.

Goodman, J. (1998) Ideology and critical ethnography, in G. Shacklock and J. Smyth (eds) *Being Reflexive in Critical Educational and Social Research*. London: Falmer Press.

Mills, C. W. (1961) *The Sociological Imagination*. London: Penguin.

Walford, G. (1987) (ed.) *Doing Sociology of Education*. Lewes: Falmer Press.

6

Reflections on Reflective Teaching

Kenneth M. Zeichner and B. Robert Tabachnick

In the last decade, concurrent with the growth of research on teacher thinking and with the increased respect for teachers' practical theories (Clark, 1988), the 'reflective practitioner' has emerged as the new zeitgeist in North American teacher education. One consequence of this phenomenon is that terms such as 'action research', 'reflective teaching', 'reflection-in-action', 'teacher as researcher' and 'research-based' or 'inquiry-oriented' teacher education have now become fashionable throughout all segments of the US and Canadian teacher education communities. Among the signs of this ascendancy are two recent national conferences in the USA focused primarily on reflective inquiry in teacher education (e.g. Clift, Houston and Pugach, 1990), a special issue of the *Journal of Teacher Education* devoted to 'Critical Reflection in Teacher Education (*JTE*, 1989) and the recent proliferation of books and monographs on reflective practice in teaching and teacher education (e.g. Grimmett and Erickson, 1988; Posner, 1989; Waxman *et al.*, 1988).[1]

It's come to the point now that we don't know very much at all about a practice if it is merely described as something aimed at facilitating the development of reflective teachers. We agree with Calderhead's (1989) assessment that the full range of beliefs within the teacher education community about teaching, schooling, teacher education and the social order has now been incorporated into the discourse about reflective practice. There is not a single teacher educator who would say that he or she is not concerned about preparing teachers who are reflective. The criteria that have become attached to reflective practice are so diverse, however, that important differences between specific practices are masked by the use of the common rhetoric.

On the one hand, the recent work of teacher educators such as Cruickshank (1987), who has drawn upon Dewey (1933) for inspiration, gives us some guidance. The distinction that is often made between reflective and routine practice is not trivial and enables us to make some important qualitative distinctions among different teachers and teaching practices.[2] Similarly, the enormously popular work of Schon (1983, 1987, 1989) which has challenged the dominant technical rationality in professional education and argued for more attention to promoting artistry in teaching by encouraging 'reflection in action' and 'reflection on action' among teachers, also directs our attention to the preparation of particular kinds of teachers and not others. These generic approaches to reflective teaching lose their heuristic value, however, after a certain point and begin to hide more than they reveal.[3]

After we have agreed with Cruickshank and Schon, for example, that thoughtful teachers who reflect about their practice (on and in action) are more desirable than thoughtless teachers, who are ruled primarily by tradition, authority and circumstance, there are still many unanswered questions. Neither Cruickshank nor Schon have much to say, for example, about what it is that teachers ought to be reflecting about, the kinds of criteria that should come into play during the process of reflection (e.g. which help distinguish acceptable from unacceptable educational practice) or about the degree to which teachers' deliberations should incorporate a critique of the institutional contexts in which they work (Richardson, 1990). In some extreme cases, the impression is given that as long as teachers reflect about something, in some manner, whatever they decide to do is all right since they have reflected about it.

> *How* to get students to reflect can take on a life of its own, and can become *the* programmatic goal. *What* they reflect on can become immaterial. For example, racial tension as a school issue can become no more or less worthy of reflection than field trips or homework assignments.
>
> (Valli, 1990b, p. 9)

One of the reasons that these generic conceptions of reflection have become so popular is that they can (and have been) employed by teacher educators of every ideological persuasion.[4] Everyone can identify with them and they offend no one, except those who seek to tightly control teachers' actions through external prescription. Despite the important distinctions between reflective and routine practice on the one hand, and between technical rationality and an epistemology of practice on the other (Schon, 1983),[5] both of which affirm the value of teachers' practical knowledge, we do not think that it makes much sense to encourage or to assess reflective practice in general without establishing clear priorities for the reflections that emerge out of a reasoned educational and social philosophy. We do not accept the implication that exists throughout much of the literature, that teachers' actions are necessarily better just because they are more deliberate or intentional.

This chapter will examine several aspects of reflective teaching practice in an attempt to push the discussion among teacher educators beyond an attempt to prepare reflective teachers in general. We hope that this analysis will encourage teacher educators to identify clearly the educational and political commitments that stand behind their own and others' proposals regarding reflective teaching so that we can move beyond the current situation where important differences in our motives and passions are hidden from view by the use of popular slogans. In the next section, various conceptions of reflective teaching practice will be described utilising a framework that has emerged out of our analysis of four traditions of reform in twentieth-century US teacher education: an academic tradition, a social efficiency tradition, a developmentalist tradition and a social reconstructionist tradition. We will then explore the relationships between these different (but also overlapping) orientations to reflective teaching practice and the descriptions of inquiry-oriented teacher education practices that are presented in the remaining chapters of the book [from which this chapter is taken]. Following this discussion, the question of the different meanings that reflective teaching practice can take on as it is acted out in classrooms will be examined through an analysis of specific examples of the teaching of social studies.

Conceptions of Reflective Teaching Practice

There are various ways in which we can distinguish particular proposals for reflective teaching from one another. One way in which we can think about differences among proposals for reflective teaching is in light of different traditions of practice in teacher education.[6] Zeichner and Liston (1990) have identified four varieties of reflective teaching practice based on their analysis of traditions of reform in twentieth-century US teacher education:

1. an academic version that stresses reflection upon subject matter and the representation and translation of subject matter knowledge to promote student understanding (Shulman, 1987);
2. a social efficiency version that emphasises the thoughtful application of particular teaching strategies that have been suggested by research on teaching (Ross and Kyle, 1987);[7]
3. a developmentalist version that prioritises teaching that is sensitive to students' interests, thinking and patterns of developmental growth (Duckworth, 1987);
4. a social reconstructionist version that stresses reflection about the social and political context of schooling and the assessment of classroom actions for their ability to contribute towards greater equity, social justice and humane conditions in schooling and society (Beyer, 1988; Maher and Rathbone, 1986).

In each of these views of reflective teaching practice, certain priorities are established about schooling and society that emerge out of particular historical traditions and educational and social philosophies.

None of these traditions is sufficient by itself for providing a moral basis for teaching and teacher education. Good teaching and teacher education need to attend to all of the elements that are brought into focus by the various traditions: the representation of subject matter, student thinking and understanding, teaching strategies suggested by research conducted by university academics and classroom teachers, and the social contexts of teaching. These elements do not take the same form, however, or receive the same emphasis within each tradition. For example, technical competence in teaching, when viewed as an end in itself apart from its ability to promote student understanding (a fairly common phenomenon in the USA)[8] is not synonymous with technical competence that is sensitive to and builds upon student understandings (see MacKinnon and Erickson, 1988). Also, the employment of teaching practices that lead to student understanding does not necessarily mean that all students share the benefits of the exemplary teaching. In fact, much evidence suggests that the continued existence of a serious 'crisis of inequality' in US public schooling corresponds to a similar situation of inequality in the society as a whole (e.g. Kelly and Nihlen, 1982; Ornstein and Levine, 1989).

Despite the differences in the emphasis given to various factors within the different traditions of reflective teaching, these traditions are not mutually exclusive. In practice, the traditions overlap in many ways and each one attends in some manner to all of the issues that are raised by the traditions as a group. The differences among the traditions of reflection are defined in terms of the emphasis and priority that is given to particular factors within traditions. For example, although social reconstructionist teacher educators are frequently critical of those from other traditions for failing to emphasise a concern for reflection about the institutional, social and political contexts of schooling, it is not reasonable to conclude (without further analysis) that individuals who express allegiance to another version of reflective teaching are unconcerned with issues of social justice and equity.[9] Similarly, although there has been frequent criticism of social reconstructionist teacher educators for their strong emphasis on institutional and societal critique as a fundamental part of reflective teaching, it is not reasonable to conclude (again without further analysis) that they are unconcerned with teaching skills and techniques. Following is a brief discussion of each of these traditions of reflective teaching.

The academic tradition of reflective teaching

The academic tradition of reform within twentieth-century US teacher education has historically emphasised the role of the liberal arts and disciplinary knowledge in teacher preparation and belittled the contribution of schools, departments and colleges of education, with the exception of practice teaching and other clinical experiences (e.g. Flexner, 1930; Koerner, 1963; Damerell, 1985). This orientation to teacher education emphasises the teacher's role as a scholar and subject matter specialist and has taken different forms throughout the twentieth century. In recent years, Lee Shulman (1986, 1987) and Margaret Buchmann (1984), among others,[10] have advocated views of reflective teaching that emphasise the teacher's deliberations about subject matter and its transformation to pupils to promote understanding. Shulman and Buchmann, unlike many others within the academic tradition who advocate merely more exposure to subject matter content for teachers, recognise the contribution that pedagogical knowledge (and professional education course work) can make to a teacher's formal education. Their views represent a challenge to historically dominant notions of academically oriented reform in teacher education (see Zeichner and Liston, 1990).

For example, Shulman (1986a) has described subject matter knowledge as the 'missing paradigm' in research on teaching and teacher education. Reacting to a neglect of this issue by scholars in the field, Shulman (1987) and his colleagues in the 'Knowledge Growth in Teaching Project' (e.g. Wilson, Shulman and Richert, 1987; Wilson and Wineburg, 1988; Grossman, Wilson and Shulman, 1989) have proposed a model of pedagogical reasoning and action and of the professional knowledge base for teaching that clearly places the emphasis on the intellectual basis for teaching and on the transformation of subject matter knowledge by teachers. Shulman and his colleagues have raised the important question of what kind of subject matter knowledge teachers need to teach in a way that leads to student understanding. Rather than assuming that more exposure to liberal arts courses, as they are currently conceived, is a solution to problems related to teachers' subject matter expertise,[11] they have proposed a model of the components of the professional knowledge base for teaching that includes three major categories of content knowledge: subject matter content knowledge, pedagogical content knowledge and curricular knowledge. A key component of the knowledge base for teaching that gives it its special identity according to Shulman and his colleagues is pedagogical content knowledge. According to Shulman (1986b), pedagogical content knowledge

> embodies the aspects of content most germane to its teachability. Within the category of pedagogical content knowledge I include, for the most regularly taught topics in one's subject area, the most useful forms of representation of these ideas, the most powerful anologies, illustrations, examples, explanations, and demonstrations – in a word, the ways of representing and formulating the subject that make it comprehensible to others . . . [it] also includes an understanding of what makes the learning of specific topics easy or difficult: the conceptions and preconceptions that students of different ages and backgrounds bring with them to the learning.
>
> (p. 9)

This group has also proposed a model of pedagogicial reasoning and action that identifies six aspects of the teaching act: comprehension, transformation, instruction, evaluation, reflection and new comprehension. One key aspect of their model of pedagogical reasoning (under the transformation process) is representation. According to Shulman (1987),

> representation involves thinking through the key ideas in the text or lesson and identifying the alternative ways of representing them to students. What anologies, metaphors, examples, demonstrations, simulations, and the like can help to build a bridge between the teacher's comprehension and that desired for the students? Multiple forms of representation are desirable.
>
> (p. 328)

This model of pedagogical reasoning and action is a good example of a contemporary view of reflective teaching that prioritises reflection about the content to be taught and how it is to be taught. While this conception of reflective teaching does not ignore general pedagogical knowledge derived from research on teaching, students' understandings and developmental characteristics, and issues of social justice and equity, the standards for assessing the adequacy of the teaching evolve primarily from the academic disciplines.

The social efficiency tradition of reflective teaching

The social efficiency tradition of reform in US teacher education, one version of progressivism in American educational thought (Cremin, 1961), has historically emphasised a faith in the scientific study of teaching to provide the basis for building a teacher education curriculum. According to advocates of this view, research on teaching has, in recent years, provided us with a 'knowledge base' that can form the foundation for the curriculum of teacher education programmes (Berliner, 1984). Feiman-Nemser (1990) has identified two different ways in which contemporary teacher educators have interpreted the social efficiency perspective. First, she describes a technological version in which the intent is to teach prospective teachers the skills and competencies that research has shown to be associated with desirable pupil outcomes. This narrow interpretation of the social efficiency view emphasises 'reflection' by the teacher about how closely their practice conforms to standards provided by some aspect of research on teaching (e.g. Gentile, 1988).

A second and broader interpretation of the social efficiency tradition in US teacher education (the deliberative orientation according to Feiman-Nemser, 1990) is one where the findings of research on teaching are used by teachers as 'principles of procedure' within a wider process of decision-making and problem-solving. According to the advocates of this deliberative orientation to the use of research on teaching, the crucial task for teacher educators is to foster teachers' capabilities to exercise judgement about the use of various teaching skills suggested by research as well as other sources:

> Because they view good teaching as good deliberation, their concern is not that teachers follow a set of rules, which could never account for all circumstances anyway, but rather that teachers view teaching as a process of constantly making choices about the means and ends, choices that can be informed by process product research, descriptive research, experience, intuition, and one's own values.
>
> (Zumwalt, 1982, p. 226)

A contemporary example of a teacher education programme that emphasises a conception of reflective teaching practice involving the intelligent (rather than mechanical) use of research on teaching is the elementary

PROTEACH programme at the University of Florida. Dorene Ross and her colleagues have, over a number of years, used the label of reflective teaching to describe an approach to teaching as decision-making where research on teaching is one among a number of factors that teachers deliberate about:

> The limits on the appropriate use of teacher effectiveness research must be understood by prospective teachers . . . the most important teacher behavior is the flexibility and judgement necessary to select the appropriate strategy for the particular goal and students involved.
>
> (Ross and Kyle, 1987, p. 41)

While this conception of reflective teaching does not totally ignore the social contexts of schooling and issues of equity and social justice, student understandings and developmental characteristics, or subject matter, the emphasis is clearly on the intelligent use of 'generic' teaching skills and strategies that have been suggested by research.[12]

The developmentalist tradition of reflective teaching

The distinguishing characteristic of the developmentalist tradition of reform in twentieth-century US teacher education (another element of progressive thought in US education, Perrone, 1989) is the assumption that the natural development of the learner provides the basis for determining what should be taught to students and how it should be taught. Historically, this natural order of child development was to be determined by research involving the careful observation and description of student' behaviour at various stages of development (Mitchell, 1931).

According to Perrone (1989), three central metaphors have been associated with the progressive/developmentalist tradition in US teacher education: teacher as naturalist, teacher as researcher and teacher as artist. The teacher as naturalist dimension has stressed the importance of skill in the observation of children's behaviour and in building a curriculum and classroom environment consistent with patterns of child development and children's interests. Classroom practice is to be grounded in close observation and study of children in the classroom either directly by the teacher, or from reflection on a literature based on such study. The teacher as researcher element of this tradition has emphasised the need to foster the teacher's experimental attitude toward practice and to help them initiate and sustain ongoing inquiries in their own classrooms about the learning of specific children to inform their practice. Finally, the teacher as artist element has emphasised the link between creative and fully functioning persons in touch with their own learning and exciting and stimulating classrooms.

One contemporary example of reflective teaching practice within this tradition is the work of Eleanor Duckworth at Harvard University.[13]

Duckworth (1987) has elaborated a constructivist view of reflective teaching that emphasises engaging learners with phenomena and then working to understand the sense they are making of those phenomena (instead of explaining things to students at the onset). According to Duckworth, teachers are both practitioners and researchers and their research is to be focused on their students and their current understandings of the area under study. The teacher then uses this knowledge of students' current understandings to decide the appropriate next steps for their learning and keeps trying to find out what sense the students are making as the instruction continues.

> The essential element of having the students do the explaining is not the withholding of all the teacher's own thoughts. It is, rather, that the teacher not consider herself or himself the final arbiter of what the learner should think, nor the creator of what the learner does think. The important job for the teacher is to keep trying to find out what sense the students are making.
>
> (Duckworth, 1987, p. 133)

This developmentalist conception of reflective teaching has become increasingly popular in recent years with the growing influence of cognitive psychology in education (Reilly, 1989). While it doesn't ignore subject matter standards emanating from the disciplines, research on teaching and the social and political context and issues of social justice, the emphasis is clearly on reflecting about students.

The social reconstructionist tradition of reflective teaching

In the fourth tradition of reform in twentieth-century US teacher education, social reconstructionism, schooling and teacher education are both viewed as crucial elements in the movement towards a more just and humane society. According to Valli (1990a), proponents of this approach (which draws upon various neo-Marxist, critical and feminist perspectives)[14] argue

> that schools as social institutions, help reproduce a society based on unjust class, race, and gender relations and that teachers have a moral obligation to reflect on and change their own practices and school structures when these perpetuate such arrangements.
>
> (p. 46)

In a social reconstructionist conception of reflective teaching, the teacher's attention is focused both inwardly on their own practice (and the collective practices of a group of colleagues) *and* outwardly on the social conditions in which these practices are situated (Kemmis, 1985). How teachers' actions maintain and/or disrupt the status quo in schooling and society is of central concern. The reflection is aimed in part at the elimination of the social conditions that distort the self-understandings of teachers and undermine the educative potential and moral basis of schooling. According to

John Elliott (1990), institutional and social critique are a natural part of the process of reflection.

> Reflective practice implies reflexivity: self-awareness. But such an awareness brings with it insights into the ways in which the self in action is shared and constrained by institutional structures. Self-awareness and the awareness of the institutional context of one's work as a teacher are not developed by separate cognitive processes, reflexive and objective analysis. They are qualities of the same reflexive process. Reflexive practice necessarily implies both self-critique and institutional critique. One cannot have one without the other.
>
> (p. 23)

A second characteristic of a social reconstructionist conception of reflective teaching is its democratic and emancipatory impulse and the focus of the teacher's deliberations upon substantive issues that raise instances of inequality and injustice within schooling and society for close scrutiny. Recognising the fundamentally political character of all schooling, the teacher's reflections centre upon such issues as the gendered nature of schooling and of teachers' work, the relationships between race and social class on the one hand and access to school knowledge and school achievement on the other, and the influence of external interests on the process of curriculum production. These and other similar issues are addressed in concrete form as they arise within the context of the teacher's classroom and school.

For example, an issue that is confronted fairly frequently by student teachers at the University of Wisconsin-Madison is disproportionate assignment of pupils of colour to the lower tracks of school programmes and to such remedial categories as 'learning disabled'. In the Madison area, pupils of colour also have higher than average school suspension rates and lower than average high school graduation rates (Ptak, 1988). All of this is fairly common across the USA (Goodlad, 1990). In a social reconstructionist conception of reflective teaching these so-called 'facts' about the context of the teacher's work which highlight racial and class differences in educational outcomes would be made problematic and examined as part of the teacher's deliberations about teaching. These reflections would then stimulate an exploration of alternative possibilities through which the painful effects of these practices could be lessened. The more usual scenario is for these and similar issues to serve as background during teachers' reflections.

The third distinguishing characteristic of a social reconstructionist conoception of reflective teaching is its commitment to reflection as a communal activity. Social reconstructionist oriented teacher educators seek to create 'communities of learning' where teachers can support and sustain each others' growth. This commitment to collaborative modes of learning indicates a dual commitment by teacher educators to an ethic where justice and equity on the one hand, and care and compassion on the other, are valued. This commitment is also thought to be of strategic value in the transformation of unjust and inhumane institutional and social structures. Specifically, it is felt that the empowerment of individual teachers as individuals is inadequate, and that the potential for institutional and social change is greater, if teachers see their individual situations as linked to those of their colleagues (Freedman, Jackson and Boles, 1986).

These four traditions of reflective teaching (see Figure 6.1) can be used to interpret various aspects of proposals for teacher education reform and descriptions of existing practices. In the final part of this chapter, we will address the important issue of the way in which reflective teaching can take on different meanings within the classroom.

Tradition	The focus of the reflection is on
Academic	The representations of subject matter to students to promote understanding
Social efficiency	The intelligent use of generic teaching strategies suggested by research on teaching
Developmentalist	The learning, development and understanding of students
Social reconstructionist	The social conditions of schooling and issues of equity and justice

Figure 6.1   *Traditions of reflective teaching*

Reflective Teaching – How Do We Know It When We See It?

In describing the classroom lives of teachers, some twenty or more years ago, Phillip Jackson presented a vision of a social environment whose intensity, complexity and insistent demands for rapid response seemed to leave little room for deliberation, weighing and choosing alternatives, or anything our common experience would label reflection (Jackson, 1968). That might come later, looking back at what happened and forward to what might be encouraged to happen next and would be desirable in the teacher's view, if it did happen next. Recently, Donald Schon has teased our interest in defining teaching to be a thoughtful enterprise by suggesting the possibility that teachers reflect-in-action (Schon, 1983, 1987), so that even the rapidly unfolding texture of classroom events is partly shaped by the teacher's intellectual intuitions, not merely by routinised or uncritical responses to instructional demands. It is appealing to find that teachers can be reflective, but it is not altogether clear what reflectiveness looks like in action or if it is something that lives in abstractions but is not recognisable as teacher behaviour.

If we want to prepare university students to become reflective teachers, it would be useful to know what reflective teaching looks like. Why should it be difficult to recognise reflective teaching when we see it?

One reason for the difficulty is that reflection is commonly considered to be a private activity, while reflective teaching, like any kind of teaching, is expected to be a public activity. Reflection, even when it is conceived to be a private activity, may have public consequences as people say or do things we can observe and that we guess are the result of reflection. In this view, thought and action are connected but separate from one another. If we want to act wisely, we think first, then deliberately do what we have decided is the best way to act.

In an alternative view (Mead, 1938), thinking and doing are inseparable parts of an act. It is not only thinking that leads to and shapes the behaviour of the wise actor, but that person's behaviour, within a particular social context, also can lead to and shape thinking. Thought and behaviour become a duality, interdependent and interactive. For this duality of thought and behaviour, it is not only language that identifies what someone believes or intends, but also the person's behaviour, within a particular social context, that expresses belief and intention.

In a study of teacher responses to contradictions between their statements of belief and their teaching behaviour, we found that two teachers, each in their first year of teaching, resolved contradictions in quite different ways (Tabachnick and Zeichner, 1986). Both teachers, Hannah and Beth, said that they intended to encourage active learning by pupils, respond to pupil interests in order to create more intrinsic motivation to learn, and to connect the school work to the lives and experiences of their pupils. As they begin the school year, both were observed teaching in rather routine ways, with almost no pupil initiatives being encouraged in Beth's room and very few in Hannah's.

As the year progressed, Hannah tried continually to change her teaching to make it more consistent with her stated intentions and by the end of the year there were noticeable differences in the way learning activities were planned, organised and implemented. As Beth's year progressed, the few instances of an open and easy approach to teaching (her term) seemed to disappear. Her teaching became more controlling and routinised. What changed noticeably were her statements of belief and commitment; by the end of the year she rejected the value of pupil participation in planning for learning and affirmed the virtues of worksheets and practice exercises that prepared pupils for tests of information transmitted by Beth or by various teaching materials. Beth and Hannah were both thinking about teaching. Are they both reflective teachers?

This question identifies a second reason for difficulty in recognising reflective teaching that was discussed earlier; that educators from a broad range of ideological persuasions embrace the term 'reflective teaching'. The message in the reform traditions framework presented earlier in this chapter is that we must be interested in more complex questions than whether teaching is reflective or not. We need to ask questions about the nature and purpose of teachers' reflections; that is, what are teachers being reflective about, and why?

Reflective teaching, like any teaching, is a social activity. Either reflective teaching looks back at social interactions and tries to make sense of them in order to plan for future teaching, or it looks forward to social interactions of teaching and learning that have not yet taken place and attempts to shape these, or reflective teaching is within the process of teaching and learning, in which ideas and behaviour interact to shape one another. Meanings for the results of teaching and learning are grounded in and confirmed by social relations within a particular social context.

Kemmis (1985), in examining the social character of reflection as a part of teaching, moves beyond its orientation to action within a social context. Kemmis identifies reflection as value-laden, expressing and serving

> particular human, social, cultural and political interests . . . it actively reproduces or transforms the ideological practices which are the basis of the social order . . . (and) expresses our power to reconstitute social life by the way we participate in communication, decision-making and social action.
>
> (p. 149)

In this activist view, thinking about teaching has consequences. Teaching itself always has some effect in terms of enhancing the life chances of students or of maintaining existing constraints to students' access to opportunity. We can see this in action when we look at reports of teaching and learning.

[. . .]

Notes

1. This growing interest in reflective practice in teacher education does not just exist of course in North America. See Handal and Lauvas (1987, Norway), Martinez (1989, Australia), Pollard (1988, UK) and Wubbels and Korthagen (1990, Netherlands) for examples of non-North American work of reflective practice in teacher education.

2. According to Dewey (1933), reflective action entails 'active, persistent, and careful consideration of any belief or supposed form of knowledge in light of the grounds that support it and the further consequences to which it leads' (p. 9). He distinguishes this from routine action which is guided primarily by tradition and authority.

3. Also see Kirby and Teddlie (1989), Stout (1989) and Osterman (1990).

4. This is not to say that these frameworks have gone without any criticism. See Grimmett and Erickson (1988) for several different kinds of critiques of Schon's work, and Gore (1987) for a critique of Cruickshank's work.

5. The characterisation of this distinction between technical rationality and reflective practice as a dichotomy by Schon is challenged by a number of the authors in the Grimmett and Erickson (1988) volume and by Harris (1989). See the chapters by Shulman (1988), Fenstermacher (1988) and Selman (1988) in Grimmett and Erickson (1988).

6. See Grimmett *et al.* (1990) and Valli (1990b) for two additional frameworks for describing varieties of reflective teaching practice. As Valli (1990b) points out, different orientations to preparing reflective teachers frequently use the same

instructional strategies, such as journals and action research. They use these strategies, however, in very different ways.

7. Grimmett *et al.* (1990) refer to this tradition of reflection as the 'instrumental mediation of action', see pp. 23–4.

8. See Zeichner (1990) for several examples of how this narrow view of technical competence is sometimes encouraged by practices in teacher education programmes.

9. In fact many of the studies which are drawn upon in efforts to promote a social efficiency view of reflective teaching (Berliner, 1984; Good, 1987) have important implications for realising social justice and equity.

10. Also see Ball, McDiarmid and Anderson (1989).

11. Shulman (1986b) has argued, for example, that 'mere content knowledge is likely to be as useless pedagogically as content-free skill' (p. 8). He has also concluded that 'instruction in the liberal arts and content areas will have to improve dramatically to meet the standards of understanding required for teaching' (p. 13).

12. As is the case in many teacher education programmes, different parts of elementary PROTEACH emphasise different traditions of practice. For example, the social efficiency tradition just described is emphasised in the Research in Elementary Education course described by Ross and Kyle. Other parts of this programme reflect a very strong emphasis on developmentalist practices which is not surprising given the 'Humanistic' teacher education programmes that immediately preceded the development of PROTEACH (Combs, 1974).

13. Also see Fosnot (1989) and Amarel (1988).

14. Each of these labels in turn (e.g. feminist) is also very diverse encompassing a range of different perspectives. See Gore (1990) for a discussion of some of the different perspectives that are included in the categories of 'critical' and 'feminist' pedagogies.

References

Amarel, M. (1988) Developmental teacher education, *Dialogues in Teacher Education* (Issue Paper 88–4). East Lansing, MI: National Center for Research on Teacher Education.

Ball, D., McDiarmid, G. W. and Anderson, C. W. (1989) Why staying one chapter ahead doesn't really work: subject-specific pedagogy, in M. Reynolds (ed.) *Knowledge Base for the Beginning Teacher* (pp. 193–205). New York: Pergamon.

Berliner, D. (1984) The half-full glass: a review of research on teaching, in P. Hosford (ed.) *Using What We Know about Teaching*. Alexandria, VA: Association of Supervision and Curriculum Development.

Beyer, L. (1988) *Knowing and Acting: Inquiry, Ideology and Educational Studies*. Basingstoke: Falmer Press.

Buchmann, M. (1984) The priority of knowledge and understanding in teaching, in L. Katz and J. Raths (eds) *Advances in Teacher Education*, Vol. 1 (pp. 29–50). Norwood, NJ: Ablex.

Calderhead, J. (1989) Reflective teaching and teacher education, *Teaching and Teacher Education*, **5**, 1, pp. 43–51.

Clark, C. (1988) Asking the right questions about teacher preparation: contributions of research on teacher thinking, *Educational Researcher*, **17**, 2, pp. 5–12.

Clift, R., Houston, W. R. and Pugach, M. (1990) *Encouraging Reflective Practice: An Examination of Issues and Exemplars*. New York: Teachers College Press.

Combs, A., Blume, R., Newman, A. and Wass, H. (1974) *The Professional Education of Teachers: a Humanistic Approach to Teacher Education*. Boston: Allyn and Bacon.

Cremin, L. (1961) *The Transformation of the School: Progressivism in American Education, 1876–1957*. New York: Vintage Books.

Cruickshank, D. (1987) *Reflective Teaching*. Reston, VA: Association of Teacher Educators.

Damerell, R. (1985) *Education's Smoking Gun: How Teachers' Colleges have Destroyed Education in America*. New York: Freandlich Books.

Dewey, J. (1933) *How We Think*. Chicago: Henry Regnery.

Duckworth, E. (1987) *The Having of Wonderful Ideas*. New York: Teachers College Press.

Elliott, J. (1990) Teachers as researchers: implications for supervision and for teacher education, *Teaching and Teacher Education*, **6**, 1, pp. 1–26.

Feiman-Nemser, S. (1990) Teacher preparation: structural and conceptual alternatives, in W. R. Houston (ed.) *Handbook of Research on Teacher Education* (pp. 212–33). New York: Macmillan.

Fenstermacher, G. D. (1988) The place of science and epistemology in Schon's conception of reflective practice, in Grimmett and Erickson, *op. cit.*

Flexner, A. (1930) *Universities: American, English, German*. Oxford, England: Oxford University Press.

Fosnot, C. T. (1989) *Enquiring Teachers, Enquiring Learners: a Constructionist Approach to Teaching*. New York: Teachers College Press.

Freeman, S., Jackson, J. and Boles, K. (1986) *The Effect of Teaching on Teachers*. Grand Forks, ND: North Dakota Study Group on Evaluation.

Gentile, J. R. (1988) *Instructional Improvement: Summary and Analysis of Madeline Hunter's Essential Elements of Instruction and Supervision*. Oxford, OH: National Staff Development Council.

Good, T. (1987) Two decades of research on teacher expectation. *Journal of Teacher Education*, **38**, 4, pp. 32–48.

Goodlad, J. (1990) *Teachers for Our Nation's Schools*. San Francisco: Jossey-Bass.

Gore, J. (1987) Reflecting on reflective teaching, *Journal of Teacher Education*, **38**, 2, pp. 33–9.

Gore, J. (1990) The Struggle for Pedagogies: Critical and Feminist Discourses as 'Regimes of Truth'. Unpublished doctoral dissertation, University of Wisconsin-Madison.

Grimmett, P. and Erickson, G. (eds) (1988) *Reflection in Teacher Education*. New York: Teachers College Press.

Grimmett, P., Mackinnon, A., Erickson, G. and Riecken, T. (1990) Reflective practice in teacher education, in R. Clift, W. R. Houston and M. Pugach (eds) *Encouraging Reflective Practice in Education* (pp. 20–38). New York: Teachers College Press.

Grossman, P., Wilson, S. and Shulman, L. (1989) Teachers of substance: subject matter knowledge for teaching, in M. Reynolds (ed.) *Knowledge Base for the Beginning Teacher* (pp. 23–36). New York: Pergamon Press.

Handal, G. and Lauvas, P. (1987) *Promoting Reflective Teaching: Supervision in Action*. Milton Keynes, UK: Open University Press.

Harris, I. (1989) A critique of Schon's views on teacher education, *Journal of Curriculum and Supervision*, **5**, 1, pp. 13–18.

Jackson, P. (1968) *Life in Classrooms*. New York: Holt, Rinehart and Winston.

Journal of Teacher Education (1989) Critical reflection in teacher education: practices and problems, **40**, 2.

Kelly, G. and Nihlen, (1982) Schooling and the reproduction of patriarchy, in M. Apple (ed.) *Cultural and Economic Reproduction in Education* (pp. 162–80). Boston: Routledge and Kegan Paul.

Kemmis, S. (1985) Action research and the politics of reflection, in D. Boud, R. Keogh and D. Walker (eds) *Reflection: Turning Experience into Learning* (pp. 139–64). London: Croom Helm.

Kirby, P. and Teddlie, C. (1989) Development of the reflective teaching instrument. *Journal of Educational Research*, **22**, 4, pp. 46–51.

Koerner, J. (1963) *The Miseducation of American Teachers*. Boston: Houghton Mifflin.

Mackinnon, A. and Erickson, G. (1988) Taking Schon's ideas to a science teaching practicum, in Grimmett and Erickson *op. cit.*

Martinez, K. (1989) Critical Reflections on Critical Reflection in Teacher Education. Paper presented at the Fourth National Conference on the Practicum in Teacher Education, Rockhampton, Australia.

Maher, F. and Rathbone, C. (1986) Teacher education and feminist theory: some implications for practice, *American Journal of Education*, **94**, 2, pp. 214–35.

Mead, G. H. (1938) *The Philosophy of the Act*. Chicago: University of Chicago Press.

Mitchell, L. S. (1931) Cooperative schools for student teachers, *Progressive Education*, **8**, pp. 251–5.

Ornstein, A. and Levine, D. (1989) Social class, race, and school achievement: problems and prospects, *Journal of Teacher Education*, **40**, 5, pp. 17–23.

Osterman, K. (1990) Reflective practice: a new agenda for education, *Education and Urban Society*, **22**, 2, pp. 135–52.

Perrone, V. (1989) *Working Papers: Reflections on Teachers, Schools and Communities*. New York: Teachers College Press.

Pollard, A. (1988) Reflective teaching: the sociological contribution, in P. Woods and A. Pollard (eds) *Sociology and Teaching* (pp. 54–75). London: Croom Helm.

Posner, G. (1989) *Field Experience: Methods of Reflective Teaching* (2nd edn). New York: Longman.

Ptak, D. (1988) *Report on the Achievement of Black High School Students in the Madison Metropolitan School District, 1987–1988*. Madison, WI: Urban League.

Reilly, D. (1989) A knowledge base for education: cognitive science, *Journal of Teacher Education*, **40**, 3, pp. 9–13.

Richardson, V. (1990) The evolution of reflective teaching and teacher education, in R. Clift, W. R. Houston and M. Pugach (eds) *Encouraging Reflective Practice in Education* (pp. 3–19). New York: Teachers College Press.

Ross, D. and Kyle, D. (1987) Helping preservice teachers learn to use teacher effectiveness research, *Journal of Teacher Education*, **38**, pp. 40–4.

Schon, D. (1983) *The Reflective Practitioner: How Professionals Think in Action*. New York: Basic Books.

Schon, D. (1987) *Educating the Reflective Practitioner*. San Francisco: Jossey-Bass, Inc.

Schon, D. (1989) Professional knowledge and reflective practice, in T. Sergiovanni and J. H. Moore (eds) *Schooling for Tomorrow*. Boston: Allyn and Bacon.

Selman, M. (1988) Schon's gate is square. But is it art? in Grimmett and Erickson, *op. cit.*

Shulman, L. (1986a) Paradigms and research programs in the study of teaching, in M. Wittrock (ed.) *Third Handbook of Research in Teaching*, pp. 3–36. New York: Macmillan.

Shulman, L. (1986b) Those who understand: knowledge growth in teaching, *Educational Researcher*, **15**, 2, pp. 4–14.

Shulman, L. (1987) Knowledge and teaching: foundations of the new reform, *Harvard Educational Review*, **57**, pp. 1–22.

Shulman, L. (1988) The dangers of dichotomous thinking in education, in Grimett and Erickson, *op. cit.*

Stout, C. J. (1989) Teachers' views of the emphasis on reflective teaching skills during their student teaching, *Elementary School Journal*, **89**, 4, pp. 511–27.

Tabachnick, B. R. and Zeichner, K. (1986) Teacher beliefs and classroom behaviors: some teacher responses to inconsistencies, in M. Ben-Peretz, R. Bromme and R. Halkes (eds) *Advances of Research on Teacher Thinking* (pp. 84–96). Berwyn PA and Lisse, W. Germany: Swets North America/Swets and Zeitlinger.

Valli, L. (1990a) Moral approaches to reflective practice, in R. Clift, W. R. Houston and M. Pugach (eds) *Encouraging Reflective Practice in Education* (pp. 39–56). New York: Teachers College Press.

Valli, L. (1990b) The Question of Quality and Content in Reflective Teaching. A paper presented at the annual meeting of the American Educational Research Association, Boston, MA.

Waxman, H. J., Freiberg, J. C., Vaughan, J. and Veil, M. (eds) (1988) *Images of Reflection in Teacher Education*. Peston, VA: Association of Teacher Educators.

Wilson, S., Shulman, L. and Richert, A. (1987) 150 different way of knowing: representations of knowledge in teaching, in J. Calderhead (ed.) *Exploring Teachers Thinking* (pp. 104–24). London: Cassell.

Wilson, S. and Wineburg, S. (1988) Peering at American history through different lenses: the role of disciplinary knowledge in teaching, *Teachers College Record*, **89**, pp. 525–39.

Wubbels, T. and Korthagen, F. (1990) The effects of a pre-service teacher education program for the preparation of reflective teachers, *Journal of Education for Teaching*, **16**, 1, pp. 29–44.

Zeichner, K. (1990) When you've said reflection, you haven't said it all, in T. Stoddard (ed.) *Guided Practice in Teacher Education*. East Lancing, MI: National Center for Research on Teacher Education.

Zeichner, K. and Liston, D. (1990) *Traditions of Reform and Reflective Teaching in US Teacher Education* (Issue Paper 90–1). East Lansing, MI: National Center for Research on Teacher Education.

Zumwalt, K. (1982) Research on teaching: policy implications for teacher education, in A. Lieberman and M. McLaughlin (eds) *Policymaking in Education* (pp. 215–48). Chicago: University of Chicago Press.

7

Discovering Our Professional Knowledge as Teachers: Critical Dialogues about Learning from Experience

Tom Russell and Shawn Bullock

Introduction

Teachers' knowledge is personal, context-rich and exclusive. This chapter approaches the issue of researching teaching by demonstrating the power of critical dialogue in naming and transforming teachers' professional knowledge. In this instance, the dialogue is made possible by the authors' shared commitment to probing the importance of pedagogy and experience in facilitating learning. Tom is an experienced teacher educator seeking the best ways to identify and encourage the learning of science teacher candidates in a programme based on early extended experience: Shawn is a teacher candidate coming to terms with his first extended teaching assignment and his pre-service education courses. Each is helping the other identify and interpret his professional knowledge as a teacher by reading and commenting on e-mail accounts of teaching–learning experiences. Sharing our personal experiences of teaching drives the process of naming our professional knowledge as teachers. By grounding our analysis in experience of teaching and critical dialogue about teaching, we demonstrate how we come to understand our knowledge and our ongoing efforts to extent, refine and consolidate that knowledge.

Setting the Stage and Introducing the Characters

We see ourselves as two actors on the stage in a learning-to-teach playhouse. Tom began teaching in 1963 and has been teaching pre-service teachers at Queens University since 1977. Shawn began the education portion of his Queen's–Waterloo concurrent education programme in 1997, after completing the first two years of his Honours Physics programme at the University of Waterloo. Shawn and Tom met at Queen's in late August 1997, when Shawn found himself in Tom's course on methods of teaching physics.

Shawn began his first teaching placement at Aurora High School on the first day of the school year in September. After eight weeks, he returned to Queen's for two weeks of courses that coincided with a two-week protest by teachers across the province of Ontario. He then returned to Aurora High School for six more weeks of teaching, until the school closed for holidays in December. In the Winter Term of the BEd programme, Shawn spent eleven weeks in courses at Queen's, with a three-week 'alternate practicum' in late February and March. He returned to his science studies at Waterloo in May and is scheduled to teach again for four months in the Fall Term of 1998.

Tom began teaching with no formal training but years of observation as a student, just as Shawn did. Tom taught for two years (in Nigeria) before entering a formal teacher education programme, and he has always paid special attention to the role of experience in learning to teach. Schon's (1983) *The Reflective Practitioner* has influenced his research over the last 15 years. The 1997–98 academic year happened to be the first full year of a revised BEd programme structure at Queen's University, a structure that can be summarised as 'extended teaching experience first'. In this programme, Tom met Shawn in several classes in late August, worked more intensely with him in a group of eleven for two weeks in late October, and then continued through the Winter Term in a class of 26. An invitation to write this paper came shortly after the curtain rose on Shawn and Tom's 'shared adventure' of preparing, exchanging, and commenting on each other's teaching notes.

The Curtain Rises

In a two-hour class on Thursday 30 October 1997, feeling inspired and empowered by his first three one-hour classes with eleven candidates and their stories of eight weeks' teaching, Tom 'makes his big move'. He had been developing an experience-rich approach to teaching science, but the group seemed ready for more. In this class Tom developed links between the new teachers' learning (to teach science) from experience, their students' learning (science), and his own learning (to teach others to teach science). Tom argued that all three categories of learning are more similar than different, and he urged that all three be seen from the vantage point of 'experience first' – a phrase that later evolved into 'the power of experience'. Several people responded positively, and this class set the tone for the remainder of the ten-hours-over-two-weeks block of classes. On 31 October, Shawn sent an electronic message to Tom that included the following, and the curtain rose on our shared adventure in dialogue about pedagogy and learning from experience:

> Although I might have been realising it at the subconscious level, the ideas we talked about yesterday [in class] finally put a lot of things into focus. The idea you

mentioned about Experience coming before Theory really makes a lot of sense to me. Last night . . . I started looking at my day book and journal from the past two months. And then the crux of what you've been saying hit me like a tonne of bricks: that experience lays a foundation to learn a concept, and theory cleans up what was floating around in one's mind after the experience. I then applied that to my own learning as a Teacher Candidate: I've been experiencing teaching, and I've had my own successes and challenges, but only by reflecting on it will I truly learn anything from my experience.

These two weeks are helping me come to some important realisations, specifically last night. Now comes the unique part: When I return in January, I, like everyone else, will be learning from experience and consolidating ideas for four months. But what I find exciting is the notion that I get to go back to Waterloo and apply what I've learned about teaching to my own learning, and then, in September 1998, I get to have another four-month 'practicum'. These two weeks are valuable, because they serve to refocus, but I get to do it on a large scale with two four-month blocks next year.

Later that Friday afternoon, Tom sent Shawn a reply that began with the following:

[Your message is] off the scale, Shawn – what pleases me most is that I think I can honestly say I 'heard' (saw!) in your earlier e-mails and writing the potential for that kind of response. One of the beauties of e-mail is that you never quite know when you will get a response (I had thought of sending a 'what's up' note earlier, just because I was truly interested, and then I reminded myself – 'give Shawn time, Tom – he's busy and has lots to do; he'll reply when he's ready!') Now I can just float home for the weekend on the good signals in your note.

With this exchange, the curtain was up and the action began on our stage of pedagogical conversations. We began with no clear purpose beyond exploring the issue of 'experience first' in the teaching of science and in the teaching of new science teachers. John Loughran's invitation to Tom to write a paper arrived just a Shawn began sending weekly reports to Tom, by e-mail, from his school. Tom extended, and Shawn accepted, an invitation to explore our discussions further by preparing this chapter. Naming our professional knowledge and interpreting its development thus became an important additional focus that fits well with the 'experience first' approach.

Act I, Scene 1: Shawn Writes and Tom Responds

In this scene, Shawn speaks in the first person about the various benefits he sees in the process of writing about his teaching experiences and engaging in dialogue with Tom about his interpretations of his experiences.

A journal of experience

First and foremost, writing creates a detailed record of experience. So much happens in teaching that it is easy to forget things, and a journal allows one to look back and say, often nostalgically, 'I remember that!' It also provides an invaluable record of successes and failures. Each time I look at my notes, the experiences I had in the classroom rush back to me. By keeping detailed records of lessons, student responses, and my own thoughts at the time, I get a palpable sense of being back in the classroom.

There are certain lessons that I conducted over my practicum where I took a pedagogical risk, in the sense that I deviated from a standard approach and took an 'experience first' approach to science teaching. The journal allows me to revisit, with remarkable clarity, the experiential science lessons that I conducted. This proved to be an invaluable tool in completing my action research report.

I think that my detailed notes for the lessons in which I discussed the concept of gravity with my 12A physics class were the best example of my journal of experience. The unit started out with a 'bang', a successful interactive demonstration activity in which I showed that all objects fall to the Earth with the same acceleration. I then set the class the task of designing experiments to determine a numerical value for the acceleration due to gravity. That particular class was one of the highlights of my practicum, in terms of being the science class I envison myself teaching in years to come.

Conversely, my notes for the class when the students conducted the experiments they designed on their own reveal the angst I felt when I 'let the reigns go'. I had hoped to be far more comfortable in an experiential setting than I actually was. The thoughts from this particular entry, upon revisiting, have helped me understand experiential learning on a deeper level, as well as providing a framework from which to shape further experiences.

> Today the physics class carried out their experiments to determine the acceleration due to gravity. I vowed to provide them with as little guidance as possible, since yesterday I emphasised that they would be responsible for writing up their own methods in the final lab report. I let them debate amongst themselves how to minimise error. It was one of the most difficult things I have ever had to do. My every impulse was to point out errors and make suggestions as they performed their experiments around the classroom. Instead, I just walked around and made sure that they weren't totally lost. I was amazed at the diligence with which they worked. Frustration levels were high, but they kept going with their labs. I expect that their frustration was due to the fact that I did not hand out a piece of paper that said 'Laboratory Instructions'. This sort of approach bears further investigation.
> Sidebar: CONTROL! CONTROL! I craved control . . .

[. . .]

Issues are explored and revisited

One of the themes I notice when I revisit my writing is that I am reminded of unresolved issues that I would like to explore in the future. Many things

happened during my practicum to inspire me to think, and there are many
teaching issues that cannot be 'answered'. Instead, they must be constantly
revisited, which is something I hope to do in the future. One of the dominant themes in my journal concerns the issues surrounding general level
education. I did not teach a general class until the last half of my practicum,
when I switched into an 11 General math class. After having a lot of
experience with the advanced level math students and the senior physics
classes, I was amazed at the different atmosphere in a general level class.

The journal record of my first day in a general math class finds me
wondering where the 'general = stupid' label comes from. I also wondered
how a level whose mantra is supposed to be one of 'experience first' seems
remarkably unconnected to the outside world, short of textbook examples.
I revisited this issue many times during my work with the math class. I
struck gold with a unit on buying a car, and I found myself making connections with the students' self-esteem as it was affected by success in math
class. I also managed to develop a technique of interactive note-taking,
which involved the students in completing the calculations in examples as
we did the 'note'. This technique came about from revisiting an observation I made on my first day, namely that general level students tend to
get 'hung up' on mechanical errors.

> The experiment came in my so-called 'note' portion of the overhead. Rather than
> finishing the examples all the way, I would set up the problem and leave the
> mechanical math for the students. It seems that general students make as many
> calculation errors as they do conceptual errors. So I ask the class to have their
> calculators out for the lesson, and I get them to finish up the examples. I empha-
> sise that we need three answers to agree to accept it. The students seem to get
> more into the lesson, and it partially solves the age-old problem of math class:
> sitting and mindlessly copying notes.

An exercise in metacognition

I am concerned with students thinking about their own learning, and not
simply being 'theory sponges'. One of the themes I took back from the on-
campus weeks was Tom's statement that 'How we teach IS the message'. I
feel that by engaging in metacognition during my practica, I can learn from
EXPERIENCE how to encourage students to think about their learning. It
is my contention that the act of keeping a written record of teaching experience is an exercise in metacognition. Tom provided a push in terms of
organising my thoughts by suggesting that I sum up key points of each
week in a separate portion of my entries. This pushed me into the new
realm of reflection-in-action.

I became convinced of the benefits of writing about learning shortly after
I began, and I even started including metacognitive exercises in student
assignments towards the end of my practicum. I asked the math students to
comment on what they learned about buying cars from the unit I created,

and I asked physics students to comment on their feeling towards experiential science. I found that asking students to write on their own learning needs to be an ongoing process, much like keeping a journal of experience myself. Perhaps the single greatest moment in metacognition came in the final instalment of my notes. I tried as best I could to sum the philosophies I had developed over the practicum. I formulated a 'big picture' to my placement, and laid the foundation for the conclusions and extensions that would become part of my action research report:

> I would argue that the nature of science is to construct your own reality of how the world works. I would also point out that most physical tasks performed in a high school laboratory could be performed by anyone (pour this, time that, measure this). High school labs should focus on 'discovering' things, not developing basic motor skills to verify facts that are already known. We as educators should remember that although it is apparent to us that, say, all objects undergo the same acceleration due to gravity near the Earth's surface, it remains a mystery to most high school students. 'Experience first' allows people to discover science rather than be information sponges.

Pedagogical sounding board

For me, the fall practicum was a place where I could build my own pedagogy. The writing task forced me to record and reflect on experience, from which I could construct theories and philosophies based on the 'So what?' of my experience. I was able to 'sound my findings off' a colleague well-versed in the subject matter, allowing me to revisit and refine my philosophies based on experiences and comments. Over the course of the writing exercise, I sent Tom 'snapshots' of my teaching experience in the form of detailed descriptions and sample lesson plans and handouts. I usually made some conclusions about how the lesson went, or how effective the material was, based on my own musings and conversations with my associates.

One of the pedagogical issues that I discussed at length with Tom was the place of labs in a science class. We both felt that labs need to be based on an 'experience first' pedagogy rather than the more traditional approach of 'theory first, lab later'. I was able to investigate the notion of labs before theory in conjunction with my action research report. We discussed at length the notion that, when asked, over half of my Grade 12 physics class preferred doing a lab first and then naming their experiences with standard physical theory (in this instance, the Law of Universal Gravitation).

In one entry I hypothesised that the ability of Grade 12 students to function in an 'experience first' approach might be due to the fact that they were used to a very structured approach to labs. I felt that this comfort level could allow them to rely on skills achieved through rote learning, and allow them to function independently. Tom asserted that there was a difference between 'experience first' and 'functioning independently'. To this end, I tried a similar 'experience first' approach with a lab in my Grade 9 class, with the help of my associate. The Grade 9s reacted quite differently to the 'experience first' approach than the Grade 12s did, although I am not sure how much those differences were due to issues inherent in the relative ages of the two groups. Tom helped me unpack much of what I learned from the two classes, and it became clear that this particular topic, like so many others, would bear further investigation.

> I tried the 'experience first' concept with the Grade 9 class. The topic was reflection of plane and curved surfaces (concave and convex). I introduced the equipment, explained very carefully how to use it, and basically turned the class loose. I insisted that they have a piece of paper out when I was explaining things, so that they could write down the experimental method I was outlining – in their own words. It was quite an interesting class, to say the least. I had to intervene more with the Grade 9s than I did with the Grade 12s. I am forced to wonder if I had to intervene more with the Grade 9s because they haven't had the years of conditioning that the 12s have had, thus making it easier for them to function independently.

[. . .]

Adding links to my map of teaching

Many times during the placement I felt like I was dancing around some central themes or issues, but I could not put my finger on what they were. Initially, I might have said that Tom assisted me in naming my experiences, but I have come to view that as inaccurate. 'Naming' implies that Tom was trying to fit what I was experiencing into a pre-moulded pedagogical genre, which was certainly not the case. He recognised that my teaching experience, like everyone's, was unique and that the key was, as Tom put it in an e-mail, 'constructing understanding from experience first'.

One of the challenges of exploring teaching pedagogy is to be speaking the same language in terms of concept naming. In our particular case, this had the potential to be further compounded by differences in experience: a university professor and a teacher candidate. Very early on, however, we discovered that we did indeed speak the same language. It started out with an 'experience first' pedagogy, something I had experienced both as a Queen's teacher candidate and as a University of Waterloo Co-op student (alternating terms of on-campus study and off-campus work experiences).

Over the course of the writing exercise, all of our writings could probably be grouped under one heading, namely, 'How we teach is the message'. It is a concept I have taken very much to heart. If I want students to construct an understanding of the world around them, I must create an environment rich in experience. Through questioning, Tom helped me create links between various ideas and philosophies that I was discovering. The final instalment of my teaching notes showed the beginning of my being able to name what I was seeing independently, when I was concerned about students being active learners as opposed to 'theory sponges'.

The road ahead

Certainly one cannot learn to be a teacher in four months alone, and through 'thinking questions' I was shown many things to explore further, both practically and conceptually, during my next four-month practicum, in fall 1998 and, indeed, during the rest of my teaching career. After concluding my writing experience for the Fall Term, I found that I had a clear route defined in terms of what I wanted to accomplish at the Faculty of Education. I saw the Faculty as a place to unpack and explore my experiences with peers and colleagues.

Act I, Scent 2: Tom writes, Shawn Observes and Responds

As our drama continues, the first person voice passes to Tom, who illustrates and interprets the researching of his teaching by recording and sharing with Shawn the notes of his teaching of the chemistry/physics methods class in which Shawn was one of 26 students.

A journal of experience

I have always wanted to keep a detailed personal account of my teaching of BEd candidates, much as I had done in my second year (1992–93), teaching one class a day of physics in a local secondary school. Shawn's notes in November–December and the commitment to prepare this chapter finally pushed me to begin. Once started, there was little chance of stopping, thanks to the commitment made to share weekly notes with Shawn. I soon realised that the replies from Shawn were invaluable. After the first six weeks of classes in the Winter Term, all candidates departed for a three-week 'alternate practicum'. While they were away, I worked on replies to questions they had left for me, and it occured to me to review the notes I had kept thus far. I was stunned by the detail in the notes, particularly by the sense that we really had done more than I could remember doing. While I have always tried to be open about my teaching, the discussions with Shawn had made that openness seem very safe, and so I posted the complete set to a website where members of the class could read them. Education programmes are often criticised for their lack of substance, and it seemed important to provide members of the class with a reminder of how much we had done. Two hours later I had the following reply from another member of the class:

> Hi Tom. Wow. I just finished reading your personal teaching notes that you put on the web. I must say I found it pretty mesmerising. It was neat to see how you perceived things. What surprised me (although it shouldn't have) was how often your perception of how the class went was in sync with ours. For example, I remember being disappointed by our last class before our practicum as well. How

quickly it is that I've forgotten how clear it should be to a teacher when a class has gone well or not. Anyway, thanks for sharing your thoughts with us.

The record of experience had already paid rich dividends.

[. . .]

Issues are explored and revisited

Time and again, the e-mail exchanges with Shawn (and our occasional conversations about this chapter) helped me understand particular features of my teaching more fully, pick up issues that had slipped out of view temporarily, and take points further than I might have on my own. Because I have never before shared and examined my teaching with a student throughout his or her time in my class, it is a challenge to describe just how our relationship developed. Once we were underway, there seemed to be no stopping us. Each of us respected the other's autonomy and independence. The common ground of 'experience first' and the shared pleasure of 'talking pedagogy' were ever-present themes.

In the first week of February, Ian Mitchell (of Monash University and the Project for Enhancing Effective Learning – PEEL) visited Queen's University and participated in my three classes and also presented an evening lecture about the PEEL project. My notes on his lecture and Shawn's comments illustrate the exploration and revisiting of issues that we both consider important in our teaching:

> *My notes about Ian Mitchell's lecture*: 45 people in the audience, including CC and her [evening] class. I think there were 11 from Chem-Physics [our class], and R has already watched the videotape. I wonder how I could find out if that evening talk made a difference. For me, it was an absolutely stunning performance of good teaching practice ABOUT good teaching practices. I need to revisit the videotape myself to take it all in. I wonder about doing a quick on-paper survey of how many times people saw Ian during the week and what insights and further questions they gained from him. I have to assume that more contact meant greater impact, particularly since extra contact would mean there was already a significant level of interest.

> *Shawn's comment closes with an intriguing speculation*: I see that you have gone with your original plan as far as the survey goes. I think it goes without saying that Ian had a remarkable impact on me as a professional. It is so rare that someone practices what they preach in the Crystal Palace. People do take notice, and that is part of the reason I think ChemPhys has been so successful. I wonder if the reason so many students do not internalise good learning behaviours is because they are not getting 'quality teaching practices'. Practise what you preach . . . hmmm . . .

Pedagogical sounding board

This section might also be titled, 'Clarifying, consolidating and refining the "so what?" of my teaching'. Our earliest exchanges about 'experience first' convinced me that I could trust Shawn with any and all thoughts about my teaching. He never let me down, and I hope he can say the same about my comments on his teaching. There are times when Shawn seems to see the big picture better than I do. His comments about what he sees me doing often show me new ways that I can 'drive home the message' with the entire class. The discussion we had following the class on 29 January 1998 illustrates how the conversation with Shawn served me well as a pedagogical sounding board. We were two weeks into a five-week block of classes, meeting for ninety minutes three times a week. I knew, from experience, that the climate established by this stage in the term is crucial, and so I was watching everywhere I could for clues about how each member of the class was responding to our 'class tone' and atmosphere. Focusing on the P.O.E. [Predict–Observe–Explain] strategy automatically (and refreshingly) reduces the importance of 'right answers' in the classroom. Yet beginning teachers often look to experienced teachers for long lists of 'right ways to teach' or 'best ways to teach'. Both the events of this class and the position of this class in our course made me particularly interested in how my pedagogical moves were affecting members of the group. After the class I sent an e-mail message to Shawn that I included in my notes for the day, which then evolved into an e-mail message to the entire class. It is convenient to pick up the storyline with Shawn's subsequent comment on part of my message and to continue with the text of my message:

> *Shawn's comment on an earlier portion of my notes*: The simple answer is something that you said at the beginning of the year (and I didn't quite grasp): 'The medium is the message.' How you teach is what inspired me to take on the challenges that I have taken on. I hope that how I teach infects students with a love for science . . . that is my ultimate goal.

> *My notes on the class of 29 January*: [part of an e-mail message to Shawn] Thanks for listening. I remember your 'So What?' comment about having someone outside the school to talk to about teaching. I'm feeling it far more dramatically than that at the moment – it makes ALL the difference to know that someone has made a commitment to being an active listener. Teaching really is a lonely profession. Now to my notes. [end of e-mail to Shawn]

> [continuing to write with Shawn as audience] Surprise, surprise, suddenly what I was going to write seemed important to put to everyone. I can't make that an every-class process, but today turned out, in hindsight, to be incredibly important to me. I think there were several turning points and leaps forward, as well as something of a sequel to that 'experience first' talk in the on-campus blocks last term. Anyway, you'll see it both ways, Shawn. Here you can insert any comments you might have!

> [start of e-mail to class] Thanks, everyone, for another class that I will certainly remember
> [. . .]
> There are several ways to think about the 'right answer' issue. I think I made one reference today that it is increasingly important to ME that you realise that I do not have right answers that I wish you to adopt as science teachers. My job teaching you is VERY different from your job teaching 9–OAC science [14- to 18-year-olds]. At the same time, if you are enjoying the relief of time to think about

practice, after a major 'dose' of it last term, I encourage you to think through how you might adopt (appropriately) features of the environment we are enjoying three times a week in 339 [our classroom]. For me, today's class was very important on two fronts: I started out, from The Stove is Hot, suggesting to at least some that Experience is the Best (and only?) Teacher. Fortunately for me, you brought me back, quickly, and I spotted some of the missing pieces. I had 'Change takes an idea, a challenge, or a puzzle' in my notes, but I didn't say it. Perhaps the extra piece is 'Change has to have experience to build on'. There's plenty of important room for telling and seeing, but both are greatly enhanced by 'feeling' – direct personal experience, whether of spinning wheels or spinning classrooms.

If I have any 'right answers' to offer you, they are about the learning process, not about how Grade 9 density should (or should not) be taught. 'Backtalk' and 'action research' and 'experience first (P.F.E.)' are all general processes that tend to be missing [unintentionally] from most classrooms. You should know that I tend to get very 'nervous' in large-group discussion such as the one that started in response to J's question (which, refreshingly, I never heard!), simply because only one person can speak at a time. But it seemed OK today and I loved the way you all kept building on each other's ideas. The climate at the moment is one that I treasure – there are no put-downs. People listen openly and respond honestly (or else I've been fooled!). This is hard to build in a class of teenagers, but if it is one of your two or three central goals from the first day, I think you can make progress.

In reply to my weekly set of notes. Shawn made the following comment: I think that the key point to remember is that teaching is NOT just about curriculum, classroom management, labs and exams. Teaching is a profession, which entails a responsibility to be a reflective practitioner. Action research, backtalk and thinking about learning are missing from most departments and staffrooms. Talking about teaching, it seems, is quite often left as how to deal with so-and-so or whether something needs to be on a test. These are important points, but there need to be more open forums for teachers to talk about teaching. I think that our e-mail conversations provide that. What concerns me is the resources that go untapped when people do not reflect. The most disturbing thing is that, back in August, I didn't even know what a reflective practitioner was. I certainly did not know it was a part of teaching. Thank you for opening my mind.

It should be self-evident that I was using my conversations with Shawn, and with the entire class by e-mail, as a pedagogical sounding board. The preceding material seems an appropriate passage to extract from our conversation because it reveals what was clearly the case – I was thinking about broader pedagogical issues ('So what?' not 'What?') and Shawn was doing much more than encouraging me. He too kept looking for the bigger picture, linking back to the start of the course in August and its initial phase in ten hours of classes in October. Shawn's comments about being a reflective practitioner were of particular interest because I do not believe I had encouraged him to use that phrase; he had found it elsewhere (in a transcript of a lecture by Donald Schon) and was using it to point to what he now sees himself doing.

An exercise in metacognition

Just as Shawn reports his concern with students thinking about their own learning, so I can report that I am always eager to learn about what my students are thinking about their learning – and learning in the 'teachers' college' setting is always complex. I was particularly successful this year in encouraging members of my class to call the Faculty of Education the 'Crystal Palace', because we are always teaching about teaching and our teaching actions can so easily contradict our words about teaching. Soon after starting to teach in the Crystal Palace in 1977, I made a 'mid-course evaluation' (free responses about strengths, weaknesses and suggestions) a regular feature of my courses, so that everyone could see what everyone else was thinking about the course and so I could attempt to clarify my purposes for the second half of the course. For the last decade, I have required a final assignment that is the 'story' of one's year learning to teach, and to those who ask 'Why?' I usually say that I want them to have a record of this year to look back to in two or five years, to be better able to judge their progress. On 19 February, as they departed for three weeks of teaching, I collected individuals' free responses about our work since early January and posted them to a website where all could read them at their convenience.

Shawn provided a number of personal comments about the comments of the entire group, and this became a very special element in our ongoing conversation about my teaching. I insert in brackets comments about my reactions as we listen to Shawn thinking about other people's thinking about their learning in my course.

> An overriding theme on the web page is people's overwhelming appreciation for you to 'talk the talk and walk the walk'. This is a crude way of saying that how you teach is the message. I think that we were all a little confused [when you said it] in August. I remember thinking, 'Is this guy for real? Does he really MEAN all the stuff he says?'
>
> The single greatest way that you proved it to us was by throwing out the assignment sheet. That sent a strong signal that you were willing to make the course based on our experiences. The other indicator was generating the topics in the first class. I remember that the class was truly shaping its own curriculum. [These are themes Shawn notices regularly, yet it is additionally helpful to have him speak on behalf of the group.]
>
> It is my feeling that one of the problems with some of the courses here is that people are simply throwing as much at us as possible, based on their experiences. There is so much to cover on the topic of teaching that it is easy to get lost in a sea of pedagogical ideas. One person said it the best: 'Russell's enthusiasm, and particularly his single-mindedness in following the path that he feels, is central (overall strategy/intent/aim/vision of what you, the teacher, are trying to accomplish when you have certain activities done in the classroom) is impressive, sobering (are there teachers, and teachers of teachers, who really do think about, and care about, these ideas?) and even inspirational.' I could not agree more. [By selecting and repeating a comment from the website, Shawn helps me see even more clearly just what he and others are noticing.]
>
> [. . .]
>
> The general consensus of weaknesses in our course rides in tandem with its greatest strength, namely the self-directed learning. Some see the lack of structure in the class as a weakness because it seems like we are spinning our wheels sometimes. Others indicate that lack of a 'plan' results in huge tangents in our work (five-minute brainstorming running over a whole class). My opinion tends to be that you have a definite goal in mind for the end of the course, but you are

willing to let us take ourselves there. It's sort of like a race where the finish line is definite but there are no lanes. [Shawn's supportive interpretation of the responses under 'weaknesses' helps me see some of the contradictions in my teaching.]

I was dismayed to see one person questioning the use of the story assignment, but I think it is indicative of the atmosphere you have created that someone feels comfortable enough to say it. [This matches my own interpretation exactly.]

The suggestions made seem to point towards the finish line. There is a desire to hear what you think on issues. Many people tend to see our class as an ideal. Now the trick is to apply what we have learned to our own classrooms (maybe even math). Although I did not understand what you meant at first, I think that how you teach is truly the message, and now the trick becomes how you close and leave us with the big picture (or perhaps more tools for us to discover it on our own.). [As he often does, Shawn concludes with a challenge and a direction. I addressed the issue of 'what I think on issues' by inviting questions and then posting responses to the class website.]

Adding links to my map of teaching

I might also give this section a title such as, 'Making connections I would not see otherwise'. When Shawn names what he sees me doing and what he sees happening in our class, I get a better sense of how to continue to develop perspectives that I believe are important to sustain new teachers through a career of science teaching. As we looked back over my teaching, Shawn was in a special position to point to what may have been unique features of my teaching to the class of which he was a member. Because I invited everyone in that class to read my recent account of how I believe my teaching of teachers has evolved to its present state (Russell, 1997), Shawn was able to draw together features of a number of classes in the following summarising statement:

> You managed to draw on your wealth of experience without giving us your résumé. I was fascinated to see you drawing links in class to your dissatisfaction with [the teaching of] undergraduate physics at university, to your experience of first teacher training, to your physics classes in 1966–67 [from which you shared students' accounts of their year in your class], to Queen's Faculty of Education and finally to us. Your teaching practice seems to have come full circle – you teach teachers in the manner that you learned.

How intriguing to have Shawn helping me to see that I have come full circle! I trust that this account supports my hope that I teach teachers as I myself learned to teach, not because I am teaching as I was taught but because I have examined my own learning and extracted a coherent set of premises and practices.

The road ahead

My teaching of pre-service science teachers has come a long way in 20 years, but most of the significant progress has come since returning to the physics classroom in 1991 and 1992 and since constructing a personal understanding of the pedagogical insights of the PEEL project (Baird and Mitchell, 1986; Baird and Northfield, 1992). Working in an 'experience first' programme structure for pre-service teacher education took me the rest of the way forward, with Shawn's insightful assistance. In the first half of 1999, a sabbatical leave at Monash University will enable me to explore the PEEL project first hand in Australian classrooms. My challenge is to extract the principles from this year's experiences so that I may enact them more fully with the next group of pre-service science teachers. After 20 years it is finally clear: teacher education can only walk its talk when it makes pedagogy its central focus.

The Curtain Falls for the Interval

We expect our pedagogical conversations to continue for some time. We continued to write through the last nine classes in Tom's course in the Winter Term, and we will resume our conversations about teaching when Shawn returns to the classroom in September 1998. On 4 May 1998, Shawn resumes his undergraduate studies in physics at the University of Waterloo; he will be awarded the BSc degree from Waterloo and the BEd degree from Queen's in May 2000. On 28 May 1998, Tom was one of two faculty members presented with the Education Student Society's Golden Apple Award for Excellence in the Education of Pre-service Teachers. This is the first time in 21 years that Tom's teaching has been recognised, and it is difficult for him not to attribute part of his success in the year's teaching to these ongoing conversations with Shawn.

So what?

This closing portion of our chapter might typically bear the heading of 'Conclusions'. In this instance, 'So what?' is consistent with our shared view that every teacher needs to pose this question at every possible opportunity. Brookfield (1995) is one of many who have noted how readily gaps can and do appear in teaching, between what teachers think they are doing and what learners see them doing: 'One of the hardest things teachers have to learn is that the sincerity of their intentions does not guarantee the purity of their practice' (p. 1). Perhaps it is only in this shared experience of supporting each other's efforts to study our professional knowledge as teachers that we more completely understand just how easy it can be for a teacher to lose a focus, misintrepret a response, or put one goal at risk by pursuing another.

We have used the following headings through Scenes 1 and 2 of Act I:

• A journal of experience
[. . .]

- Issues are explored and revisited
- An exercise in metacognition
- Pedagogical sounding board

[. . .]

- Adding links to my map of teaching
- The road ahead

These headings worked well for both of us, and we will probably continue to research our teaching in terms such as these. These headings point more to the process than to the content of our research into our teaching, and they have worked well across two different teaching contexts. While our contexts are different, we are pleased to have confirmed that 'experience first', personal learning from experience, and metacognition help us see the similarities, particularly in terms of learning processes.

We offered this shared study of two individuals' teaching as a contribution to a collection titled *Researching Teaching*. This provides the inspiration to ask what others may ask as they read this chapter: Is this research? and Is this real research? We believe it is, in terms of the following aspects of our professional knowledge:

- The personal accounts of our teaching, with each other's comments embedded, enable us to revisit our experiences and remind ourselves how we interpreted them at the time.
- We better understand our teaching and the responses of our students to our teaching.
- We better understand the pedagogical perspectives and values that we share, and we are encouraged to pursue them further to understand and enact them more fully.
- We better understand how we think about our teaching and about our professional learning as teachers.
- We realise more fully that powerful perspectives on teaching may take years to understand and develop in our teaching.
- We realise that a shared dialogue such as this involves risks and trust, trust in each other as well as the process to which we committed ourselves. We recommend such dialogue to others willing to take similar risks to overcome the invisible and private nature of most teaching and thinking about teaching.

When we began this research, we put our faith in a process with little sense of the possible outcomes. The risk of unknown outcomes is inherent in all research, just as it is inherent in teaching. While many of the details of our teaching may be unique to our personal classrooms, we are pleased to have discussed both the science classroom and the science teacher education classroom in one piece of research. We will be pleased if others interested in 'experience first' teaching approaches that value personal learning from experience find meaning for their own science or teacher education classrooms. The process we have followed is one that we have tried to illustrate as openly as we revealed the content of our discussions. We both find strong meaning in saying that how we teach *is* the message that we want our students to hear. As we conclude this account of our study of our teaching, we hope that readers will understand us when we say that how we research teaching is also the message.

References

Baird, J. R. and Mitchell, I. J. (eds) (1986) *Improving the Quality of Teaching and Learning*. Melbourne: Monash University Printery.

Baird, J. R. and Northfield, J. R. (eds) (1992) *Learning from the PEEL Experience*. Melbourne: Monash University Printery.

Brookfield, S. D. (1995) *Becoming a Critically Reflective Teacher*. San Francisco: Jossey-Bass.

Russell, T. (1997) 'Teaching teachers: How I teach IS the message', in J. Loughran and T. Russell (eds) *Teaching about Teaching: Purpose, Passion and Pedagogy in Teacher Education* (pp. 32–47). London: Falmer Press.

Schon, D. A. (1983) *The Reflective Practitioner: How Professionals Think in Action*. New York: Basic Books.

8

Critical Phases and Incidents

Patricia Sikes, Lynda Measor and Peter Woods

The question is raised, if the teacher career consists of phases, how does one move from one to another? The progress it seems is not always smooth and inevitable. Sometimes there are sharp discontinuities and enormous leaps in such passages. These phenomena are the subject of this chapter.

In the research of life history and sociological biography the issue of 'critical phases' has already emerged as an area of importance. Strauss and Rainwater (1962, p. 105), for example, discussed 'periods of strain' in the lives of the chemists they were researching. During these critical phases, particular events occurred which were important for their careers and identities. Strauss (1959, p. 67) referred to these transformations of identity as 'critical incidents' (see also Walker, 1976). Our research also indicates 'critical incidents' being key events in an individual's life, and around which pivotal decisions revolve. They provoke the individual into selecting particular kinds of actions, which lead in particular directions. Becker wrote of 'these crucial interactive episodes, in which new lines of individual and collective activity are forged . . . and new aspects of the self brought into being' (1966, p. xiv); and Strauss (1959, p. 67) of 'turning points' and the 'frequent occurrence of misalignment – surprise, shock, chagrin, anxiety, tension, bafflement, self-questioning – and also the need to try out the new self, to explore and validate the new and often exciting or fearful conceptions'. Critical incidents are a useful area to study, because they reveal, like a flashbulb, the major choice and change times in people's lives. Here, we aim to pinpoint the 'critical incidents' in some teachers' biographies and to give detailed descriptions of them. We can then consider whether there are any, common patterns in different biographies, and so work towards 'the developmental, generalised formulation of careers' that Glaser called for (1964, p. xv).

'Critical incidents' are most likely to occur during the 'periods of strain' that Strauss and Rainwater (1962) identified. We term the latter 'critical phases', and we noted among our teachers three particular types: (i) extrinsic; (ii) intrinsic; and (iii) personal. 'Extrinsic' critical phases can be produced by events occurring in society. In the biographies of the older teachers we interviewed, the Second World War was a prominent example. It had forced decisions on people that had had a profound effect upon career development. At another level, policy innovations, for example comprehensivisation, could also have a dramatic effect.

'Intrinsic' critical phases occur within the natural progression of a career. Again, the individual is confronted by choices and decisions. We identified the following intrinsic critical phases within the careers of teachers:

1. Choosing to enter the teaching profession.
2. The first teaching practice.
3. The first eighteen months of teaching.
4. Three years after taking the first job.
5. Mid-career moves and promotion.
6. Pre-retirement.

Family events, marriage, divorce, the birth or illness of a child, can also provoke 'personal' critical phases, and project an individual in a different career direction from that held formerly. For older, female, unmarried teachers, parental demands and pressures had profoundly influenced their actions and choices.

It is during these periods of changing and choosing that critical incidents are most likely to occur. The incident itself probably represents the culmination of a decision-making process, crystallising the individual's thinking, rather than being responsible of itself for that decision. We take as our focus in this chapter the kind of 'critical incidents' that occur in one 'critical phase' – the first eighteen months of teaching.

The majority of teachers we interviewed said they had had serious trouble controlling the pupils they taught during their first eighteen months of teaching. This, of course, is nothing unusual (see, for example, Hannam, Smyth and Stephenson, 1971; Hanson and Herrington, 1976). Discipline difficulties are one of the defining characteristics of this critical phase. The problems are moreover experienced in the context of an extreme form of exhaustion. Mr Shoe's (63, retired, science) comments were typical:

> I must admit that the first six months of my real teaching was very, very hard.

Mr Quilley (67, retired, art) agreed. He had begun his career in an elementary school in the North of England in the late 1930s, and both times and pupils were exceptionally hard:

> I think your worst feelings about discipline were in your first job. I went through hell, for about five or six weeks.

Teachers who taught male pupils seemed to have most difficulty. Women teachers in girls' schools faced comparatively few such problems. Miss Coal (65, retired, science) recalled:

> Oh yes. I mean the children were a bit naughty, but it was alright.

The background against which critical incidents occurred revealed the pressures and constraints upon the young teacher entering the profession. The young teacher was usually under the tutelage of a more experienced member of staff. The older teacher exerted pressure to show a 'heavy hand' to pupils. Mr Shoe described the experience of teaching in a small rural school, staffed by himself, and a much older Headmaster, A glass partition was all that separated their classrooms, and Mr Shoe (63, retired, science) remembered the eagle-eyed observation with horror:

> He kept popping in to tell me how to do it . . . He was one of the old school, strong disciplinarian, no nonsense, he was the boss in his school. His advice to me was, if you have any trouble with any of the kiddies, impose your authority. Smack them down. He'd got a very hard, horny, hand there.

This graphically portrays the context of the critical incident, which in this case involves a confrontation between teacher and pupils. Quite frequently that confrontation is violent, and leads to the involvement of senior members of staff at the school. One account, from a Glasgow woman teacher, gives a particularly clear view of the character of such episodes.

The woman began her career in a tough elementary school in Glasgow in 1939. During her first year there she experienced considerable discipline difficulties, which culminated in the following incident. One day, the teacher entered the classroom to find that each of her male pupils had displayed their genitals on the desk in front of them. She told the pupils to put them away, and then frog-marched one of the boys out of the classroom. Her classroom was on a first-floor balcony, and somehow she pushed the boy in such a way that he fell over the balcony and on to the floor some distance below. A now carefully buttoned group of boys watched his fall in a hushed and respectful silence. The woman had no further discipline problems. This incident, while perhaps particularly colourful (blue?), is a good example of many of the issues involved. The general properties are that a class is disruptive over quite a long period of time. At some point, a particular potent threat is made by pupils, bringing a response from the teacher, and a violent outcome.

These incidents have long-term effects. The Glasgow teacher reported that as a result of the above event, she established a reputation which enabled her to gain reasonable discipline in the school from then on. It is significant that the accounts we collected of these kinds of encounters had successful outcomes for the teachers – presumably those who fail such tests give up teaching. Even so, their response to incidents varied considerably, and as a result, the teachers established quite different kinds of reputations. But we can still see some common patterns, as the following two accounts illustrate:

> And I've been bashed by kids about a quarter my size, and one of them got bashed back (laughter) and I ended up on the mat about it . . . It was near the end of the lesson, and I walked past a child who was working, and he'd take a swing at you. In the tummy, or even further down . . . well what do you do? Wop them one then and there? At least I did that, and so I was sent for. Eventually the Head said I mustn't bash them up. I wasn't a bully, but I said, personal violence, foul-mouthed cheek is not on, because most of the staff were wopping them one occasionally, or taking them to be wopped . . . Eventually the Head said, 'No more, that's it. The next time and you're going in front of the Director' (Laughs). And I thought, My God, my old man, teaching in town, me in front of the Director, this will be terrible . . . This will be ghastly, because my father was running two departments in the local tech (Said in a highly animated way) . . .

Well I went to see my NUT bloke. Anyway there came a time when a bloke was absolutely terribly disobedient, so I said 'Come out here, I'm gonna cane you in front of, everybody.' And I rushed into my store room, and I had lots of little sticks in there, and I unfortunately grabbed the first, and it happened to be the black one, and it was about twelve inches long, and I came out, and I said . . .

(Mr Quilley, 67, retired, art)

We had some difficulty in transcribing Mr Quilley's account from the tape. The problem was in getting down what he had said. This appeared to be because he increased the pace of delivery of his sentences, which were shortened and forceful, piling them up in a staccato fashion. This style of talking, which is difficult to represent in print, emphasised the drama of his narrative:

and I came out and I said 'Hold your hand out lad; now you know what you're getting this for?'
Yes.
'Do you deserve it?'
I don't know.
'Yes you do; hold your hand out.' So he held his hand out and as I struck him, he turned it upward, so I bashed him across the thumb. So I said 'Serve you right. And the other hand, and this one again, and that one.' And I sent him back to his seat.
(Draws a proper breath for the first time and relaxes the pace of' the narrative.) And nothing happened, the next day the Head yanked me out and said 'You're as good as fired.' 'Got to go and see – the what's his name, Director – in the town hall, but I'm washing my hands of it, the only hurdle you've got to get past is the boy's father, he's coming to see you. You'd better watch it . . . but I've washed my hands of you, I'm speaking against you.' So the father came up, about the boy, and I thought Ughm this is it, and the boy's father came in, and we had quite a nice conversation, we got on quite well, and to cut a long story short, I gave him ten bob – at his request (pause) lots of money in those days . . . I only got paid £14 a month – but, er, he said er, next time Mr Quilley, get him out of school, and knock his head off, I don't want him bashed in school. And that was the end of it.

Mr Tucks (29, scale 2, science) gave an account of a very similar incident. However, his reaction to it was very different:

Mr Tucks: Well . . . there was a very significant incident on the . . . last day of the first half term . . . when I actually came to blows with a student. Yeah, and . . . he wasn't a student of mine, but he'd interrupted a lesson and gone out, and slammed the door, and various things (mutters) and, and didn't seem to (mutters, and his voice becomes quiet and indistinct) work at the time (mutters again).
R: Were you teaching him?
Mr Tucks: No, no, no? No – (takes a deep breath in).
R: He just came in and interrupted your lesson?
Mr Tucks: Yeah, yeah, yeah (mutters, sighs). Er mmm! And in fact I was reprimanded by the Head, for that . . .
R: What did you do?
Mr Tucks: I chased him and then I clocked him over the head . . . yeah . . . I completely lost control of myself . . . I hesitate to repeat it, I can't, I don't know what . . . you know, . . . it's difficult to repeat it, don't like it. Well that was crucial. I suddenly got the wrong sort of reputation amongst students who didn't know me, for some time the ones who knew me well, didn't learn

anything from it. At least – well not – but it had the effect . . . these students could perceive, from afar that I was slightly different style . . . they weren't prepared to sort of it . . . test it. I was prepared to be very informal with students I was teaching, but I was sufficiently unsure of myself to regard an assumption of students I wasn't teaching, of that informality as a threat,

R: What effects has it had? Do you hit kids now?
Mr Tucks: Noooh! Not at all.

For Mr Tucks the experience had been personally distressing. His facial gestures and tone of voice expressed his discomfort, and he openly stated that he did not like even talking about it. The pace of his delivery slowed down discernibly, and the researcher had to push for the full story. Mr Tucks' response to the critical incident was different from Mr Quilley's. The discovery of such personal anger in himself discomforted Mr Tucks quite considerably and determined his future course of action. He sought to avoid any repetition of such incidents.

Mr Shoe (63, retired, science) gave an account of a similar 'critical incident'. The details were the same – in a moment of exasperation he 'just banged their heads together you know'. He was able to draw out what was crucial in the experience for him:

I did it once – it was a salutary lesson, so I learned that if I ever wanted to hit out, I never did. I learned from that, and I think one of the things I learned was the fact that one of the worst things you can do is deal with a child in anger, when he's provoked you. I think I learned, too, that if you begin to shout and you begin to rant and rave with the class, you lose your authority anyway.

Mr Shoe gives an indication of one of the elements which make such incidents 'critical'. It is the discovery that a display of real anger in the classroom is genuinely counter-productive, and that teachers need to 'stage manage' a 'front' of anger if they are to cope as 'proper teachers'. Being provoked into a display of real anger by pupils represents not 'coping', but rather a breakdown in classroom interaction rules. Mr King (65, retired, art) recognised this:

I think you have to pretend to be angry with children, but never to lose your temper. Once you lost it, they sense it, something's transmitted, salt or something is sent across the atmosphere. They know it, just like an animal, a horse will gallop through a wood, if you're frightened of him, and brush you off. If you really hold the reins he won't. So children are like that, they react intuitively or whatever, instinctively is better.

These incidents caused 'trouble' (Furlong, 1977) for the teachers, in which they faced punishment or embarrassment of some kind as a result of their loss of control. The intervention of senior colleagues escalated the affairs beyond the privacy of one's own classroom, so, there is both a public and private loss of face involved.

As a result of the 'critical incident', the teachers involved reached a number of decisions.

R: Did you go on hitting kids?
Mr Shoe: Not really, no . . . It wasn't my way really.

The teacher came to a decision about his own teaching style, and about the way he wanted to do things. When the teachers described this process, they usually employed a negative model, to help define their own choices. Mr Shoe, for example, compared himself with the 'horny handed Headmaster':

> I learned by observing him in many ways . . . In his lessons there wouldn't be any messing. You hadn't got to think, now how can I make sure I've got their interest. What he did was purely imposing his will on them, that was that really.

Mr Redford (33, scale 4, art) used the same tactic, in reference to his first Head of Department:

> I quickly ditched any set rules he was passing on to me, and just taught in my own sort of way.

Hanson and Herrington (1976) discuss the ways that senior members of the teaching profession put pressure on younger teachers to conform. Heads of departments in particular may act as 'critical reality definers' (Riseborough, 1981). The 'critical incidents' show how such pressures work, but also how teachers find their way through them. The incidents are 'critical' in that they force a major leap in the process by which new recruits become the kind of teachers they want to be.

We offered this analysis of 'critical incidents' to some of the teachers being interviewed. This was part of an attempt to get respondent validation, but also to involve teachers more fully in the work of analysis. It was suggested to Mr Redford (33, scale 4, art) that a 'critical incident' had set the style of teaching and discipline he had held ever since:

> Yes, I think it probably did, although I don't think it came as a great shock to me, do you know what I mean, I think I'd perhaps, I'd actually reached that stage earlier, but my lack of experience had encouraged me to, under the pressure of the situation, to accept the urgings of the Head of Department to take on *his* operations. Plus I was supply at that point. If I'd started in September, perhaps I wouldn't have done that you know, but er . . . in fact . . . er

This suggests that the critical incident does not necessarily introduce anything totally new into the practices of the teacher. Rather, it probably acts to crystallise ideas, attitudes and beliefs that the teacher has more generally or less consciously held up to that point.

Teachers gave an account of another kind of incident, which occurred usually soon after the 'critical incident'. We have termed these 'counter incidents'. The 'counter incident' also involved a challenge from the pupils, but brought a different response from teachers which reflected 'their way', and the sort of teacher they wished to be. Mr Shoe (63, retired, science), for example, offered an account of another confrontation situation he had encountered, during his first six months teaching, but this time he had stayed in control, successfully stage-managing the interaction:

> I would have felt dreadful, I think, if I felt that I was losing the control and some kiddies wouldn't do what I wanted. I don't think I could live with that, and I think the worst occasion I had, or the best occasion maybe, and that was, with one lad, he had a widowed mother, a very fine lady really, but John, her son, was not

particularly able, but tending to be a bit difficult at times and I know one day I had to remove him; I said 'Well if you're going to behave like this, I've had enough of this. it's going to be to the Headmaster.' And we were in a dining room then with a central corridor and this was used as a classroom, and he'd played and played, and he'd been funny and difficult and I thought – well I'd better get rid of him, and he wasn't going to go if I just said 'Go'. So I think one of the best ways, really, you get them at a disadvantage very quickly, to get them by the scruff of the pants and scruff of the neck, and you've got them then and they will go, I got hold of this lad and he was pretty big and heavy, and I said 'Well are you going out?' and he said 'No, I'm not'. 'Oh, you are!' and he said 'No, I'm not'. 'Oh, you are!' Well, of course, he went down the middle of the passageway, and hitting desks and chairs as he went, there was an almighty crash, bang. wallop, doors open, out he went, and he was seen to go straight through, like that, across the playground and in front of the Headmaster's study. I said. 'Now you can tell the Headmaster what you've seen.' The kiddies had seen all this; heard the noise and kerfuffle 'What a tiger we have!' But I didn't do that very often, just that one occasion I think. You learn, well I'm not standing any nonsense, so I'm not sure it works on every occasion . . . actually end of the day, John Dewhurst and I were the best of pals. He didn't sort of resent me, no; I told him I wanted him out, and certainly I tried to tell the kids that 'Alright you misbehaved, but I assure you that I'm not one to bear grudges', and I would hope that teachers would, once they've chastised or corrected, are not going to hold it against you – 'I'll remember you in future' – As far as I'm concerned if you accept punishment and it's accepted gracefully, and most of them did, as far as I'm concerned, then it's finished. 'I'm not going to treat you now any different from anybody else.'

Mr Shoe's 'critical' and 'counter' incident stories were told, closely following each other in the same interview. They were used to highlight the teacher's choices of teaching and discipline style, and indicate the values and attitudes he chose for himself as a teacher. In Mr Shoe's case, his style did not entirely exclude a physical approach. Nevertheless, Mr Shoe learned from his 'critical incident' to pick both his pupil and the form of trouble quite carefully. In the counter incident, the events are staged to show 'what a tiger we have'. In the second episode, there is noise, excitement, spectacle, and a mass audience. Yet there was no real physical violence or pain. Mr Shoe was in control of the counter incident, unlike the critical one. His comment that John and he were later 'the best of pals' was also significant. No such reconciliation would have been possible after the first incident.

A 'counter incident' in which rather different values were made clear is illustrated in the following story:

I had another quick incident. There was a cupboard, with the stock in, and some of the big fifth years, they were quite toughies, were in the cupboard, and I said 'Come out!' and the whole class went silent. And I said, 'Right, empty your pockets' and this lad said 'No'. [The first 'empty your pockets' was said quite gently.] So I said 'Empty your pockets.' [Mr Redford repeated the order, even more quietly and with real gentleness in his account.] He said 'No', and you know you've got this immediate confrontation, this lad was about six foot tall, and there's me – looking up at him. And he said 'You'll have to make me.' It was an *awful* situation, but I knew I couldn't back down. He walked towards me, and I put my hand out, and he slipped, his feet shot front under him, and he fell flat on his back. He said, 'Right then!' (his tone very aggressive) and I said 'OK come on' (Mr Redford's tone was very gentle). I realised he needed a way out. He said, 'Alright, I'll empty my pockets, but if you don't find anything, I want an apology.' He got up and emptied his pockets, and there was nothing in there, and I apologised, and after that my relationship with the whole group was completely different.

(Mr Redford, 33, scale 4, art)

This incident was important to Mr Redford because it showed his preferred way of dealing with discipline difficulties. He attempted to leave violent confrontation completely out of his teaching style. While he could not always avoid confrontation in an all-boys' comprehensive school, he did attempt to meet it when it occurred in a calmly rational way, refusing to allow himself to be influenced by the culture of aggression that, in his view, is current in such schools. He told of a third incident, in which another individual reinforced the identity he was seeking. A pupil approached him:

'Ere Sir,' he said, 'Ey, you're alright.' So I said 'Oh, thanks a lot.' 'Yeh,' he said, 'Yeh, what I like about you,' he said, 'You don't try and be tough like the other guys, some of the other teachers.' And I said, 'Well I'm not', an' you could have heard a pin drop. And he said, 'What did you say?' I said, 'Well, I'm not tough', and he said (loudly) 'Did you 'ear what he said', you know. And I was intrigued, and it seemed to me that a lot of teachers, you can get drawn into a situation, where – if you're not careful, where you have to act tough, and you're pushing and pushing and pushing, and you never allow them to see that there's no harm in not being tough, which probably contributes to the tendency for them all to be little tough guys.

Mr Quilley also described a 'counter incident' which reveals some particular features about his teaching style, which were in direct opposition to those of Mr Redford. When Mr Quilley related his 'critical incident' he had shown none of the remorse about his experience of violent confrontation which the other teachers had. He did not suggest that he avoided violent confrontations from then on in his career. Other data gathered in the project supported this conclusion. [. . .] we thought it would make for useful cross-referencing if we chose teachers for interviewing who knew each other, either from working in the same school, even at different times historically, or because they taught the same subject in the same town. Thus Mr Tucks knew Mr Quilley – he had done his student teaching practice at his school. He laughed when Mr Quilley was mentioned, 'Oh he was renowned that guy, everyone knew him.' Mr King declared, 'He was a bully', and Mr Redford told tales of Mr Quilley's monstrous mass canings, that had shocked pupils, parents and peers alike. Nevertheless, this was not the full picture. Mr Quilley (67, retired, art) did not provide a specific 'counter incident' to reveal his teaching style, but he did make a series of comments which showed there was another side to him. He was anxious to indicate that he did achieve good relationships in some areas, with at least some of the pupils.

Colliers' sons, wonderful in the playground, great on the football pitch, and in the swimming pool. I had no trouble with them there, but in the classroom, you were a different person, to be got at, if you were gottable at.

In addition, Mr Quilley provided long accounts of the expeditions and trips he had organised, for pupils to go skiing or to visit art galleries abroad, or sailing small boats. Mr Tucks (29, scale 2, science) confirmed this view of a two-sided figure.

> He was extraordinary, such a mixture, he'd organise all these super trips, skiing and painting, the kids loved it, and yet all this violence too. I don't know if the story is apocryphal, but there are tales of him playing games with knives, you know boys had to splay their fingers out, and you dot between them with a big knife.

In all three sets of 'critical' and 'counter' incidents that we have described, the teachers are indicating what choices they took at a particular phase, and trying to show what kind of teacher they became. But the communication of identity is no easy matter. We have considered this elsewhere (Measor and Woods, 1984a), taking Lewis' (1979) argument that values, attitudes, roles and identity are things which are very difficult for people to talk straightforwardly about. Indeed, in Lewis' view, they are precisely the things that people need symbols for. We suggested that adolescents employed myths to signal acceptable role models and identities for themselves. We also documented the ways that adolescent girls personified values into particular people around them, and used them as positive or negative role models.

The same mechanisms appeared to be at work in these teachers' biographies. We have already seen how negative role models were employed. The 'critical' and 'counter' incident accounts were another device, where symbols are used to reveal choice and identity preferences. The 'critical' incident is described, the reaction to it is identified, and the confusion it engendered is emphasised. The choices that resulted from it are then made clear. The 'counter' incident, when told, acts like a contrastive shadow, reinforcing the choices that resulted from the 'critical' event, and confirming the identity.

Critical incidents set teachers off on a path, looking for a new way – 'their way' – to do things. Mr Shoe (63, retired, science) indicated the importance of discovering positive role models at this phase:

> I think one of the teachers that perhaps interested me was a lady, Deputy Headmistress, and I used to admire her in some ways. She always used to seem to have – the kids in her class always seemed to be well occupied, always interested. I used to think, well – I used to see her sometimes coming to school in the morning, she'd get off her bike, and she'd be snatching a sample of this, a flower of that, and she'd come in armed with that, and suddenly you'd see that these were being used in a lesson. She always seemed to, never had discipline problems with the boys that I was having you see. It was just the fact that her lessons were interesting.

As a result, Mr Shoe discarded his old role model, the Headmaster of his first school. He decided he had been wrong, that there was another way and that he was going to follow it!

> I think the first thing is that you've got to get the kiddies interested . . I think bringing in a certain sense of humour, if you can break it up, have a laugh.

Involve them . . . (by) . . . talking, even though it wasn't necessarily relevant. Football, if they're a Chelsea supporter, or something. And 'Top of the Pops'. Knowing their interests, whether it be roller skating, or skateboarding or any other interest.

Mr Shoe had, by the time he had been in teaching three or four years, found his own 'way' in school, and it was one that was markedly different from the first role models he had encountered.

There were clear gender differences involved in critical incidents for teachers. All of the incidents we have described here, except for the first, occurred when male teachers confronted male pupils. The women teachers we interviewed who had taught in girls' schools did not report comparable experiences, although women teachers involved in teaching boys or mixed classes did. The Glasgow woman teacher's story has already been told. Another woman, Mrs Castle (64, retired, art) also had difficulties and experienced violence in her first teaching job. She taught in a selective grammar school in a South Wales mining village. Mrs Castle described the school as 'nicely disciplined'. Nevertheless, there were many challenges to her discipline, and once she cracked.

> *Mrs Castle:* I did hit a pupil once, in a temper, hit a boy of six foot . . . I felt ever so silly afterwards, very upset, I apologised.
> *R:* What had he done?
> *Mrs Castle:* I don't know, he was probably being a bit cheeky or something. I was horrified. I think I apologised almost straight away. He tried to cheer me up then.

Mrs Castle gave further accounts of the challenges she received:

> *Mrs Castle:* As I say the boys did play me up at Christmas. I got chased round with the mistletoe and shut in the art room with some of the sixth form and they said things like 'Why don't you give in gracefully, or are you going to call for Sir.'
> *R:* Which did you do?
> *Mrs Castle:* I gave in gracefully of course.

There are gender differences, it seems, not only in the ways boys and girls misbehave (Ebbutt, 1981; Measor, 1984; Measor and Woods, 1984a), but also with regard to the teacher's effect on the nature of classroom deviance (Walkerdine, 1980).

One of our teachers felt he had never had any real discipline problems, and could recall no 'critical' experience of violent confrontation. But there were certainly critical incidents elsewhere in his life, and these might hold the key to his comparatively smooth professional development:

> . . . Well I was blown up, as I told you and was asked if I would go into a garrison regiment, because that's for downgraded physique. In theory you strut about with a revolver at your hip, and look after a town as opposed to fighting. But no, this garrison unit piled into boats and sailed over to the Channel Islands, we were the liberating force. I remember being in the first landing boat, not a German in sight, but girls galore. I suppose I had been there about three or four weeks, the civic authorities had a big dinner, they invited some officers, I sat next to the Education Officer and he said 'Why don't you come to Jersey, you're just the sort

of man we want' I said 'I don't care to teach in the Channel Islands.' I saw myself with a good job in a public school. Or painting portraits in a posh studio of posh people.

(Mr King, 65, retired, art).

However, Mr King agreed to take the job. His military background was to have a profound effect on his career and identity as a teacher:

The Channel Islands' public schools had suffered like hell, because the Germans had imprisoned a lot of the teachers that that hadn't escaped, so it was more or less run by the locals and senior boys. I remember being shown around by the HM and the first room he opened, he, not me, was hit in the face with a book, and he spread it around that I was an ex-commando, which I wasn't, and of course boys immediately moved to the other side of the corridor and said 'Morning Sir', and that was what I was really enrolled for, to impose discipline, there was none. I never hit a boy. I would grab him by the scruff of the neck and the trousers and pick him up, and say 'Now what are you going to do?' It didn't matter if he was eighteen years of age, because I was very strong then, I would put him down and say, 'Now, *behave yourself.*' I never needed to hit the boys.

Mr King had finished up as the senior tutor at his school, in charge of discipline. He had a reputation in the school and wider community, for excellent discipline. He felt that these early incidents were crucial in enabling him to build a confident front. They had set his image and given him his teacher style.

What is it then which makes these incidents critical for the teacher telling the story? The account involves a set of claims about the self. For the individual particular claims are made about their ability to maintain discipline, and their authoritative image. It represents a claim to the identity of being 'a proper teacher'. The critical incident involves a challenge to this identity. As a result some of the claims are dropped, others are made real. Some parts of the identity are confirmed, others renounced. In addition, the critical incident can involve a discovery about parts of the self hitherto unknown, about, for example, one's capacity for anger, and this can be difficult to cope with. The incident provokes a series of choices, as the individual sorts out which kind of behaviour and which parts of the self are appropriate for display in the teacher role. Strauss (1959) discussed the way a particular event can change the things an individual wants, or sees as important, thus changing the trajectory of a career. The critical incident works in this way. It involves a reassessment of priorities. By examining such incidents, therefore, we gain an insight into the processes by which identities are built by individuals at particular points in their life cycle. Hankiss wrote of the way 'people endow certain fundamental episodes with a symbolic meaning, by locating them at a focal point of the explanatory system of the self' (Bertaux, 1981, p. 205). The individual chooses 'a way' and by so doing, makes a self.

It is open to question whether these changes remain permanent. Hankiss felt that 'key events' were important because 'they constantly lead or force that person to select new models or a new strategy of life' (*ibid.*, p. 206). However, coping with such 'critical incidents' 'constantly', or even quite often, would be extremely exhausting, probably destructive. Critical incidents occur at fairly lengthy intervals, probably during critical phases, and they have momentous consequences for the self.

Critical incidents then have a far-reaching effect upon teachers' careers, but there are a number of critical phases in any biography. Teachers, if they survive this kind of test, find others later on in their careers. They have to negotiate their way through promotion hurdles once they are established in their role, and this calls for increasingly sophisticated strategies in the current economic situation. They always have to cope with senior colleagues, and have to set their own ambitions and career interests alongside those of their family. They may experience a 'mid-life crisis'. Finally, as the teacher comes up to retiring age, another critical period ensues. More adjustments are made as the teachers look forward to retirement, and back over what they have and have not achieved.

References

Bertaux D. (ed.) (1981) *Biography and Society: the Life History Approach in the Social Sciences*. Beverly Hills: Sage.

Ebbutt, D. (1981) Girls' science: boys' science revisited, in Kelly, A. (ed.) *The Missing Half*. Manchester: Manchester University Press.

Furlong, J. V. (1977) Anancy goes to school: a case study of pupils' knowledge of their teachers, in P. Woods and M. Hammersley (eds) *School Experience*. London: Croom Helm.

Glaser, B. (1964) *Organizational Scientists: Their Professional Careers*. Kansas: Bobbs-Merrill.

Hannam, C., Smyth, P. and Stephenson, N. (1971) *Young Teachers and Reluctant Learners*. Harmondsworth: Penguin.

Hanson, D. and Herrington, M. (1976) *From College to Classroom: the Probationary Year*. London: Routledge and Kegan Paul.

Lewis, M. (1979) *The Culture of Inequality*. New York: New American Library.

Measor, L. (1984) 'Gender and the sciences: pupils' gender-based conceptions of school subjects', in M. Hammersley and A. Hargreaves (eds) *Curriculum Practice: Some Sociological Case Studies*. Lewes: Falmer Press.

Measor, L. (1985) 'Interviewing in ethnographic research', in R. Burgess (ed.) *Strategies of Educational Research: Qualitative Methods*. Lewes: Falmer Press.

Measor, L. and Woods, P. (1984a) *Changing Schools: Pupil Perspectives on Transfer to a Comprehensive*. Milton Keynes: Open University Press.

Measor, L. and Woods, P. (1984b) 'Cultivating the middle ground: teachers and school ethos', *Research in Education*, 31 May.

Riseborough, G. (1981) Teacher careers and comprehensive schooling: an empirical study, *Sociology*, **15**, 3, pp. 352–81.

Strauss, A. L. (1959) *Mirrors and Masks*. San Francisco: The Sociology Press.

Strauss, A. L. and Rainwater, L. (1962) *The Professional Scientist*. Chicago: Aldine Press.

Walker, R. (1976) Innovation, the school and the teacher (1), Unit 27 of Course E203 *Curriculum Design and Development*. Milton Keynes: Open University Press.

Walkerdine, V. (1980) Learning, language and resistance. History Workshop Conference, Brighton.

Introduction to Section 3: Investigating Professional Development

The chapters in this section of the book focus on teachers investigating their own practice. The main themes of this section are:

- teachers as researchers;
- reflective cycles;
- using autobiography;
- investigating professional identity.

Donald Schon's notion of the reflective practitioner came to the notice of teacher educators and educationalists in the 1980s. It was often seen as a new discovery rather than a revisiting of Dewey's notion of reflection. In the years since Schon wrote *The Reflective Practitioner* (1983) there have been increased attempts to encourage reflective practice in professional development and teachers' research into their practice. The teacher-as-researcher movement has gained popularity in recent years. Readings in this section critically explore the notion of the 'teacher-researcher' and its potential for enabling educators to analyse and investigate their own professional development. This view led proponents of the reflective practitioner movement to argue that the teacher should be able to develop professional knowledge from their own professional experiences. This principle is also the basis for the movement's claim that the teacher should act as a researcher who generates and tests out educational theories. The notion of teachers as researchers is a powerful one for the teaching profession especially when it informs approaches to professional development. If research is only conducted by experts from outside the profession, the potential for teachers to contribute and control the development of knowledge and practice can be very limited.

The first chapters in this section discuss the theoretical and practical issues identified in the literature associated with this movement and provide examples of teachers engaging in investigation of their own practice. These readings investigate concepts and issues associated with the reflective practice movement and its implicit aim of valuing teachers' experience and expertise. These chapters also illustrate how reflective practice cycles can be organised for individual and collaborative facilitation of professional development.

There are examples of research into teachers' careers and practice, which emphasise self-reflection, and the need for the individual to engage in reflective practice. This literature utilises approaches such as biography, life history and narrative to investigate personal ideas, thoughts and perceptions about teaching practice and professional development. These writers and researchers tend to focus upon the individual and self-knowledge. The later chapters in this section give examples of teachers and researchers utilising methods from the self-study and reflective practice literature to research their own teaching practice. These chapters focus upon the methods and issues associated with using biography and narrative as a tool for investigating professional development. They also indicate the complexities and depth of understanding of the formulation and construction of teacher identities that emerge when the process of professional development is investigated from the teacher's perspective.

Chapter 9 by Roger Hancock focuses upon issues for teachers who attempt to investigate their own teaching. Hancock explores the reasons why teachers have not become teacher-researchers in the past. He signals the need to effect change in traditional attitudes which regard teaching and research as separate activities as well as highlighting the practical issues which have often prevented teachers becoming researchers. The traditional approach to viewing teaching and researching teaching has perpetuated the gulf between theory and practice so that teachers' experience and insights have not been seen as valid factors in developing educational theory. Hancock concludes by arguing that teachers' views, experiences and insights must be valued if teaching is to become a research-based profession.

In Chapter 10 Andy Convery provides an example of a teacher identifying the issues he met when attempting to investigate his own teaching. This chapter explores the implications of utilising the notion of reflective practice to inform his own professional development. This chapter focuses specifically upon the issue of a teacher-researcher attempting to change his own practice through utilising and exploring Schon's notion of 'reflection-in-action'. Convery argues for the use of collaborative discussion in developing reflective action in order to change and inform practice.

The eleventh chapter of this book provides a model of professional development that can help address the issues raised in the first two chapters. Michael Huberman explores models for professional development beyond traditional in-service based activities to include self-study and research-based projects. Like the preceding chapter by Convery, Huberman draws upon the literature based upon Donald Schon's notion of the reflective practitioner. He argues that there is a need to develop approaches to professional development that take into account the 'artisan' model of teaching. In arguing for a recognition and accommodation of an 'artisan' or teacher experience driven model of professional development, Huberman emphasises the need to build reform from the bottom up rather than implement reform through professional developments programmes in a linear fashion from the top down. Huberman suggests teachers should be encouraged to form experimenting teacher networks to confront and re-solve problems and generate new initiatives.

The final chapters of the book look at autobiography as a tool to investigate professional development. In Chapter 12, Peter Clement discusses the use of autiobiography – a specific method which teachers and education practitioners can use to critically analyse their practice and professional lives. Clement's chapter initially draws attention to the advantages of auto-biographical memory as a method teachers can use to discover the values and beliefs they bring to teaching. He then raises the difficulties for teachers relying upon memory to objectively investigate and research their teaching. He concludes by suggesting ways in which these methodological approaches can help teacher-researchers use autobiography to assess changing and enduring features of their professional practice.

Chapter 13 by Maggie Maclure provides an example of the use of auto-biography in a research project investigating professional identity. Using autobiography to look at this issue through the eyes of the participating teachers revealed the power these teachers had to change their practice. Maclure's chapter also highlights the complexities that surround profes-sional development and the construction of professional identities. The use of autobiography enabled Maclure to show how teachers' professional identities are constructed from a variety of aspects which include their career, home life, curriculum and pedagogy. The research also indicated that teachers' identities are not necessarily stable and coherent, and high-lighted a crisis surrounding teachers' identities and careers.

References

Schon, D. 1983) *The Reflective Practitioner: How Professionals Think in Action.* New York: Basic Books.

9

Why are Class Teachers Reluctant to Become Researchers?

Roger Hancock

Introduction

> To date, the United Kingdom's new Teacher Training Agency has been able to identify only a small, if significant, body of research findings directly focused on classroom practice and enhancing it; more is needed.
>
> (TTA, 1996a, p. 1)

There have been important developments in the past 20 years with regard to Lawrence Stenhouse's (1975) vision of teachers integrating research into their classroom practice. Teachers have contributed as practitioners, researchers and writers to some classic collaborative action research projects like, for instance, the 'Humanities Curriculum Project' (e.g. Stenhouse, 1968, 1971; MacDonald, 1973), the 'Girls into Science and Technology (GIST) Project' (Smail, Whyte and Kelly, 1982; Kelly, Whyte and Smail, 1984) and the 'Pupil Autonomy and Learning with Microcomputers (PALM) Project' (Somekh, 1991). Teacher research has been generated by award- bearing courses and higher degrees (e.g. Lewis, 1988; Falkner, Swann and Streddle, 1992) and some of this work has been published in journals, bulletins, local collections and edited books gathered together by experienced researchers (e.g. Vulliamy and Webb, 1992; Bell, Stakes and Taylor, 1994). Teacher, research has also been greatly supported by research networks like the pioneering CARN (Classroom Action Research Network) (e.g. Ryan and Somekh, 1991) and by institutions like, for instance, Kingston University (Lomax and Jones, 1993) and Canterbury Christ Church College (Frost, 1995).

These are all very significant and desirable developments and I have no wish to devalue the importance of what appears to be a gathering teacher research movement. However, as my title suggests, my impression is that the great majority of classroom teachers remain uninvolved. They shy away from seeing themselves as researchers and they are reluctant to write about their teaching practice. Writing in the mid-1970s, Stenhouse anticipated the difficulties:

> I concede that it will require a generation of work . . . if the majority of teachers – rather than only the enthusiastic few – are to possess this field of research.
>
> (Stenhouse, 1975, p. 142)

119

If more teachers are to become involved then it seems crucial to have a good understanding of the basis of this teacher reluctance. This chapter offers four areas of explanation – teachers' status, teachers' working conditions, teachers' confidence and, lastly, the difficulties that teachers experience when they try to integrate outsider research methodologies into their day-to-day practice. I then conclude by highlighting some of the ways in which teacher research might be effectively supported.

Teacher Status and Public Expectations

> . . . wise parents and wise children know that growth, education and enrichment depends on a deep collaboration between the natural God-given knowledge of parents and the professional knowledge of teachers – there's a complementarity here. Alas, what we have is a teaching profession which feels itself to be not trusted by government and which feels that government is almost setting the parents against the teachers. This cannot be constructive.
>
> (Milroy, 1992)

The history of the teaching profession is a history of a struggle for status. Teacher professional association activity, although often focusing on front-line issues like pay and workloads, can be seen, at a deeper level, to be about 'building up public appreciation of the value of education and the worth of the teacher' (Tropp, 1957).

Traditionally, class teachers have never been expected to comment on the theory and practice of their work and very few have done so. Those who research classroom practice tend to be former classroom teachers working in higher education, educational psychologists and those in advisory or inspection posts. To a large extent, classroom teachers' skills and knowledge are, at best, underestimated, and at worst, disregarded – by parents and the general public, by politicians, by the children and, curiously, by many teachers themselves. A further downgrading of an already poorly regarded workforce has been particularly in evidence over the past ten years when there has been a sustained period of political and public criticism of teachers. This continues unabated as I write, with, for instance, a concentration on getting rid of a very small percentage of inadequate teachers by both Labour and Conservative political parties and also by Her Majesty's Chief Inspector of Schools, Chris Woodhead.

There never has been a public expectation that teachers would write about the theory underpinning the classroom craft. Indeed, it can be argued that there is a tradition of public and political questioning about the very existence of any significant educational theory at all – an anti-intellectual and anti-professional stance. For instance, in the early 1990s, Kenneth Clarke, as Education Secretary, frequently referred to teachers' concerns as 'silly' and applauded a 'common-sense', uncomplicated approach to educational practice and decision-making. It should, nevertheless, be recognised that even common sense has a theoretical base – 'useful is good theory' (Brook, 1992).

Professionals who are able to integrate research with practice – e.g. doctors, educational psychologists, architects, management consultants – do not find themselves on such shaky theoretical ground. They are seen as possessing a body of knowledge that is not easily acquired by others and, generally speaking, they are held in some regard by the public. In contrast, there is a lack of agreement about the knowledge needed for teaching and a 'yawning gap between theory and practice' (Hargreaves, 1996, p. 2). Teaching children (particularly primary aged children) is something that many people feel they can do without any professional training or experience.

In short, teachers' understanding of teaching and their insights into the way in which children learn has generally not been recognised as a valid form of professional knowledge which is worthy of very much respect. Teachers, therefore, have not been made to feel they do something that merits research and dissemination.

Teachers' Working Conditions

Teachers, as a class, work under less-than-professional conditions with increasingly complex demands for academic, social and psychological expertise in demographically diverse settings.

(Hollingsworth, 1994, p. 51)

A class teacher's work is intensely social with a heavy investment of 'self' (Nias, 1993). This arises from the historically determined context in which teachers find themselves – one adult managing the behaviour and learning of a large group of children – but also from the interactive nature of teaching. Teachers teach classes of children but they are also expected to build relationships with individuals. Teaching is probably as much about teachers 'giving' their personalities as it is about teaching the curriculum – a substantial amount of 'what gets taught is the teacher' (Nias, 1989, p. 14).

The great outnumbering of children to teachers results, understandably, in a professional preoccupation with control and the skills that maintain classroom order. Much teacher energy and creativity is directed towards managing and controlling the class. Many teachers, particularly those in the early stages of their careers, live daily with the thought that they might – at some point in the lesson, the week or their careers – lose control.

An orderly classroom learning environment is achieved through a delicately balanced cluster of skills which includes a preparedness to make ongoing adjustments to teaching plans and intentions. However, the relationship between teacher and taught is best understood as a refracting rather than a transmitting medium (Hamilton, 1973, cited in Stenhouse,

1975). This gives rise to curious educational paradoxes, like, for instance, the fact that different pupils can learn different things from the same event and well-planned lessons can fall flat whilst unplanned lessons can go well. This 'illogical' and unpredictable dimension to teaching is professionally very bewildering and testing. Certainly, it is not generally taken into account by those outside teaching, most of whom subscribe to the 'illusion of causality' (Crites, 1986) – i.e. teachers teach and pupils therefore learn what is taught.

Hofkins (1994) captures a core element of a teacher's role when she talks of a teacher being a 'ringmaster ensuring all performers are on task'. Successful 'crowd' management requires close monitoring of individuals, subgroups and the collective mood of the class. Although, if only for sanity's sake, teaching has to have routines, it also needs to be spontaneous and sometimes prepared to 'go with the flow'. These are subtle skills demanding well-developed professional abilities and intuitions which are built up over many class teaching encounters. In any one day, a teacher handles multiple child interactions with their attendant voices, emotions and volume levels. Indeed, teaching is a highly emotional, if not passionate, enterprise and this has been a neglected dimension in recent years. Williarn Lodge Paley, a National School teacher in 1824, captures the extent to which feelings are involved:

> (I am) so teased with teaching that my soul feels heaviness and my spirits dullness.
>
> (Mitchell, 1991, p. 32)

For the classroom teacher, teaching is overwhelmingly a 'doing' activity. It requires constant attention to the here and now of pupil life – a 'shifting, unpredictable, capricious world' (Nias, 1989, p. 13). The teaching day has a very crowded skyline. Although many teachers find themselves working through their lunch breaks, they still come to the end of a day with outstanding items on 'the list of things to do'. Teachers encounter difficulties finding time when they urgently need to telephone a doctor or the bank and those outside schools often find it difficult to make telephone contact with teachers.

Teachers have little timetabled time for preparing teaching resources, liaising with parents, writing up records, consulting with colleagues or simply thinking about their work. Such essential professional activities have to be squeezed into tightly marked daytime moments or confined to evenings, weekends and holidays. And yet, many teachers will say they wish they had more time with their pupils in order to meet their learning needs (see Lortie, 1975). There is increasing evidence to suggest that government reforms have resulted in further work overload for many classroom teachers (Hargreaves, 1993; Campbell and Neill, 1994).

Teachers' working conditions militate against any activity that is not contributing to the 'hands on' work with pupils. Two teachers involved in a collaborative research project on children's thinking make this clear:

> Anyone who has experienced the concentrated action a teacher faces daily will ask: Why would a teacher further complicate life by trying to collect information on a very complex area of educational theory?
>
> (Hull *et al.*, 1985, p. 92)

Any slack in the system is quickly taken up by an ever-present surplus of pupil-related work. In short, the nature of class teachers' working conditions is excluding of all other activities, particularly an activity as demanding as research. It seems pertinent to ask why teachers were ever adopted as researchers (see Lawn, 1989). Research is another level of work requiring its own time, training, creative energy and commitment, and understandably, most teachers are too fatigued to contemplate it.

Confidence and Having Something to Say

> What came through to the National Commission was the extent to which teachers' own self-confidence had been undermined by the way in which they had been undervalued by government and by the media.
>
> (Kennedy, 1996)

If teaching has always been short-changed in the public's ranking of worthwhile occupations, then a case can be made for thinking that things have become considerably worse for teachers in recent times. The way in which the Education Reform Act (1988) was conceptualised and imposed runs counter to some of the most basic principles regarding ownership of change, and as Sikes (1992, p. 48) reminds us – 'imposition generally implies criticism'. Teachers have been left feeling reproached, challenged, besieged and 'grieving' (Nias, 1993) for lost practices and professional identities. In their study of 400 infant teachers, Campbell and Neill (1994) concluded that recent educational reforms rode on the back of teachers' conscientiousness and almost 50 per cent of those studied felt their own sense of professionalism had been damaged. The National Commission on Education (NCE, 1993, p. 195) commented, 'Morale is low in the teaching profession.'

The radical nature and restless speed of government reforms and their various revisions and adjustments have disoriented many in the profession, particularly the more experienced – those who had developed, over time, personalised ways of doing the job, those with 'experientially-based confidence' (Sikes, 1992, p. 49). The National Curriculum and its assessment structure has required that teachers learn a new pedagogic language in order to 'deliver' a politician's curriculum. The government has challenged teachers' professional experience, judgement and expertise and the net effect is that teachers are left with an overwhelming impression that they must try a lot harder in order to be better. Such was the level of professional confidence and dignity that most have done as they were told, often, as Campbell and Neill (1994) suggest, at the expense of their self-image as competent and effective professionals.

Meanwhile, despite an official recognition that a period of calm is needed, government tinkering, and gathering opposition party proposals for tinkering, continue unabated with a string of 'first-aid' ideas and reforms. Speaking of proposals for a new national curriculum for teacher training, Doug McAvoy, general secretary of the National Union of Teachers, commented:

> It's change upon change without any consultation. The government is about to reform it's own reforms.
>
> (McAvoy, 1996)

The effect on a beleaguered profession is to reaffirm the message that politicians are the professional educators and teachers are 'marginalised victims' of reform (Hargreaves and Goodson, 1995). Innovation no longer resides within a professional domain; it is now delivered to schools by a political bureaucracy. Teachers have little part in drawing up an agenda for change (Nixon, 1989).

Interestingly, government reforms have probably led to a considerable increase in the amount of planning and writing done by teachers. However, this has not been writing of a spontaneous or creative kind – writing by one who wants to write because there is something burning to say. It is the equivalent of the dubious classroom practice which requires children to write to a title that has suddenly appeared 'out of the blue' on the blackboard.

To a very considerable extent, teachers have been usurped as creative and thinking professionals. It is now possible that they believe less in themselves than they ever did – less in themselves as professionals with something worthwhile to say about children's learning and development. Truly, teachers have had their wings clipped and the idea that they should research their practice in a grassroots way has lost much ground.

Research and the Class Teacher

> I became a writer partly because I was slightly detached from my family.
>
> (Mason, 1992)

For a number of years, doubt has been cast on the extent to which the more traditional (academic) forms of educational research are relevant to classroom teachers who work in the diverse and variable settings of classrooms (e.g. Nixon, 1981; Carr and Kemmis, 1986; Pollard and Tann, 1987; McNiff, 1988; Elliott, 1988). Nevertheless, teachers have been encouraged to take a research stance on their practice through the use of alternative approaches. For instance, Carr and Kemmis (1986) write, 'teachers must be researchers'. McNiff (1988, p. xiii) comments, 'Action research presents an opportunity for teachers to become uniquely involved their own practice' and Pollard and Tann (1987, p. 23) believe that 'critical reflection and systematic investigation' of teaching practice should be an integral part of classroom life. Such writers have recommended 'teacher friendly' forms of research like self-evaluation, reflection, action research, action enquiry, and case study. And, as indicated at the beginning of this chapter, many teachers have successfully researched educational issues using these approaches.

A noteworthy feature of the teacher research movement is the role of outsiders. Elliott (1991, p. 47) has drawn attention to this:

> One of the interesting things about the school-based action research movement is that it has been led and sustained by academic teacher educators operating from the higher education sector.

If most teacher research depends upon outsiders in order to get off the ground, then there is reason to question whether even the alternative methodologies are feasible in the classroom situation.

Jackson (1968) and Taylor (1970) provide examples of early insights into teachers' professional behaviour in classrooms. Jackson studied a group of American elementary teachers and was struck by the immediacy of life in the classroom and the way in which this made teachers look for quick solutions to complex classroom issues. Jackson commented:

> Were she [the teacher] seriously to try untangling the web of forces that combine to produce reality as she knows it, there would be no time for anything else.
>
> (p. 159)

In his study of the way teachers plan their teaching, Taylor (1970) provided similarly interesting insights when he wrote:

> It may well be that the planning is undertaken instinctively, governed by rule-of-thumb, drawing on successful experience, by feel and intuition rather than by reference to explicit criteria employed in a systematic manner.
>
> (p. 71)

Hull *et al.* (1985), in a collaborative research project between teachers and a small team of university staff, found the school staff were at first very tentative about getting involved and surprisingly unfamiliar with the 'culture' of research. They write, 'the professional teacher community does not embrace a research tradition' (p. 99).

Brown (1989) is concerned that outsiders' models have dominated the thinking on teaching in classrooms and asks the question: what does classroom teaching look like from a teacher's perspective? She found that teachers work spontaneously from their own situations and that this does, not tally well with a more systematic 'define objectives – plan activities – evaluate achievement of objectives' approach. Recently, Hammersley (1993) suggests that the rigour inherent in most teacher research approaches could militate against the actual practice of teaching and the way in which teachers need to 'operate under great pressures of immediacy and complexity' (p. 438). He believes that we should be concerned to raise the status of teaching as an activity *per se* and not necessarily through associating it with research.

Some writers, like, for instance, Armstrong (1980) and Rowland (1984) have advocated 'observational' approaches to researching classroom life. These are inspiring studies and, on the face of it, they contain replicable methodologies for teachers. However, it needs to be noted that they were possible because the authors had time to observe. They were not carrying a full teaching load as well as observing, researching and writing.

Action research has received a high profile as a friendly methodology for teachers wishing to study and improve their practice. Reporting on their experience of action research in a community college, Cooper and Ebbutt (1974, p. 70) found it 'possible' to participate in action research although the 'constraints of the day-to-day secondary school situation' reduced its effectiveness.

Elliott (1991), who has long been a leading protagonist of the method, draws into question the logic of established action research ways of approaching issues in schools:

> When one is faced with a practical problem, it is better to take the calculated risk of getting it wrong, and adjusting one's action strategy retrospectively, than that of not doing anything about the problem until one has fully understood it.
>
> (p. 24)

Elliott argues that the above approach to classroom problems is more reflective of the 'natural logic' of teachers' practical thinking.

Johnston (1994) questions if action research is a 'natural' process for teachers. She identifies the barriers which prevent teachers from carrying it through on their own. She mentions teachers' strong orientation to practice, their continued belief that research is done by professional researchers, the isolation of individual class teachers which makes collaborative research difficult, and their lack of time and training in the necessary research skills. Echoing Hammersley (1993), she is concerned that teachers might be seen as lacking because they appear to need outside help in order to engage with action research. She concludes that there is a dissonance between action research and teaching:

> Teachers' reluctance to take on action research may arise because action research, although appearing on the surface to be a natural part of what is considered to be good teaching, actually does not fit with the processes that reflective, inquiring teachers use.
>
> (Johnston, 1994, p. 43)

Dadds (1995) observes that teachers experience action research very differently from the way in which it is represented theoretically in the literature. She offers a penetrating account of the potential value of action research to a committed teacher-researcher; however, she is also honest about the difficulties and sees success to be dependent upon the 'fortitude of teachers working . . . within severe time constraints' (p. 169).

So, although many teachers have been able to integrate research into their classroom teaching, there is reason to think that recommended outsider methodologies, like action research, are by no means straightforward.

Perhaps this dissonance is part of a larger difficulty related to the research role itself. Smetherham (1978, p. 98) suggests that the very act of doing research separates one 'from the thoughts and interests of those cohabiting the observed social world'. The maintenance of a research identity necessarily results in a degree of detachment from the here and now being studied. Participants who carry out 'insider' research have to grapple with this. Good professional practice requires that teachers give full attention to children's ongoing needs – the 'ethic of care'. However, observing the situation and collecting data must, to some extent, take them away from this interpersonal engagement. So, there is a sense in which research may actually conflict with good teaching practice.

Summary and Conclusions

Nothing exists until we write about it.

(Ross, 1995)

This chapter has addressed class teachers' lack of enthusiasm for classroom-based research. (A more 'playful' approach might have involved asking why researchers are reluctant to become class teachers!)

I have identified four areas of difficulty:

- the lack of expectation that teachers should research and write about their professional practice;
- the demanding nature of teaching which leaves little time and energy for research;
- the current lack of professional confidence and marginalisation of teachers from government change agendas;
- the mismatch between many available research methodologies and teachers' professional ways of working in classrooms.

My purpose in revealing these difficulties is not to be discouraging of teacher research. As I said at the beginning of this chapter, I am committed to making teachers' understandings more widely available than they are at present. However, I think there is a need to develop clearer insights into teachers' reluctance in order to offer more effective support. And I do feel strongly that teachers need (and should expect) support if they are to take on research in addition to teaching.

By way of concluding, I want to look briefly at the idea of support. From the very beginning of the teacher-as-researcher movement there have been enterprising approaches to teacher involvement; however, there is now a particular need for imaginative and effective help.

I have argued that recent educational reforms have not been encouraging of grass roots practitioner research. Much has happened to make teachers feel powerless and disinclined to take the initiative. There is now a need for creativity with regard to establishing promising 'points of entry' for teacher research in a climate of imposition.

Three examples serve to show the sorts of measures that are needed. At Kingston University, lecturers have supported teacher research in the somewhat unpromising area of National Curriculum assessment and testing (Lomax and Jones, 1993). The authors state, 'teachers can work within the apparently strangling framework of national assessment to create something that is educationally worthwhile' (p. 2). At the University of Greenwich there has been recognition of the potential for research that is offered by the Government's GEST-funded 'Special Educational Needs Parent Partnership Programme'. A lecturer is providing school-based support to teachers in Tower Hamlets to assist them in developing and writing up projects in the area of home–school relations (Harland and Gale, 1997). Thirdly, the Teacher Training Agency (TTA) has recently announced a wish to bring teaching and research closer together and has made available small research grants for classroom-focused projects with a particular emphasis on effective dissemination of findings.[1]

In addition to their creativity, these three initiatives illustrate an important principle with regard to establishing appropriate foci for teacher research. This is the need to achieve a high degree of overlap between the researched themes and classroom concerns. Given the difficulties of finding time for research, it makes a considerable difference if teachers feel that time spent on research is also *directly* benefiting their classroom work.

Given that research is an extra layer of work for teachers, it is important to provide the kind of practical support that will enable lift-off. Clearly this will vary from teacher to teacher but it seems that 'hands on' help is particularly welcomed. For instance, in the above example, the University of Greenwich offers teachers the choice of writing up their projects independently, writing them jointly with the tutor or delegating the writing-up to the tutor. Although most teachers are involved in teaching children to develop as writers, it seems that many teachers lack confidence as writers themselves.

As already noted, staff from higher education have traditionally carried the main support load so it seems important to look for other people who can increase the size of the 'support service'.

Headteachers are very well placed to encourage teacher research. However, headteachers (possibly even more so than class teachers) have experienced huge changes and increased work pressures in recent years (NAHT, 1993; Judd, 1996). It is difficult, therefore, to imagine that many could take on this facilitating role at this point in time; nevertheless, it is important to recognise that they could play a key enabling role in the development of a teacher research culture.

Most local education authorities (LEAs) still have a number of support, advisory and inspection staff (albeit much reduced) who can do much for the cause of teacher research. Such staff can provide an important service to class teachers by drawing attention to any exciting and innovative practice that they see from the 'privileged' position of a peripatetic observer. (It is actually very hard to be aware of successful practice when you are a class teacher who is very close to it and particularly when you are working in a climate in which many of those outside schools are suggesting that you are ineffective.) Teachers continue to hold to the view that research is an activity which is done by professional researchers based outside schools. Teachers therefore need support in order to see themselves as researchers and to see their practice as 'worthy' of research.

Many teachers feel the gap between their practice and research lift-off is very wide and video can be a very effective way of breaching this imagined divide. Videos create 'curiosity and reaction' (Anning, 1990, p. 16) and help initiate the process of reflection. Video can be used to help teachers look objectively at their practice and can generate discussion and writing (see Hancock, 1995; Ferris and Hancock, 1997). A further benefit is the increased possibility of a research/practice overlap. Children are very motivated by video – to become both video makers and evaluators of classroom events. Parents can also be drawn in as videos can make the life and learning of schools more visible to the wider community (Hancock *et al.*, 1996).

With regard to choice of methodology, it seems desirable that no research approach is ruled out providing teachers feel motivated and involved. Golby (1989) believes that methodology relates to the research situation and its aims and is a matter of what is appropriate and possible. However, it seems important that there is acceptance of teachers' subjective and intuitive ways of understanding classroom processes – what Hart (1995) has termed 'interpretive modes' of enquiry. Teachers should be helped to cultivate personalised styles of writing which are likely to be more consistent with their professional ways of operating in classrooms and the nature of teachers' 'schoolwork' (see Lawn, 1989). Case study has long been popular. Walker (1980) suggests that teachers make educational judgements on the basis of particular instances rather than referring to research findings and this makes them 'natural case study workers'. In recent years, a number of other teacher-centred approaches to inquiry, writing and research have become available. These include: 'narrative inquiry' (Connelly and Clandinin, 1990); the study of 'critical events' (Woods, 1993) and 'biography' (Thomas, 1995). All seem to offer teachers potentially meaningful ways of examining their implicit 'craft' understandings.

Finally, Eisner (1988, p. 19) has written:

> Researchers are beginning to go back to schools, not to conduct commando raids, but to work with teachers.

Although one hopes there have been less 'commando raids' in recent years, I feel these words continue to offer sound advice to all who are in a position to promote teaching as a research-based profession. It seems crucial that teachers' insights into children's learning are valued, captured in writing and made more widely available than they are at the present time.

Acknowledgements

I would like to express my thanks to Edward Korel, Titus Alexander, Harry Torrance, David Brook, Linda Harland and Margaret Meek Spencer for their interest in many of the ideas contained in this paper.

Note

1. The TTA made available a first round of small grants of up to £2,000 per application in recognition of the need to stimulate teacher research.

References

Anning, A. (1990) *Using Video Recording for Teacher Professional Development.* Leeds: University of Leeds, School of Education.

Armstrong, M. (1980) *Closely Observed Children: the Diary of a Primary Classroom.* Oxford: Writers & Readers.

Bell, G. H., Stakes, R. and Taylor, G. (eds) (1994) *Action Research, Special Needs and School Development.* London: David Fulton.

Brook, D. (1992) Personal communication.

Brown, S. (1989) How do teachers talk about and evaluate their own teaching? *Spotlight 12.* Edinburgh: Scottish Council for Educational Research.

Campbell, J. and Neill, S. (1994) *Curriculum Reform at Key Stage 1: Teacher Commitment and Policy Failure.* London: Longman.

Carr, W. and Kemmis, S. (1986) *Becoming Critical: Education, Knowledge and Action Research.* Lewes: Falmer Press.

Connelly, F. M. and Clandinin, D. J. (1990) Stories of experience and narrative enquiry, *Educational Researcher*, 19(5), pp. 2–14.

Cooper, D. and Ebbutt, D. (1974) Participation in action research as an in-service experience, *Cambridge Journal of Education,* Vol. 4, pp. 65–71.

Crites, S. (1986) Storytime: recollecting the past and projecting the future, in T. R. Sarbin (ed.) *The Storied Nature of Human Conduct.* New York: Praeger.

Dadds, M. (1995) *Passionate Enquiry and School Development: a Story about Teacher Action Research.* London: Falmer Press.

Elliott, J. (1988) Educational research and insider–outsider relations, *Qualitative Studies in Education*, Vol. 1, pp. 155–66.

Elliott, J. (1991) *Action Research for Educational Change.* Milton Keynes: Open University Press.

Eisner, E. W. (1988) The primacy of experience and the politics of method, *Educational Researcher*, Vol. 20, pp. 15–20.

Falkner, D., Swann, J. and Streddle, K. (1992) Professional Development in Action Module E621, Certificate of Professional Development in Education. Milton Keynes: Open University Press.

Ferris, A. and Hancock, R., with Nicholson, A. and Maples, C. (1997) Nursery Education. A Video. Bilingual Primary Pupils Project/Hackney PACT, Queensbridge Buildings, Albion Drive, London E8 4ET, United Kingdom.

Frost, D. (1995) Networking, *Educational Action Research*, Vol. 3, pp. 249–51.

Golby, M. (1989) Teachers and their research, in W. Carr (ed.) *Quality in Teaching: Arguments for a Reflective Profession.* London: Falmer Press.

Hamilton, D. (1977) At classroom level. Unpublished PhD thesis, University of Edinburgh.

Hammersley, M. (1993) On the teacher as a researcher, *Educational Action Research*, Vol. 1, pp. 425–45.

Hancock, R. (1995) The Chinese Independent School of Tower Hamlets. A video about the life and learning of a Chinese Saturday School. PICC Project, Tower Hamlets Learning Design Centre, English Street, London, E3 4TA, United Kingdom.

Hancock, R., with O'Connor, A. Jenner, H., Østmo, G. and Sheath, G. (1996) Making school more visible to parents: an evaluation of the Harbinger video project, in J. Bastiani and S. Wolfendale (eds) *Home–School Work in Britain: Review, Reflection and Development*. London: David Fulton.

Hargreaves, A. (1993) Time and teachers' work: an analysis of the intensification thesis, in R. Gomm and P. Woods (eds) *Educational Research in Action*. London: Paul Chapman/Open University.

Hargreaves, A. and Goodson, I .(1995) Let us take the lead, *The Times Educational Supplement*, 24 February, p. 15.

Hargreaves, D. H. (1996) Teaching as a research-based profession: possibilities and prospects. Teacher Training Agency Annual Lecture. TTA, Portland House, Stag Place, London SW1 STT, United Kingdom.

Harland, L. and Gale, S. (1997) *Developing Home–School Links*. Learning by Design, English Street, London E3 4TA, United Kingdom.

Hart, S. (1995) Action-in-reflection, *Educational Action Research*, Vol. 3, pp. 211–32.

Hofkins, D. (1994) Mentors 'ignored' trainees, *The Times Educational Supplement*, 23 November, p. 13.

Hollingsworth, S. (1994) Feminist pedagogy in the research class: an example of teacher research, *Educational Action Research*, Vol. 2, pp. 49–70.

Hull, C., Rudduck, J., Sigsworth, A. and Daymond, G. (eds) (1985) *A Room Full of Children Thinking: Accounts of Classroom Research by Teachers*. York: SCDC Publications-Longman.

Jackson, P. (1968) *Life in Classrooms*. New York: Holt, Rinehart & Winston.

Johnston, S. (1994) Is action research a 'natural' process for teachers? *Educational Action Research*, Vol. 2, pp. 39–48.

Judd, J. (1996) Heads quitting profession in record numbers, *The Independent*, 23 May, p. 7.

Kelly, A., Whyte, J. and Smail, B. (1984) *Girls into Science and Technology Final Report*. University of Manchester, Department of Sociology.

Kennedy, H. (Member of the National Commission on Education) (1996) Keynote Address at the Helping Children to Succeed Conference at Swanlee School, Tower Hamlets, London, United Kingdom, 27 April.

Lawn, M. (1989) Being caught in school work: the possibilities of research in teachers' work, in W. Carr (ed.) *Quality in Teaching: Arguments for a Reflective Profession*. London: Falmer Press.

Lewis, I. (1988) Learning together: issues arising from outstation MA course experience, in J. Nias and S. Groundwater-Smith (eds) *The Enquiring Teacher: Supporting and Sustaining Teacher Research*. London: Falmer Press.

Lomax, P. and Jones, C. (eds) (1993) *Developing Primary Schools through Action Research*. Bournemouth: Hyde Publications.

Lortie, D. (1975) *School Teacher: a Sociological Study*. Chicago: University of Chicago Press.

MacDonald, B. (1973) Humanities Curriculum Project, in *Schools Council Research Studies Evaluation in Curriculum Development: Twelve Case Studies*. Basingstoke: Macmillan Education.

McAvoy, D. (1996) Speaking on the *Six o'clock News*, BBC 1, 12 June.

Mason, G. (1992) *In the Psychiatrist's Chair*, BBC Radio 4.

McNiff, J. (1988) *Action Research: Principles and Practice*. London: Macmillan.

Milroy, Father Dominic (1992) Headteacher of Ampleforth School and Chair of the Headmasters' *(sic)* Conference. Interviewed for *Hard Words in the Classroom*, BBC Radio 4.

Mitchell, W. R. (1991) *Mr. Elgar and Dr. Buck: a Musical Friendship*. Settle: Castleberg Publications.

National Association of Head Teachers (1993) Press Release on resignations due to ill-health, 14 July.

National Commission on Education (1993) *Learning to Succeed: a Radical Look at Education Today and a Strategy for the Future*. London: Heinemann.

Nias, J. (1989) *Primary Teachers Talking: a Study of Teaching as Work*. London: Routledge.

Nias, J. (1993) Changing times, changing identities: grieving for a lost self, in R. Burgess (ed.) *Educational Research and Evaluation: for Policy and Practice?* London: Falmer Press.

Nixon, J. (ed.) (1981) *A Teacher's Guide to Action Research*. London: Grant McIntyre.

Nixon, J. (1989) The teacher as researcher: contradictions and continuities, *Peabody Journal of Education*, Vol. 64, pp. 116–27.

Pollard, A. and Tann, S. (1987) *Reflective Teaching in the Primary School*. London: Cassell.

Rowland, S. (1984) *The Enquiring Classroom*. Lewes: Falmer Press.

Ross, B. (1995) Said by Dr Zeigler, a prison psychiatrist, in the film *The Young Poisoner's Handbook*, directed by Benjamin Ross. An Electric Pictures/ Polygram Filmed Entertainments.

Ryan, C. and Somekh, B. (eds) (1991) *Processes of Reflection and Action*, CARN Publication 10B. Norwich: University of East Anglia.

Sikes, P. J. (1992) Imposed change and the experienced teacher, in M. Fullan and A. Hargreaves (eds) *Teacher Development and Educational Change*. London: Falmer Press.

Smail, B., Whyte, J. and Kelly, A. (1982) Girls into science and technology: the first two years, *School Science Review*, Vol. 63, pp. 620–30.

Smetherham, D. (1978) Insider research, *British Educational Research Journal*, Vol. 4, pp. 97–102.

Somekh, B. (1991) Pupil autonomy in learning with microcomputers: rhetoric or reality? An action research study, *Cambridge Journal of Education*, Vol. 21, pp. 47–64.

Stenhouse, L. (1968) The Humanities Curriculum Project, *Journal of Curriculum Studies*, Vol. 1, pp. 26–33.

Stenhouse, L. (1971) The Humanities Curriculum Project: the rationale, *Theory into Practice*, Vol. 10, pp. 154–162.

Stenhouse, L. (1975) *An Introduction to Curriculum Research and Development*. London: Heinemann.

Taylor, P. H. (1970) *How Teachers Plan their Courses*. Slough: NFER.

Thomas, D. (1995) *Teachers' Stories*. Buckingham: Open University Press.

Tropp, A. (1957) *The School Teachers*. London: Heinemann.

Teacher Training Agency (1996a) *Teaching as a research-based profession: promoting excellence in teaching*. TTA Information Section, Portland House, Stag Place, London SW1E STT, United Kingdom.

Vulliamy, G. and Webb, R. (eds) (1992) *Teacher Research and Special Educational Needs*. London: David Fulton.

Walker, R. (1980) The conduct of educational case studies: ethics, theory and procedures, in W. B. Dockrell and D. Hamilton (eds) *Rethinking Educational Research*. London: Hodder & Stoughton.

Woods, P. (1993) *Critical Events in Teaching and Learning*. London: Falmer Press.

10

A Teacher's Response to 'Reflection-in-Action'

Andy Convery

Introduction

In 1991 I began researching my teaching for a PhD study. Two years into the study I experienced a particularly frustrating period when I seemed unable to engage in reflective practice in the classroom research phase. To try and better understand my research difficulties, I read more widely, but reading about reflection generated further confusion, with writers (often following Schon) using the term 'reflection' to describe a wide range of thinking processes, from spontaneous reaction through to deliberation. From my experience, it seemed that although Schon's promotion of reflective practice has a genuine appeal to the teaching profession, his associated analysis of the reflective process had limited application for resolving teachers' difficulties. Whereas Schon differentiates between 'reflection-in-action' and 'reflection-on-action' with confidence, such categories were not helpful for improving my understanding of classroom decision-making or the planning of sessions. In this chapter I argue that for reflection to fundamentally influence practice it is necessary that such reflection is informed by collaborative discussion, as individual reflection tends to focus on immediate rather than underlying problems.

The Reflective Practitioner and the Role of the Teacher

Schon's text *The Reflective Practitioner* (Schon, 1983) argues that professional development through 'reflection-in-action' is necessary as we live in an increasingly complex world in which individual problems require particular rather than generalised responses. Professionals can no longer rely on an accepted body of knowledge as being applicable to the diverse human challenges which they encounter, rather, they must consider a response to each individual problem in relation to the ends they hope to achieve and the means which are available for this response. Schon argues that if a student fails to demonstrate understanding of a principle in a lesson, the teacher should not (and cannot) resort to an authorised volume of teaching techniques or learning theories to definitively identify both the impediment and appropriate solution. Instead, the professional educator should attempt to explore the presented problem from the learner's perspective and evaluate the teacher's own practice as it relates to the learner. From this reflective exploration the teacher may generate a unique personal theory to explain the learner's problem and to provide a guide to remedial action. If teachers research their practice and 'reflect-in-action', i.e. deliberate about their professional decision-making in order to implement appropriate changes to their practice, then students will have improved learning experiences and teachers will develop improved self-awareness and become more experienced at exercising autonomous professional judgement. Whilst this seems a desirable mode of self-development for teachers, offering an attractive image of 'teacher-as-professional' to the practitioners themselves, I suggest that an examination of how teachers interpret Schon's writings may lead us to agree with Munby and Russell's (1989) conclusions that Schon offer's 'very full accounts of where we might wish professional education to go, but very little in the way of how we might get there'. Schon's model of the reflective practitioner may have limited application in the teaching context.

Defining and Interpreting 'Reflection-in-Action'

Schon explains that the tacit knowledge of our practice which we intuitively demonstrate can become unthinking and routine. Reflection enables us to examine our practices and underlying assumptions and identify why these tacit practices may no longer be adequate to deal with new situations. Such reflection may either be after the event or at a time when it can still influence the event.

> Practitioners do reflect *on* their knowing-in-practice. Sometimes, in the relative tranquillity of the post-mortem, they think back on a project they have undertaken, a situation they have lived through, and they explore the understandings they have brought to their handling of the case. They may do this in a mood of idle speculation, or in a deliberate effort to prepare themselves for future cases.
>
> But they may also reflect on practice while they are in the midst of it. Here they reflect-in-action, but the meaning of this term needs now to be considered in terms of the complexity of knowing in practice.
>
> A practitioner's reflection-in-action may not be very rapid. It is bounded by the 'action-present', the zone of time in which action can still make a difference to the situation. The action present may stretch over minutes, hours, days, or even weeks or months, depending on the pace of activity and the situational boundaries that are characteristic of the practice.
>
> (pp. 61–2)

From my own experience, 'reflection-in-action' seems the norm in teaching; I rarely experience 'the relative tranquillity of a post-mortem' in which I am unable to act in order to make a difference to the situation. The busyness of the classroom is marked by its continuity and consequence – it becomes difficult to separate events into individual cases that do not have repercussions either for the individual teacher or learner or for those with whom these individuals interact. Thus there is a particular problem of interpretation for teachers considering 'reflection-in-action'. Schon's broad definition can seem to embrace all of a teacher's planning, delivery and evaluation; during the teaching year, at any stage of preparation, implementation or retrospection, teachers can usually act to influence the situation, so they are almost always in the 'action present'. Consequently, because 'reflection-in-action' encompasses almost all of a teacher's activity, I suggest that teachers may reinterpret 'reflection-in-action' by imposing a particular understanding which suits both their situation and interests. I would argue that Schon's frequent use of the terms 'action' and 'practice' invites teachers to concentrate on their immediate classroom performances. Certainly, in my own research, my response was to give 'reflection-in-action' a specific interpretation and focus narrowly on aspects of my classroom activity.

In one example, taken from my own practice, I wanted to introduce more student-centred activities with my class of adult learners. Consequently, I experimented with a variety of strategies and approaches which created more student-controlled classroom experiences, yet my fixation with planning, implementing and evaluating these student-centred activities blinded me at the time to my working assumption that I should focus exclusively on students' autonomy *within* my classroom, rather than student autonomy both inside and outside my classroom. Over a number of sessions I tinkered with methods for improving the students' social classroom experience and perhaps lost sight of the fundamental needs of adults wishing to develop greater independence beyond the classroom. Adults could and should have been helped to learn independently of my controlled lessons, but in busying myself with attending to the short-term needs of the impending sessions I was neglecting the underlying aims of their learning programme. My attention to specific classroom strategies tended to limit reflection to deliberations on technical strategies. My efforts to implement actions that could make a difference to the situation in the 'action-present' meant that the ends or values that I was trying to achieve remained unquestioned. Reflective practice concentrated on my teaching practice and ignored the emancipatory potential which I could have stimulated for my learners beyond my immediate teaching environment.

Now this is obviously not what Schon intended, but I suggest there are a number of factors which invite teachers to claim allegiance to Schon's ideal of reflective practice whilst remaining locked into limited and immediate problem-solving and engaging in reactive rather than reflective practice. These factors include his rhetorical appeal, his lack of appropriate practical examples from teaching, and the individualistic response which he invites.

The rhetoric of The Reflective Practitioner

Part of Schon's appeal lies in his broad welcome to aspiring professionals which invites positive identification from a very wide audience. He states that when professionals 'go about the spontaneous intuitive performance of the actions of everyday life, we show ourselves to be knowledgeable in a special way' (p. 49). This celebration of intuitive 'knowledge-in-action' must find favour with teachers whose claim to expertise cannot be justified by reference to a given body of knowledge, but is founded on tacit craft wisdom borne from experience. Schon thus seems to make a virtue from Lortie's (1975) criticism that teachers lack a technical culture based on a shared empirical knowledge base. Schon reassures teachers, offering them professional salvation from their marginal role as 'minor' professionals; he argues that the established 'major' professions are becoming obsolescent, restricted by their inability to respond flexibly to change and he elevates those minor professions – which are distinguished by practitioners' contin-uous exercise of their developing professional judgement – above those traditional professions which are based on privileged access to a relatively permanent body of specialised knowledge. It is difficult to resist Schon's appeal as he offers teachers the opportunity to rediscover their profession-ality, emancipated from the dominance of expert outsider theorists. A particular reading of *The Reflective Practitioner* enables teachers' everyday activities to be celebrated as examples of intelligent 'knowing-in-action' from which unique theory can be generated. For a hard-pressed teacher it becomes increasingly tempting to claim allegiance to Schon and identify oneself as a reflective practitioner.

Oversimplified examples of reflective practice

Schon's accommodating language and style are complemented by simplis-tic examples which encourage the readers to position themselves as reflec-tive practitioners. He describes how baseball pitchers and jazz musicians demonstrate 'reflection-in-action' when they are successful in their pursuits and such undemanding practical comparisons enable teachers to identify easily with the process of 'reflecting-in-action'. Schon offers us such an uncomplicated description of the process:

> Much reflection-in-action hinges on the experience of surprise. When intuitive, spontaneous performance yields nothing more than the results expected for it, then we tend not to think about it. But when intuitive performance leads to surprises, pleasing or promising or unwanted, we may respond by reflecting-in-action.

(p. 56)

Here reflection-in-action is portrayed as natural, relating strongly to the serendipity that is frequent in teaching. From a teacher's perspective, Schon is not making demands of his audience, but enabling the audience to reconstruct their everyday practices as the practice of reflective professionals. However, these uncomplicated descriptions and examples of 'reflection-in-action' might actually reduce the potential that reflection-in-action has to stimulate professional self-development, as such examples can invite the conclusion that the ends of one's practice are unproblematical and can be taken for granted. Now whereas in baseball the ends may be relatively uncontroversial – winning the game according to agreed rules and regulations – education does not enjoy such a consensus about means and ends. Although the above description of 'reflection-in-action' could lead to teachers re-evaluating their practices and questioning their taken-for-granted values, it is by no means inevitable that such would occur. Thus, in my own situation, whilst I was improving student control of the immediate classroom, I was ignoring more fundamental opportunities for developing autonomy outside the classroom. Although Schon's emphasis is on resolving those problems that fall outside the established technical knowledge of a profession, reflection-in-action may nevertheless invite practitioners to focus on the immediate solution to the new problem and to concentrate on what 'works', rather than on the assumptions and underlying values of the practitioner.

Whereas investigating why our implicit 'knowing-in-action' has let us down in a situation could lead us to appreciate that our practices are frustrating our espoused underlying values, I would also argue that Schon's writings encourage us to focus on the *situation* rather than the *professional* as the source of the problem. In the examples which Schon provides he emphasises the importance of individuals reframing problems in 'one-to-one' situations. These illustrations may ignore the self-conscious, often defensive dimension of 'reflecting-in-action', for example, the teacher's concern with managing complex situations in front of multiple audiences. Thus a teacher (such as myself) may unconsciously select a particular strategy because it enables me, the teacher, to retain control of a situation. If the underlying personal interests of the teacher are not considered when engaging in reflection, then the implicit values of the teacher are also unlikely to be questioned in the reflective endeavour and the potential of reflective practice is unlikely to be realised.

Reflecting in isolation

Perhaps the critical reason why *The Reflective Practitioner* may be an inappropriate text for teachers hoping to improve their practice is that Schon offers professionals the illusion of independent self-improvement. However, for many teachers, the central impediment to fundamentally improving their practice is their self-protective individualism. Teaching is often a way in which individuals find opportunities for self-expression (see Nias, 1984, 1989; Woods, 1985), but the identity which is invested in the professional role becomes a barrier to accepting the need for change

(Elliott, 1991). In my experience I was concerned to maintain and defend my self-image as being the individual who could create and control a classroom environment in which mature individuals would experience significant personal development. In my daily practice I was too close to the action to question the motivation for my behaviour and consequently my reflective practice remained at a technical, problem-solving level.

Because my teaching practice was founded on personal values which were implicit (and therefore above examination), I did not investigate whether my values were being realised in practice or being frustrated by my other fundamental needs, such as the need to be a significant influence in my students' development. My argument is that individual teachers are unlikely to make essential changes to their practice if they are not supported and guided through the reflective process. Individuals defending their teaching identity are unlikely to progress beyond a short-term, instrumental reflective practice. They will tend to be *reflective* rather than *reflexive,* asking 'what works?' and 'why and how does it work?', but still failing to confront the questions 'why am I trying to make this work?' and 'are my actions in "making it work" realising or frustrating my espoused values and intentions?' Schon's writings are too respectful of the existing craft culture which has evolved from coping strategies rather than educational philosophies. Reflection-in-action implies that some personal tinkering or some individual problem-solving can activate the professional in the teacher. Although Schon seeks a professional renaissance, the force of his argument becomes diluted in a text which can be perversely interpreted to sanction short-term individualism. In my experience, solitary reflective practice did not lead to self-awareness of my inhibiting defensive behaviours; maintaining and protecting my self-image as a competent professional became paramount and I unconsciously avoided examining whether my aims had been realised in practice.

The Importance of Collaboration

In my experience collaboration was crucial in helping me develop beyond a reflective practice which focused on techniques for improving classroom experiences, to a reflexive appreciation of my actions. Schon seems to invite an individualistic response to problematical situations, but such individualism can allow self-defensiveness. He encourages professionals to challenge accepted practices and evolve new and more relevant responses, but he does not necessarily require the reflective practitioners to critique their interests, needs and values in constructing new understandings. Personal needs and insecurities may well be fundamental to the behaviour of teachers, but teachers will not willingly acknowledge such immature and unprofessional emotional influences. I argue that for constructive self-critical reflection, teachers need to believe they have the support of others who will sufficiently respect the integrity of their enquiry to enable awkward and uncomfortable self-revelations to be identified. This provides the basis for teachers to engage in more productive alternative behaviours. In my experience the knowledge of such support, from both a colleague and supervisor, meant that I could acknowledge my defensiveness, even in the process of writing for these audiences. Addressing a sympathetic audience enabled me to 'reframe' the problem; writing helped me to objectify my personal situation, to anticipate critique and to explore my self-defensiveness. I would argue that reflection is not a cognitive activity which can be imposed on the social and emotional experience that is teaching; reflection must be recognised as an activity that can only be developed in conducive social and emotional circumstances.

Aspects of my personal experience as a teacher-researcher have been confirmed by other teacher-educators; for example, Day (1993) argues that

> reflection is a necessary but not sufficient condition for learning. Confrontation either by self or others must occur. Teachers need challenge and support if their professional development is to be enhanced.
>
> (p. 88)

Elliott (1989) has explored the difficulties of establishing the conditions which enable teachers to develop their reflexive powers; he argues that 'expert' intervention can be resisted and self-reflection can be inhibited in the presence of an authority figure. Confrontation must therefore involve a sensitive balance between challenge and support, with the outside facilitator acknowledging that the teachers' reflections and professional development constitute a significant educational process for the teacher-educators themselves. Those supporting teachers must relinquish their expert status and adopt partnership roles as facilitators and collaborative learners. Thus reflection needs confrontation and collaboration, but collaboration requires the appreciation that

> studying one's own professional work is no straightforward matter and adopting the reflective mode is not simply a cerebral activity. As we study our teaching, we are studying the images we hold of ourselves as teachers. Where these established self-images are challenged, questioned and perhaps threatened in the learning process we may experience feelings of instability, anxiety, negativity, even depression. This is especially so if the 'self' we come to see in self-study is not the 'self' we think we are, or the 'self' we would like to be. Thinking about our work in self-evaluation can thus be a highly charged emotional experience, one from which we may be tempted to retreat, thus endangering further learning. If on the other hand, we have the support of caring, sensitive and interested critical friends to help us through the potentially dangerous processes of self-evaluation, we are more likely to remain open to further learning and professional development.
>
> (Dadds, 1993, p. 287)

Dadds' experience of facilitating reflective learning complements my experience of attempting reflection on my teaching. Knowing that I was in a relationship where my inadequate teaching behaviour could be examined, without having to be defended or justified, meant that areas for improvements could be identified rather that avoided. Being valued by my critical friends as a teacher-researcher rather than as a failing teacher validated my changing self-image and provided both encouragement and direction. Critical friendship enabled social acceptance and self-acceptance as a precondition for change as a teacher.

In conclusion, I would argue that reflective teaching requires an approach that is social and collaborative rather than individually introspective. Schon's *The Reflective Practitioner* has proved a useful stimulus for teachers' professional development, but it must not be allowed to dictate how teacher reflection should consequently develop. Identifying subtle differences between 'reflection-in-action' and 'reflection-on-action' may be inappropriate in a teaching context and unnecessary concentration on these definitions can disorientate teachers who attempt to adapt their experience to conform with the fashionable paradigm. Focusing on such distinctions can distract from the potential of teachers to reflect and improve their students' experience. Perhaps some in teacher education have been overwhelmed by the uncritical welcome which Schon's approach has received throughout the professional development world, and have channelled all their energies into ensuring teachers profess allegiance to reflective-in-action, rather than exploring the extent to which Schon's text was proving appropriate for teachers. The power of Schon's credentials and his rhetorical appeals should not restrain teachers and teacher-educators from evolving their own approaches to reflexive practice, ones which acknowledge the value of collaborative support for stimulating critical self-consciousness and sustaining subsequent improvement in practice.

References

Dadds, M. (1993) The feeling of thinking in professional self-study, *Educational Action Research*, Vol. 1, pp. 287–303.

Day, C. (1993) Reflection: a necessary but not sufficient condition for professional development, *British Educational Research Journal*, Vol. 19, pp. 83–93.

Elliott, J. (1989) Educational theory and the professional learning of teachers: an overview, *Cambridge Journal of Education*, Vol. 19, pp. 81–107.

Elliott, J. (1991) *Action Research for Educational Change*. Milton Keynes: Open University Press.

Lortie, D. C. (1975) *Teacher: a Sociological Study*. Chicago: University of Chicago Press.

Munby, H. and Russell, T. (1989) Educating the reflective teacher, *Journal of Curriculum Studies*, Vol. 21, pp. 71–80.

Nias, J. (1984) The definition and maintenance of self in primary teaching, *British Journal of Sociology of Education*, Vol. 5, pp. 267–80.

Nias, J. (1989) *Primary Teachers Talking*. London: Routledge.

Schon, D. (1983) *The Reflective Practitioner*. London: Temple Smith.

Woods, P. (1985) Conversations with teachers: some aspects of life history method, *British Educational Research Journal*, Vol. 11, pp. 13–26.

11

Networks that Alter Teaching: Conceptualisations, Exchanges and Experiments

Michael Huberman

Introduction

The literature on professional development has become voluminous (Lieberman, 1988; Lieberman and Miller, 1990; Little, 1990a; Hargreaves and Fullan, 1992; Darling-Hammond, 1994; Guskey and Huberman, 1995). Its conceptual predecessor, 'staff development', was a less ambitious, less institutional call for many of the same components: ongoing collaboration between teachers, upgrading of pedagogical repertoires, higher levels of content-matter mastery, tighter connections between school districts and external sources of knowledge and technical support (in particular, the university), compensation for inadequate pre-service education and connections between the improvement of teachers' capacities and school restructuring. All that has shifted to a broader, more systemic mandate in which 'professional development' plays a prominent role (Little, 1993; Talbert and McLaughlin, 1994).

The reasons for this shift in terminology are only partly visible largely because the 'school restructuring' movement is in full flux, and its demands on and by practitioners are still volatile. Let us, however, go over this ground more deliberately before presenting the modal forms which professional development has taken.

First, there has been widespread dissatisfaction with the *organisational aspects* of conventional 'staff development' (Fenstermacher and Berliner, 1983; Wade, 1985; Huberman, 1985). In particular, most offerings have been one-shot seminars or workshops, with little follow-up and, therefore, few remaining traces when researchers verify enduring effects (e.g. Henderson, 1978; Daresh, 1987). Even in the case of longer sessions, there is no dramatic increase in *content-matter mastery* (Borko and Putnam, 1995), especially in mathematics and science, unless a continuing or more intensive model is designed. Next, staff development has been an almost wholly *individual process,* placed under the responsibility of the teacher concerned, with little concern for the potential of collaborative work before, during and after the event. The development process, in fact, is seen more as making up for intrinsic deficits than for realising one's professional potential (Lieberman and Miller, 1990). Nor has 'staff development' been explicitly *connected to the broader reorganisation of the school curriculum or infrastructure,* such that within-school articulation between grades or connections between schools and outlying constituencies have been adequately taken into account (cf. Fuhrman and Elmore, 1990; Tafei and Bertani, 1992; Prestine and Bowen, 1993).

What has changed, fundamentally, can be resuméd in two general points. First, in the US context at least, the more 'systemic' analysis of school reform calls for greater professional integration, instructional and content-matter upgrading, local autonomy – but also responsiveness to higher standards – and mastery of a less prescriptive curriculum while aiming for higher-order cognitive operations. In parallel, almost in counterpoint, the teacher professional as an 'empowerment' community, represented foremost by the teacher-researcher movement (e.g. Cochran-Smith and Lytle, 1992), has asserted that the capstone to reform are initiatives managed largely by teachers themselves, and involving dedicated school time and resources for co-operative experimentation, access to external expertise, the conduct of teacher-initiated research, and participation in local decision-making when questions of goals and resources are on the table. Lieberman and Miller (1990) have provided a catalogue of professional development activities that emphasises this tendency:

- teacher study groups – in an informal setting;
- curriculum writing – teacher-led and teacher-initiated;
- teacher research projects, with the focus on initiation to the collection and analysis of data;
- peer observation: in pairs, usually with activities and students specified in advance;
- case conferences – a group of teachers meeting to discuss individual students;
- programme evaluation and documentation;
- 'trying out' new practices;
- teacher resource centres;
- participation in outside events and organisations.

A Critical Look at Some Underlying Assumptions

Although the Lieberman and Miller repertoire is wider, most designs have two defining characteristics I would like to examine. First, they are mainly *school-based*; they situate 'systemic change' locally, not least at the level of a minimally 'collegial' teaching staff (Nias, Southworth and Yeomans 1989; McLaughlin, Talbert and Bascia, 1990; Johnson, 1990). My argument here is that the vision of a schoolhouse as a bonded community of adults and children is an unlikely one, with a few hundred children in the same place by virtue of living in the same neighbourhood, tutored by adults brought together more by the vagaries of their career paths and the central office than by affiliation or purpose. Others, too, have evoked the within-school constraints of 'cliques' (Bruckerhoff, 1991), 'contrived collegiality' (Hargreaves and Dawe, 1990), and 'the persistence of privacy' (Little, 1990b) in trying to enact collaborative reforms. On the other hand, there have been counterarguments (e.g. Nias, Southworth and Yeomans, 1989; Rosenholtz, 1989) and a trend toward 'disaggregating' effective collaboration to the department or grade-levels (Lichtenstein, McLaughlin and Knudsen, 1991). Similarly, the more affective, supportive role of peers has been put into evidence from several sources (see the review by Little, 1990a).

A second aspect of these trends is more inferential. My analysis is that these are essentially structural or organisational changes that do not directly affect instructional life in the classroom. For one thing, they may eat up the time that teachers need to master the new maths modules or reading enrichment activities to be introduced in order to meet the newly formulated set of schoolwide goals (e.g. Hyde and Sandall, 1984). For another thing, to get from a peer discussion on co-operative learning to its enactment in one's classroom is a phenomenal leap, and there is scant evidence that it is taken. In fact, the changes implied in instructional repertoire, classroom organisation, pacing, use of materials, rehabituation of students' habits and expectations, emergence of unknowns and uncertainties, initial – and sometimes enduring – impressions of ineptitude compared to one's 'usual' practice, etc., are collectively dissuasive. Empirical studies of the enactment of major and minor innovations (e.g. Huberman and Miles, 1984; Miles and Louis, 1990; Anderson, 1995) have documented this pilgrimage. We thus have a 'discussion culture' among teachers and in the many forums of organisational reforms, interspersed with timid attempts at the level of actual implementation. As collaborations intensify, linkages take shape, and teachers' self-defined professionalism bears its fruits, we may well note changes to what is now a modal pattern. Even more devious is the phenomenon brought to light by Cohen (1990) in his nownotorious study of Mrs Oublier: the impression on the part of many teachers that they *have*, in fact, modified their instructional practices, whereas external observers see few changes, even on a long-term basis. Finally, Anyon (1994) has shown trenchantly how little a difference professional development in particular *and* educational reform more generally can make in an inner city marked by poverty and social marginalisation. This calls for greater humility in our pretensions on both counts.

Towards an Alternative Model

This raises the obvious question of alternatives. A few years ago, I wrote a contentious chapter about 'teacher bricolage' in the classroom (Huberman,

1993) by which I referred to an 'artisan model' of teaching. By this I meant principally that the links between instruction and outcome remained obscure, no matter how robust our conceptual base. There are not enough strong generalisations to override apparently minor variations in pupils, teachers or instructional situations (cf. Snow, 1974). Thus, professional development cannot repose forcefully on a stable, replicable or highly codified knowledge base – cannot be transferred early. Much of our actual knowledge as we learn and perfect our profession is 'embodied', the result of swings between experimentation and the search for constants (cf. Pratte and Roury, 1991). The classroom teacher remains essentially a 'tinkerer' or 'instructional handyman', who can put together a host of materials lying around at various stages of a construction or repair job. These materials meet the particular need that emerges at a specific point and are fashioned to fit that purpose (cf. Harper, 1987, for a wonderful example in another domain).

Gradually, our teacher builds up an increasingly differentiated and integrated set of procedures, representations and algorithms for 'reading' the next task and for knowing which materials will be required at the outset. Adapted from Lévi-Strauss, this image of the 'bricoleur' (Hatton, 1987; Yinger, 1987) entails a continuous dialogue with the instructional situation as it evolves; it is inherently personal and pragmatic, and makes both technical communication between teachers and changes in instructional procedures a difficult exercise. As one of our teachers put it in an ongoing study of micro-level innovations (Hubermarn, Karlen and Middlebrooks 1995), 'I didn't know what to do with my body.'

The 'artisan' model has other characteristics worth mentioning briefly. First, it often works by ongoing improvisation, in what Yinger (1987) calls 'a conversation on practice'. There is a general plan, as in the Comedia dell'arte or in jazz groups, but within it are nested a series of not-yet defined 'moves', should the course of events prove unworkable or less interesting than the challenges one fashions for oneself (for details, see Huberman, 1993). This is a virtually idiosyncratic practice, yet it is loosely harmonised with others, and it sets up the following paradox: as we tighten articulations between classrooms in order to ensure children's progression through the curriculum, we need to co-ordinate that institutional-level planning with large zones of instructional latitude in the classroom for individual teachers.

Given that profile, how do artisans construe professional development? When do they seek out peers in relation to their craft? Typically, they are more interested in fellow artisans who are slightly farther along than they or who have fashioned a new procedure (e.g. a fellow 9th grade physics teacher with promising materials in plane geometry; a fellow 2nd grade teacher experimenting with activity corners). Unless one teaches in a very large school, these people will be in other buildings, or they will be in centralised services (universities, resource centres).

In particular, cross-school groups may afford more insight and expertise than is available in one's own institution, but this knowledge may not be known. Then, too, we have 'guilds' of the same subject matters or grade levels, units providing a form of social glue which facilitates communication and common work. These groups can be so organised as to allow for – in fact, push towards – both exchange and experimentation, with less static or potential humiliation than a longer co-habitation in the same building may trigger. Finally, they allow for the circulation of more conceptual information from outside, but at the times and in the directions dictated by the group.

Outline of an Experimenting Teacher Network

It is well-known that, most of the time, we learn alone. We confront a problem, reach for the solutions at hand, and try to resolve the problem. There is strong evidence that the procedure in the classroom is no different, even for more consequential dilemmas we may confront with children or instructional sequences (Dreeben, 1973; Lortie, 1975; Little, 1990a; Huberman, 1985). In a Swiss study of some 160 secondary-level teachers (Huberman, 1989), the most frequent scenario was the 'lone wolf' scenario. It resembles, in many ways, the procedures initially described by Schon (1983, 1987). (Segments of the models that follow are adapted from Guskey and Huberman, 1995)

The scenario is not without its pleasures, as Schon so well describes, along with others (cf. Harper, 1987), who have described solitary problem-solving through iterative chains of reasoning and direct action. In fact, in the Swiss study mentioned earlier (cf. Lowther *et al.,* 1982), we were able to predict 89% of the cases of 'disenchanted' or 'dissatisfied' older teachers and 97% of the cases of 'satisfied' teachers. Put briefly: teachers who invested consistently but mostly alone in classroom-level experiments – what they called 'productive tinkering' with new materials, different pupil grouping, small changes in grading systems – were more likely to be 'satisfied' later on in their career than most others, especially those involved in large-scale reforms.

In reviewing this constellation of 'predictors' of professional satisfaction in teaching, we approximate the 'mainstream' literature on the quality of work life. Ashton and Webb (1986) put it simply and well, noting that 'work is likely to be satisfying when we value what we do, when it challenges and extends us, when we do it well, and when we have ample evidence confirming our success' (p. 162). The secondary-school teachers in this sample presumably thrive when they are able to tinker productively inside their classrooms or with two to three peers in order to obtain the instructional and relational effects they are after (cf. Lowther *et al.,* 1982). McLaughlin and Yee (1988) have delineated more precisely some of these requisite conditions, under the rubrics 'level of opportunity' and 'level of capacity'.

Let me now move from the 'lone wolf' paradigm described above to a more continuously 'innovating' model. First, some assumptions. I assume that, structurally, the 'lone wolf' model of solitary experimentation and reflection will remain entrenched, much in the 'artisan mode', and that whatever skill-enhancing mechanism we devise will have to be grafted, at least partially, on that model. In the current organisation of schooling, teachers will remain, for some time at least, 'professional artisans', working primarily alone, with a variety of new and scrounged-together materials, in a self-tailored work environment. Like good craftspeople, they are active tinkerers, intent on developing an instructional repertoire that responds to – even anticipates – most contingencies in the classroom.

The closed individual cycle

Let us now thread our way from the 'lone wolf' to the 'innovating' paradigms. Figure 11.1, the 'closed individual cycle', depicts the way many teachers contend with the instructional challenges they face. Let us take, for example, an official biology unit that has shown itself to be too difficult for much of the class. The problem is felt, diagnosed and experimented with (photocopies of 'easier' texts, work in mixed-ability groups, increase in exercises and 'debriefing' sessions). If this suffices, the same strategy will be used again. If not, another strategy will be pursued. Literally dozens of instructional matters are resolved – or not – this way in classrooms and they correspond closely to the more 'provincial' artisan mode of instructional management.

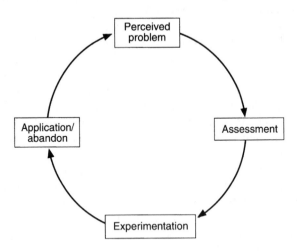

Figure 11.1   *'Closed' individual cycle*

The open individual cycle

To gain time, let us assume the same situation – an inadequate biology text. The cycle depicted in Figure 11.2 is similar, except that, at the moment of

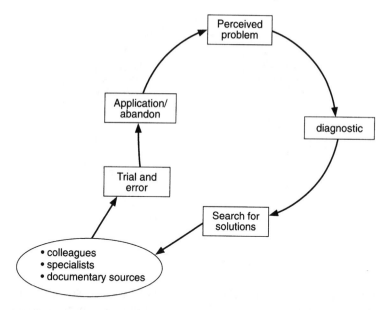

Figure 11.2   *'Open' individual cycle*

looking for solutions, the teacher reaches outside the classroom, as it were, and turns to fellow biology teachers, people at the local teacher education facility or to a wider span of biology materials. This is a primitive, but often successful, form of outreach, given the knowledge acquired, the new re-sources made available and the consultations furnished. Still, the success of the enterprise depends almost entirely on the social network of our biology teachers and their willingness to make something of the information and expertise provided. We are still in a 'lone wolf' paradigm and the key ques-tions are still outstanding: how high is the quality of this easily accessible knowledge, and how do they manage to turn it into durably modified class-room practice, when the available data suggests a high rate of discontinuity?

The closed collective cycle

The next cycle (see Figure 11.3) brings us closer to a collective enterprise, but one without resources from outside the group. Note that we are not in a school here (although we could be), but among teachers from several schools who share the same discipline, interests, preoccupations, level or type of pupil. An important premise here, at least beyond the elementary-school level, is that a biology teacher has more to learn and to give, profes-sionally speaking, in a group of fellow biology teachers from several schools than with the one to two peers who teach biology in that person's own building. In any event, these are 'professional craftspeople', and they are traversing a cycle that goes from exchange to experimentation.

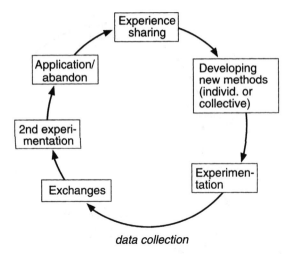

Figure 11.3   *'Closed' collective cycle*

Let us stay with the 'biology' example, although we could easily focus on evaluation, lab work, differences in pupils' ability and motivation, and so forth. In the 'experience-sharing' phase, there is an exchange of 'case' material ('In my class . . .'). There is also, however, a strong dose of more explanatory or diagnostic discussion: reflection on one's work and discussion of seminal issues about learning and teaching science in different contexts. In other words, this is one version of the 'communities' for teacher research that are fast springing up in the literature (e.g. Cochran-Smith and Lytle, 1992), and that are built into our later models. This version sensitises teachers to the fact (a) that their theories have been largely derived from their practices, (b) that their experiential base is only one of several possible and equally legitimate ways of construing the same events or the same learning patterns, and (c) that the language of exchange is an imperfect and frustrating vehicle until there has been protracted interaction, mutual experience and the gradual capacity to imagine other perspectives than one's own from the inside out. This is a key component. It entails both 'de-centring' and a growing psychological commitment to members of the group and their individual enterprises.

This combination of experience-sharing and reflection is a core component of this and the next cycle. As we know, school scheduling provides very little slack time for exchanges that are not purely functional. Most conversation has to do with what Yinger (1987) calls a 'language of practical action,' as opposed to a forum for representing practice 'in larger, more visible patterns' that are accessible to all, and that combine meaningful units of thought and action. It is from the 'teacher empowerment' movement that more collective 'reflection' is now in demand, incorporated into the school year rather than conducted on a voluntary basis.

'Experience-sharing' leads to the conclusion that new texts and new experiments are called for. Some of the experiments can be done individually; others will call for collaborative work in class. Our biologists work up a series of both, and agree to try them out. They come together to discuss these experiments and to make revisions.

The group then decides, let us say, to collect some pupil work samples ('data collection' in Figure 11.3) in order to see how well the new procedures worked. This is a qualitatively different, decisive part of the cycle. First, it involves some ongoing monitoring. Next, it renders more *public* and *visible* what has gone on in each class relative to this experiment. We are no longer in a verbal exchange mode, a 'discussion culture', with nothing on the line. These professional exchanges, carried on around what are presumably real data collected in the class of each member, set up a situation of clarification and comparison, and they only work when the group, in its earlier phases, has come to a level of mutual comfort and complicity in one another's company.

Practically speaking, the idea here is to set up exchanges around specific products or performances so that the next round of experimentation can be more successful, notably that risk-taking can be a more tolerable exercise . . . Ideally, some of these experiments are carried on together – as exchanges in action and not exchanges on action (Schon, 1983). Still, at worst we are looking at real-life data, coming from attempts to change the learning environment. How did the experiments go? Which constellation of groups worked best? Which of the children's representations arose most often? In what form? At the same time, some group cohesiveness has taken hold. The evidence is fairly clear that minimal cohesiveness increases performance, and vice versa. As Mullen and Copper (1994) conclude from a set of integrated studies, what distinguishes groups that perform well is not necessarily that their members interact with smooth co-ordination, nor that they like each other that much, nor that they are proud of their group, but that 'they are committed to successful task performance and regulate their behaviour toward that end' (p. 225). Both dimensions, however, the affective and the technical, are probably important in educational settings.

Finally, the remainder of the model shows that a group of this nature can remain together, either to refine the biology module or to work on other issues. We are in the realm of more prolonged 'teacher action research' or 'collaborative inquiry' (Lambert, 1989; Baird, 1992), both informed, however, by collective development and experimentation. And we are there, it should be noted, with virtually no recourse to external expertise or direction from external specialists. We are relying, as it were, on the collective wisdom – or lack thereof – of individual participants.

The open collective cycle

Before going on, let us have a look at Figure 11.4. There are a few core premises to bear in mind:

- In this illustration, the group comes from several schools, but shares a subject-matter, discipline, grade-level, problem or activity to be worked on.
- The 'cycle' is managed by the group, not by a consultant or specialist. In some instances a 'process facilitator' might be useful. However, external specialists are called in at various moments in accordance with the kind of issue with which the group is contending at that moment. These consultants are people of different kinds, including more experienced peers, something which is foreign to most in-service work. Also, their intervention can be brief, varying from a couple of weeks to 2–3 months, and depending on the evolving goals or pace of the group. They are there at specific moments for specific purposes, to discuss cases or to provide conceptual foci. They are resource people, not group leaders.

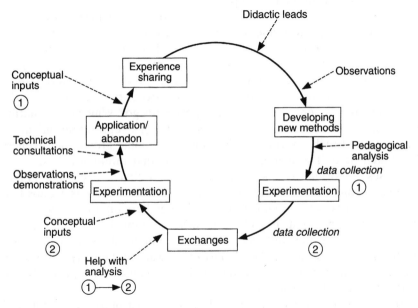

Figure 11.4   *'Open' collective cycle*

Now for the successive stages of the cycle. Let us try a new example, say, experimental science in the 5th and 6th grades. These teachers have come together because the materials at hand are purely workbook oriented, and the basic text calls more for memorisation than for active problem-solving.

Conceptual inputs. The cycle can begin virtually anywhere. In the example below, we have started with some conceptual inputs (11 o'clock on the model), although a strong case could be made for beginning with what we have called 'experience-sharing'. These are the two most likely points of entry. The conceptual inputs might come from a university psychologist who has worked on social constructivist perspectives in math and science. She provides a frame or sensitisation for conducting and monitoring experimentation in class in small groups, for the kinds of cognitive confrontations and eventual shifts one might observe, for the relationship between the conduct of small experiments and what actual scientists do, and for the possible links between science and math curricula at the upper elementary level.

If we go rather from exchanges back to the conceptual inputs the group has just received, what do they signify? How well do they illuminate the cognitions and performances one has observed over the past years? What exactly is a social constructivist perspective of teaching in real-time, in garden-variety classrooms? Presumably, some reading may be done and discussed at this phase of the cycle. It will be in the ongoing shifts from practical experience to more formalised knowledge that we can hope for the descriptions, discussions and debates that constitute for teacher-researchers the 'joint construction of knowledge through conversation' (Cochran-Smith and Lytle, 1992, p. 309).

There is some question here about the relative *timing* of conceptual inputs. It is a topic which authors from the social constructivist school have studied closely. A strong argument is made by Ross and Regan (1993), for whom sharing and conceptual inputs should be mixed, to demonstrate how 'sharing with dissonance' (the confrontation of points of view, with continual interruptions to relate the theory to one's practice, trade versions, make explicit one's point of view, stay open to another perspective), are particularly beneficial.

Experience sharing. This step has two functions The first is to make acquaintance via one's own experience with science teaching in the upper elementary grades. This is the reason for the group, and the sharing of experiences has primarily a technical, initiating function (the more social, convivial moments will come in the interstices). At one level, there is the matter of what each person has experienced with the official science curriculum. At another, all members of the group have a professional biography in science teaching that explains why they are dissatisfied and which alternatives would be both appealing and, given one's own pedagogy, acceptable. It is here that the wealth of experience accumulated through the career cycle can be shared. Shared, but, as we just saw, not necessarily aligned. The idea is not to come to agreement on a set of pedagogical beliefs, but to get as much understanding of one another to continue working together, including dissonant viewpoints and exotic perspectives.

Didactic leads. These too, are provided in part by outsiders to the group, most likely by science educators from a neighbouring resource centre or university. Their function is to build on the conceptual inputs and sharing of experiences by providing alternative scenarios, in class. For example, many hands-on science programmes have groups of pupils acting as scientists: making hypotheses, collecting and weighing evidence, drawing conclusions. Common projects have to do with measuring acidity levels in the water, building rain collectors, understanding the conditions under which pH levels can be lowered, etc. Talking through didactic leads puts flesh and bones on the conceptual inputs and suggests small, manageable experiments one has imagined or done oneself in class. Bringing along materials – or skipping directly to the discovery and observation compo- nents – could also be beneficial.

Observations. These are observations of places in which some of this novel didactic activity is ongoing. These classrooms are identified, typically, by the didactic specialist, and they have the merit of allowing visiting teachers to see 'in the flesh' how their peers enact new practices under everyday conditions. In terms of learning scenarios, of combining conceptual with didactic elements, this is one of the most powerful vehicles for moving from a conventional practice to a novel one. In effect, few modes of learning have shown themselves to be as consequential as observational learning, when the observations are focused and related to one's own experience. In actual fact, it is seldom practised, perhaps because it is (wrongly) associated with mimicry. Also, again typically, there will be a thousand questions to be asked afterwards, and, through the more informal contacts, a possible widening of the network of science teachers in the region. Once again, the observations can come elsewhere in the cycle – even the beginning – if participants are eager to see them as initial sensitisers.

Developing new methods. It is here that the group begins to construct some modest alternatives to the science text and workbooks. These are tentative procedures and materials that have been cobbled together, but they are a start. Some members of the group will want to work on different modules, some on the same.

Pedagogical analysis. The figure also shows that an external analysis might be useful. By this is meant the entry of a specialist – who may well be a more experienced peer – who can take a sympathetic but rigorous look at the procedures and materials that have been put together. Alternatively, one can invite back the person(s) providing the conceptual and didactic leads, asking for a more fine-grained look. Or one might skip this compo- nent altogether.

Experimentation. By this point, we could assume that a shared technical culture and some interpersonal complicity have developed within the group – at least for those that are still active. Our premise is that the preceding steps will have consolidated the group, as is the case in most task-centred group dynamics efforts of this type. What happens now is that each member tries out the materials and sequences that have been elabo- rated. Conceptually, this is an important moment. Group dynamics theory suggests that if a public commitment to change is made – as in this instance – there will be follow through. Otherwise, the magnitude of effort is likely to be highly variable and, in the mean, trivial. The same lines of research also suggest that groups of this type are more likely to take risks than would the same individuals left alone in their classrooms (Wallach, Kogan and Bem, 1962). Also, in keeping with social identity theory, individuals come gradually to comply with the demands and expectations of other group members, owing to the subtle powers which reward or punish individual members. Identifying with the group thus increases accountability to the group (members move to action) and reduces social loafing (Steiner, 1966). Groups with these characteristics are more often what Little (1990a) calls 'subject subcultures' (p. 197): teachers of the same discipline, or at roughly similar grade levels, or sharing a similar pedagogical perspective.

Another facet of group dynamics is the facility, in groups drawn from different schools, of giving and asking for help and advice. This turns out to run counter to the still-prevalent norms *within* schools (Glidewell *et al.*, 1983; Huberman, 1993). There, one does not readily solicit help (in order to preserve one's sense of competence and status equality), nor does one typically offer advice (for fear of appearing arrogant). One can, however, swap experiences in which help is latent, tell a story in return which contains advice ('I once had the same kind of "droop" just after Easter . . . So what I tried . . .'). There is evidence that these norms are changing, but not rapidly. Note that in the cycle we are discussing here, help and advice are literally built into the discussions. Also, since what is being tried out is new to all, temporary difficulties, even failures, are socially legitimate. Everyone is stumbling, and feels free to talk about it.

Exchanges. The figure also shows another constraint on the group. Each member will collect pre-test data and, after the experimentation, will collect post-test data. The figure also shows that external help can be provided for the analysis of pre-test (1) and post-test (2) data. These data are less there as evaluative instruments than as *an obligation to actually conduct the experimentation* and to debrief with other members in the group in ways that are not purely anecdotal. Ideally, these exchanges will also include work samples, test results, final products, and, in so doing, will make for a more concrete, technical exchange of information. But they can be more informal. The core function of the exchanges is the clear evidence of embarking on an adventure together, one in which each member has actually taken some risks, instructionally speaking, but with the expectation that there will be uncertainties and dead ends.

Conceptual inputs (2) and experimentation

Following on the first experimentation, the analysis of its results in terms of pupils' engagement, productivity or performance, and ongoing exchanges about the mass of small mysteries, epiphanies and tragedies, the cycle calls for another visit from a conceptual specialist. It is clear that the discussion at this point will be different from the initial one (conceptual inputs (1)). There will have been a conceptual articulation of individual frames, didactic and pedagogical leads, the creation and execution of an experiment and the analysis of its results. For example, one will be talking less about social constructivism in science than about what happened, and especially why, when teachers' expectations were foiled in the first part of the different experiments tried out. We would expect, in fact, that the effects of this second conceptual component, built as it was on an experiment with common features and thoroughly discussed, would be a strong one – would knit theory a bit more to the varieties of learning. As Figure 11.4 shows, these inputs lead to a revision of the same kind of experimentation or to the design of new ones.

The moments of conceptualisation are decisive. First, they stave off the rush to action – the eagerness to get the next experiment 'right'. Next, as the constructivists like to say, they give the time needed for one's confusion. Gradually, members will be still better able to consider their own views and practices from the perspective of other group members. At the same time, common knowledge is gradually broadened (seeing more various ways of acting in one setting) and deepened (conceiving more aspects of the situation).

Demonstrations and consultations. This is a delicate point. We might well imagine that the next experimentation cycle resembles the first one. There is, however, a more 'intrusive' scenario, as shown in Figure 11.4. The figure suggests, in effect, that group members will scan more actively for teachers more experienced than they are, or for teacher educators familiar with the kind of project they are working on. Why this emphasis on 'technical assistance'?

Joyce and Showers (1982, 1988) have shown convincingly, I believe, that we think magically about the mastery of complex instructional procedures – about what learning psychologists call 'enactive mastery'. It is not simply by trial-and-error, observation and verbal exchanges with colleagues that complex skill learning occurs, in the classroom or elsewhere. In effect, in other areas of expertise – law, medicine, social work, athletics – there are periods of focused observation, demonstration and at-the-elbow consultation while the novice runs through the successive components of the new practice. They are guided apprenticeships. In education, by contrast, we seem to have come to believe that no rigorous technical support is needed for durable pedagogical change by falsely extrapolating from the principle that each teacher has a unique instructional and interpersonal style. Because, in so many cases, teachers effectively teach themselves to teach, they may assume that they can teach themselves to teach otherwise. This turns out, in many ways, to be harder. Nor is practice in isolation an adequate solution, not only because it 'grooves' errorful activity, but also because it affords so little opportunity for conceptual clarification allowing teachers to make sense of their cumulative experience.

In fact, most evidence points in the opposite direction; demonstration by experts, systematic observation of teachers undertaking new practices, interventions on the spot in the form of 'coaching' and two-tiered apprenticeship (Schon, 1987) seem to be required for any major shift in the learning environment created by the teacher – required and, in most instances, appreciated. The same trends appear in the 'implementation' literature (Fullan, 1991). Teachers tend to remain 'stuck' at lower levels of mastery for lack of explicit counsel from external experts or from experienced peers – but from peers who know how to respect and integrate the 'artisanry' of the teacher they are advising. In his meta-analysis of in-service training, Wade (1985) concluded clearly that models which incorporate observation, feedback and practice are more effective than programmes that do not use those methods. Note that this does *not* assume imitation of expert models, but rather a more thoroughgoing, self-conscious application of individual styles and modes of 'bricolage'.

In effect, the kind of problem-solving built into this cycle *assumes* that the process of learning, experimentation and change will be moderately complex, novel, ambiguous, contradictory and conflicting. *These are, in effect, the ideal conditions for significant learning, be it for adults or for children* (see Salomon and Globerson, 1987). Oftentimes, too, they can trigger self-doubts in more than one sector at once: in one's sense of content mastery, in one's implicit theory of learning, in one's comfort with instructional management. But just as the group literally sets off these unsettling feelings in its members, it also provides a safe haven to experiment with them (Abrams *et al.*, 1990). This is achieved through the interpersonal bonds that build up gradually among members and which outlive the group itself, creating thereby a more durable network for later contacts.

All this is pertinent to our science teachers. What is unusual, perhaps, in this model is that we have *both* a self-directing group and a set of external interventions. In many respects, it is like other 'rational' models that have demonstrated their efficiency, like that of Stallings (1989): try, evaluate, modify, try again. At the same time, it respects some of the key 'collaborative' canons laid out by Lieberman and Miller (1990): (1) a culture of support for teacher inquiry; norms of colleagueship, openness and trust; (2) opportunities and time for disciplined inquiry; (3) teacher learning of content in context; (4) reconstruction of leadership roles; (5) networks, collaborations and coalitions.

Application/abandon

We have come to the end of the cycle shown in Figure 11.4. The group, singly or collectively, will adopt some of the new science approaches they have constructed together. Others will be discarded. More important, perhaps, an enlarged network will have been created: a network of upper-elementary science teachers, itself connected to specialists in neighbouring universities and resource centres on a longer-scale basis. One knows now where to call, where to visit, how to mitigate an enduring uncertainty or obstacle. We have, then, a plausible scenario for the professional development of teachers.

Conclusion

This scenario has more general rewards. As noted earlier by Ashton and Webb (1986), it combines community of effort with a greater certainty of practice and a more solid sense of teaching efficiency, often in the sense of having learned to listen and minister to pupils in more differentiated, challenging ways. It respects a more particularistic vision of the teaching career, what we have earlier called the 'artisan model'. It is also clear how much this kind of enterprise can bring to professional educators at day-to-day grips with the enactment of instructional change in their classrooms.

The question remains: how likely are such networks to spread? Are they already in operation? The answer to both questions is clearly 'yes' (e.g. Rogers, 1979; Gray and Caldwell, 1980; Cusick, 1982; Popkewitz and Myrdal, 1991; Lieberman and McLaughlin, 1994). Most, however, correspond to our Figure 11.3, the 'closed collective circle', or have introduced only fragments of Figure 11.4. There remains a somewhat magical assumption that discussion and sharing will translate into masterful classroom practice without the necessary consultations, observations, demonstrations and staged conceptual inputs or didactic leads. Nor do we have anything like rigorous empirical studies of follow-through in existing networks. They are seen largely as low-key, easy access to trusted forms of expertise and support.

Finally, this model does not preclude interactive work at the level of the school building. In some respects, in fact, this model could be converted to an action research project within an establishment. The differences are three-fold. First we have centred on teachers of similar grade levels or subject-matters, not on institutional problems. The network design lends itself to both, but is more powerful in instances where I may be the only science or math teacher around, and I can go only as far as my best student pushes me.

Next, we have assumed that there is ongoing work at the school level, and that this is a complementary, not competitive, mechanism. It may have to vie with school-level projects for resources, or tie school-level agendas to network priorities, which is a realistic – and probably enriching – objective. Also, a small but critical mass of teachers from one school that joins such a network, for example a group of secondary-level science teachers, can provide follow-up support and resources for one another locally far better than is possible through a more episodic mechanism.

Finally, we have centred our analysis on one key segment of school life: the instructional process. Ultimately, this is where cognitive activity is situated, where skill mastery, academic attitudes and conceptual growth are engaged – or not. Structural changes alone do not translate directly to this level (Elmore, 1992). Had we both exemplars, cross-school experimenting groups and within-school restructuring groups, we might better advance the agenda of professional development and, thereby, affect the environments of learning more rapidly and with greater understanding for the conditions which teachers are actually confronting in modifying their instructional practices.

References

Abrams, D., Wetherell, M., Cochrane, S., Hogg, M. and Turner J. (1990) Knowing what to think by knowing who you are: self-categorization and the nature of norm formation, conformity and group polarization, *British Journal of Social Psychology,* Vol. 29, pp. 97–119.

Anderson, B. (1995) *Case Studies of Innovations in Science and Mathematics Education.* Fort Collins, CO: InSites.

Anyon, J. (1994) Teacher development and reform in an inner-city school, *Teachers College Record,* 96(1), pp. 15–31.

Ashton P. and Webb R. (1986) *Making a Difference: Teachers' Sense of Efficacy and Achievement.* New York: Longman.

Baird, J. (1992) Collaborative reflection, systematic inquiry, better teaching, in R. Russell and H. Munby (eds) *Teachers and Teaching: from Classroom to Reflection,* pp. 33–48. London: Falmer Press.

Borko, H. and Putnam, R. (1995) Expanding a teacher's knowledge base: a cognitive psychological perspective on professional development, in T. Guskey and M. Huberman (eds) *Professional Development: New Paradigms and Practices,* pp. 35–66. New York: Teachers College Press.

Bruckerhoff, C. (1991) *Between Classes: Faculty Life at Truman High.* New York: Teachers College Press.

Cochran-Smith, M. and Lytle, S. (1992) Communities for teacher research: fringe or forefront? *American Journal of Education,* May, pp. 298–323.

Cohen, D. (1990) A revolution in one classroom: the case of Mrs Oublier, *Educational Evaluation and Policy Analysis,* Vol. 12, pp. 311–29.

Cusick, R. (1982) *A Study of Networks Among Professional Staffs in Secondary Schools.* East Lansing, MI: Institute for Research on Teaching, Michigan State University.

Daresh, J. (1987) (Research trends in staff development and in-service education, *Journal of Education for Teaching,* Vol. 13, pp. 11–16.

Darling-Hammond, L. (1994) *Professional Development Schools: Schools for Developing a Profession.* New York: Teachers College Press.

Dreeben, R. (1973) The school as workplace, in R. Travers (ed.) *Handbook of Research on Teaching,* 2nd edn, pp. 450–73 Chicago: Rand-McNally.

Elmore, R. (1992) Why restructuring alone won't improve teaching, *Educational Leadership,* April, pp. 44–9.

Fenstermacher, G. and Berliner, D. (1983) *A Conceptual Analysis for the Analysis of Staff Development.* Santa Monica, CA: Rand Corporation.

Fullan, M. (1991) *The New Meaning of Educational Change.* New York: Teachers College Press.

Fuhrman, S. and Elmore, R. (1990) Understanding local control in the wake of state education reform, *Educational Evaluation and Policy Analysis,* Vol. 12, pp. 82–96.

Glidewell, J., Tucker, S., Todt, M. and Cox, S. (1983) Professional support systems: the teaching profession, in A. Nadler, J. Fisher and B. DePaulo (eds) *New Directions in Helping*, Vol. 3, pp. 189–212. New York: Academic Press.

Gray, J. and Caldwell, K. (1980) The Bay Area Writing Project, *Journal of Staff Development*, 1(1), pp. 31–9.

Guskey, T. and Huberman, M. (1995) *Professional Development: New Paradigms and New Practices*. New York: Teachers College Press.

Hargreaves, A. and Dawe, R. (1990) Paths of professional development, *Teaching and Teacher Education*, Vol. 6, pp. 227–41.

Hargreaves, A. and Fullan, M. (eds) (1992) *Understanding Teacher Development*. London: Cassell.

Harper, D. (1987) *Working Knowledge*. Chicago: University of Chicago Press.

Hatton, E. (1987) Levi-Strauss Bricolage and theorizing teachers' work, *Anthropology and Education Quarterly*, Vol. 20, pp. 74–86.

Henderson, E. (1978) *The Evaluation of In-service Teacher Training*. Beckenham: Crook Helm.

Huberman, M. (1985) What knowledge is of most worth to teachers? A knowledge-use perspective, *Teaching and Teaching Education*, Vol. 1, pp. 251–62.

Huberman, M. (1989) The professional life cycle of teachers, *Teachers College Record*, Vol. 91, pp. 31–58.

Huberman, M. (1993) The model of the independent artisan in teachers' professional relations, in J. Little and M. McLaughlin (eds) *Teachers' Work*. New York: Teachers College Press.

Huberman, M. and Miles, M. (1984) *Innovation Up Close*. New York: Plenum Press.

Huberman, M., Karlen, J. and Middlebrooks, S. (1995) *A Multiple-case Study of Technology-based Innovations: Voyage of the Mimi and Kidsnet*. Andover, MA: Network.

Hyde, N. and Sandall, C. (1984) *The Impact of the Primary Schools Programme in 12 Primary Schools*. Perth, Australia: Research Branch, Educational Department of Western Australia.

Johnson, J. (1990) The primacy of the department, in M. McLaughlin, J. Talbert and N. Bascia (eds) *The Contexts of Teaching in Secondary Schools: Teachers' Realities*, pp. 167–84. New York: Teachers College Press.

Joyce, B. and Showers, B. (1982) The coaching of teaching, *Educational Leadership*, October, pp. 4–10.

Joyce, B. and Showers, B. (1988) *Student Achievement Through Staff Development*. New York: Longman.

Lambert, L. (1989) The end of an era of staff development, *Educational Leadership*, Vol. 18, pp. 78–83.

Lichtenstein, G., McLaughlin, M. and Knudsen, J. (1991) *Teacher Empowerment and Professional Knowledge*. Stanford, CA: Center for Research on the Context of Secondary School Teaching, Stanford University.

Lieberman, A. (ed.) (1988) *Building a Professional Culture in Schools*. New York: Teachers College Press.

Lieberman, A. and McLaughlin (1994) Networks for educational change: powerful and problematic, *Phi Delta Kappan*, Vol. 63, pp. 673–7.

Lieberman, A. and Miller, L. (1990) Teacher development in professional practice schools, *Teachers College Record*, Vol. 92, pp. 105–21.

Little, J. (1990a) Conditions of professional development in secondary schools, in M. W. McLaughlin, J. Talbert and N. Bascia (eds) *The Contexts of Teaching in Secondary Schools: Teachers' Realities*, pp. 187–18. New York: Teachers College Press.

Little, J. (1990b) The persistence of privacy: autonomy and initiative in teachers' professional relations, *Teachers College Record*, Vol. 91, pp. 509–36.

Little, J. (1993) Teachers' professional development in a climate of education reform, *Educational Evaluation and Policy Analysis*, Vol. 15, pp. 129–51.

Lortie. D. (1975) *Schoolteacher: a Sociological Study*. Chicago: University of Chicago Press.

Lowther, M. *et al.* (1982) Job satisfaction among teachers: a multi-survey, multivariate study. Paper presented at American Educational Research Association Meeting.

McLaughlin, M. Talbert, J. and Bascia (eds) (1990) *The Contexts of Teaching in Secondary Schools: Teachers' Realities*. New York: Teachers College Press.

McLaughlin, M. and Yee, S. (1988) School as a place to have a career, in A. Lieberman (ed.) *Building a Professional Culture in Schools*, pp. 23–44. New York: Teachers College Press.

Miles, M. and Louis, K. S. (1990) Mustering the will and skill for change, *Educational Leadership*, 47(8), pp. 57–61.

Mullen, B. and Cooper, C. (1994) The relation between group cohesiveness and performance: an integration, *Psychological Bulletin*, Vol. 115, pp. 210–27.

Nias, J., Southworth, G. and Yeomans, R. (1989) *Staff Relationships in the Primary School: a Study of Organizational Cultures*. London: Cassell.

Popkewitz, T. and Myrdal, S. (1991) *Case Studies of the Urban Mathematics Collaborative Project*. Madison, WI: University of Wisconsin at Madison.

Pratte, R. and Roury, J. (1991) Teachers' professionalism and craft, *Teachers College Record*, Vol. 93, pp. 59–70.

Prestine, N. and Bowen, C. (1993) Benchmarks of change: assessing essential school restructuring efforts, *Educational Evaluation and Policy Analysis*, Vol. 15, pp. 298–319.

Rogers, E. (1979) Network analysis of the diffusion of innovations, in P. Holland and S. Leinhardt (eds) *Perspectives on Social Network Research*, pp. 137–64. New York: Academic Press.

Rosenholtz, S. (1989) *Teachers' Workplace: the Social Organization of Schools*. New York: Longman.

Ross, J. and Regan, I. (1993) Sharing professional experience: impact of professional development, *Teaching and Teacher Education*, Vol. 9, pp. 91–106.

Salomon, G. and Globerson, T. (1987) Skill may not be enough: the role of mindfulness in learning and transfer, *International Journal of Educational Research*, Vol. 11, pp. 623–38.

Schon, D. (1983) *The Reflective Practitioner*. New York: Basic Books.

Schon, D. (1987) *Educating the Reflective Practitioner*. San Francisco: Jossey-Bass.

Snow, R. (1974) Representative and quasi-representative designs for research on teaching, *Review of Educational Research*, Vol. 44, pp. 263–91.

Stallings, J. (1989) School achievement effects and staff development: what are some critical factors? Paper presented at American Educational Research Association Meeting, San Francisco.

Steiner, I. (1966) Models for inferring relationship between group size and potential group productivity, *Behavioral Science*, Vol. 11, pp. 273–83.

Tafei, L. and Bertani, A. (1992) Reconceptualizing staff development for systemic change, *Journal of Staff Development*, 13(4), pp. 42–45.

Talbert, J. and McLaughlin, M. (1994) Teacher professionalism in local contexts, *American Journal of Education*, Vol. 102, pp. 122–53.

Wallach, M., Kogan, N. and Bem, D. (1962) Group influence on individual risk-taking, *Journal of Abnormal and Social Psychology*, Vol. 65, pp. 75–86.

Wade, R. (1985) What makes a difference in in-service teacher education? A meta-analysis of research, *Educational Leadership*, Vol 42, pp. 48–54.

Yinger, R. (1987) Learning the language of practice, *Curriculum Inquiry*, Vol. 17, pp. 293–318.

12

Autobiographical Research and the Emergence of the Fictive Voice

Peter Clements

Introduction

As educational practitioners reflect critically on their practice over time, it is often difficult for them to re-create their actual educational practice as opposed to what might be termed the rhetoric of courses they have taught. Unless careful and thorough records from the varying courses and periods were kept, what actually went on in practice may remain elusive. Using the example of classroom practice for example, documentary evidence, such as lesson schemes, mark books and all the paraphernalia of the teaching record, may be available. However, these cannot in themselves re-create accurate memory of such varying issues as what was taught and learned, what changed or remained the same in terms of pedagogical practice over time, what enduring and changing values the teacher brought to his/her craft over time and how different the practitioners' classrooms have been over the course of or part of a career. Extant evidence may well be useful in acting as an aide-mémoire, but a proposition of this chapter is that critique of memory itself will act as an important stimulus – indeed possibly the main stimulus – in allowing the educational practitioner to reflect on his/her practice over time. Memory is, however, problematic and the growing body of psychological research into what has been termed its veridicality (or truth content) (for an overview of research on veridicality see Conway, 1990, pp. 9–11; Groeger, 1997) seems not yet to have been fully disseminated within the field of biographical research in education. The aim of this chapter, in arguing that critical autobiographical research should be encouraged among reflective practitioners, is to offer a bridge between developments in psychological research and an exhortation for more educational practitioners to engage in critical autobiographical research in education, as distinct from the growing body of biographical work on teachers' lives; then go on to discuss psychological research into autobiography. It will begin with an analysis of the advantages of autobiographical memory; and, finally, to link the two in offering possible ways forward from the outcomes of a personal investigation in the field of autobiographical research into educational practice over time.

Autobiography in education is no new phenomenon, although most work has been done in the USA (see, for example, Grumet, 1980, 1990;

Pinar, 1980, 1981; Butt, Raymond and Yamagushi, 1988; Krall, 1988). In the UK, however, Abbs was stressing its importance in Initial Teacher Training (ITT) as long ago as 1974 (Abbs, 1974). Writing primarily about teacher trainees, he argued that they should be encouraged to investigate their memories and values. Autobiography, he believed, was an inward quest to discover one's own values which one would inevitably bring into one's teaching. Abbs gives a useful definition of the process of educational autobiography as 'an act of writing perched in the present, gazing backwards into the past while poised ready for flight into the future' (Abbs, 1974, p. 7). Here one could talk of learning through hindsight. However, as has already been suggested, memories can be fraught with difficulty (they can, for example, be unreliable and subjective in their partial and partisan perspective on events). If memories can be tested against other criteria, however, for example others' perspectives on the same events or extant documentary evidence, they may approach, but will still not necessarily be enough in themselves to arrive at, an acceptable level of empirical reliability or truthfulness. Teachers contemplating autobiography have, for example, been advised to keep journals which can be used as aide-mémoires for or tests against memory (Grumet, 1990), but as will be argued, this will not in itself enable one to accurately recreate the past.

There seem in fact few widely disseminated classroom teacher critical autobiographies (it is important to draw a distinction here between memoirs and critical autobiographies of teachers' professional careers). Most of the North American research referred to would appear to involve those in teacher education or higher education teachers trying to encourage their students to undertake the same sort of exercise as Abbs promoted for the same sort of reasons. Krall, for instance, noted that graduate students' studies and discoveries of new goals in life led them naturally to introspection, 'but students are usually advised to . . . distance themselves from personal perspectives, or to develop a critical attitude that ignores their own participation in social questions' (Krall, 1988, p. 467). She, on the other hand, encouraged graduate students to undertake autobiography in order 'to reconstruct their past experiences into a more unified and comprehensible and thus a more harmonious and integrated view of the present' (Krall, 1988, p. 479).

Grumet similarly encourages autobiography 'in the aspiration that it will enable the student to become the active interpreter of his past as well as heighten his capacity to be the active agent of his own interests in a present he shares with the community' (Grumet, 1980, p. 157). Pinar advocated life history through a hypothesis that 'to the extent these bonds (the bonds of academic work to personality, to physical and psychic structure) are shrouded from view is the extent to which they are rigid and arrest movement' (Pinar, 1981, p. 286)

It might appear, therefore, that only when we recognise our own personal baggage can we arrive at objective truth about our work. Here then is the challenge for educational research; if the writers cited are correct, autobiographical research would not only help answer central questions in terms of educational practice, but would also facilitate the practitioner's ability to research his/her enduring and changing values over time; the varying personal baggage he/she brought to tasks over time, his/her own 'architecture of self'.

One must, however, discuss problems of procedure here. Of course, teachers' life histories had been undertaken, particularly since teachers have been widely regarded as crucial in the change process. Fullan, for example, argued that 'Educational change depends on what teachers do and think – it's as simple and complex as that' (Fullan, 1991, p. 117), while Hargreaves agreed:

> The teacher is the ultimate key to social change and school improvement. Reform is worthless if it doesn't take the teacher into account. Teachers define, develop, reinterpret the curriculum – what teachers think ultimately shapes the kind of learning students get.
>
> (Hargreaves, 1993, p. vii)

Lortie (1975) conducted a major sociological survey of teachers in the USA in the 1970s and Huberman in Europe 20 years later (Huberman, 1993). In the UK, Goodson (1992) and Sikes, Measor and Woods (1985) have written teacher biographies. Two entire editions of the *Cambridge Journal of Education* have been devoted to studying teachers' lives, albeit in different ways (Vol. 20, no. 3 (1990) and Vol. 27, no. 3 (1997)). However, these works, even the biographies, undertaken by researchers are written about (as opposed to written by) teachers, the data relating to their lives being processed and ultimately interpreted by someone else to meet their own, possibly differing agendas. Cole, for example, sought to disprove the stereotype of teachers as conservatives who often, despite the introduction of new ideas into their training programmes, revert to pedagogies they experienced during their own schooling during their probationary year and then maintain these old methods throughout their teaching (Cole, 1985, pp. 89–104), while others may have been interested in teachers' life cycles, aspirations and careers (e.g. Goodson, 1992, p. 41; Huberman, 1993, pp. 1–21, particularly pp. 12–13). Indeed, the biographer may be interpreting the case through his/her own baggage, his/her own 'architecture of self', his/her own 'second record' (Hexter, 1972, pp. 104–11). It is important then to draw a distinction between this body of work which, valuable as it is, represents the teacher's voice through a filter as it were, a 'collaborative' venture (Goodson, 1992, p. 6) and the critical autobiographical research which I would advocate.

Problems of Memory in Autobiographical Research

Autobiography is 'first hand' in a way that biography cannot be; it is after all the work of the subject reflecting the agenda set by the autobiographer for his/her own purpose. However, autobiography is problematic in that the subject may find it difficult to be objective about him/herself and, in viewing ourselves from the perspective of the present, it may be difficult to create oneself as one was in the past. This is why it is vital to check one's analysis against the extant evidence and the remembrances of others, but then perhaps subject it to further critique in the ways offered later in this chapter.

Even if there is a determination to be as honest as possible about our past, there is a particular methodological problem with autobiography and autobiographical research that must be addressed at the onset; this is the problem of veridicality and it will be necessary to discuss this within the context of research into autobiographical memory in order to demonstrate how it might be addressed.

The issue can be summarised as follows.

1. Memory fades with time. The academic research to support this assertion is varied and much depends on the types of information to be
   recalled, but generally studies agree on this phenomenon. Wagenaar
   showed, for example, an approximate 70% accurate recall of events
   after 6 months, falling to 29% after 5 years (cited in Brewer, 1986, pp.
   49–50); Linton 99% after 18 months and 68% after 6 years (Conway,
   1990, pp. 46–7).

   [. . .]

   Most of what actually happened and when can be relatively easily
   verified by resource to the documentation, but the 'how' issues, such as
   how one felt, how such and such a decision was arrived at and implemented and, furthermore, the 'cost benefit analyses', questions such as
   what alternatives were considered and why they were rejected, may be
   more difficult. This is, moreover, a crucial issue for historical research.
   Diaries, memos and so on cannot in themselves give the looks and sighs
   and body language that really may tell the truth about any given situation.
2. False information given after the event can distort memory. If, after
   witnessing an event, misinformation is later given about that event,
   people tend to remember it falsely (Searlemann and Herrmann, 1994,
   pp. 252–3).
3. We have self-schematas on how we view ourselves (Conway, 1990, pp.
   98–9; Searlemann and Herrmann, 1994. p. 250). These self-schematas
   can affect our autobiographical memory processes by causing us to remember an event in such a way that it is consistent with our present self-
   image. We do then tend to remember events in terms of our own perceptions of them; often too we quite naturally place ourselves in the
   centre because it is our part in or our perception of the event (or process
   or situation) that we are remembering. This means, for example, that we
   could, in the process of remembrance, either exaggerate our own role or
   drag our part, which may only in fact have been peripheral, into the
   centre as it were. I can, for example, remember my cousin's wedding

from my perspective; I would find it impossible to remember it from hers – although I could imagine what she was feeling, this could have no claim to veridicality.

4. There is also a rather speculative hypothesis that if our self-schemata changes over time then our autobiographical memories may change too (Searlemann and Herrmann, 1994, pp. 250–1). According to this thesis, memories are not fixed but can be variable depending on time and circumstance, in the interpretive stages. It has been argued, for example, that the reflective memory attempts to control what happened to us in the past. Put simply, we remember things differently from how they actually occurred, usually in the best light to ourselves.

[. . .]

Addressing Problems of Memory in Autobiographical Research

If the above issues are some of the principal problems in terms of ver-idicality in deploying autobiographical memory as a methodology, we must now turn in some detail to the ways in which these can be addressed. As discussed above, the most obvious way, of course, is to test one's memory against the extant record, where that record exists. It would be easy for me, for example, to demonstrate that I was a PGCE student at the University of Bath during the academic year 1977/1978 and that I did indeed pass the course. One can test against extant evidence the course outline and indeed the components I completed. The re-creation of what I actually felt about the course is, however, more difficult. I may have copious notes, lesson plans and preparations and copies of assignments. In the absence of a personal reflective diary in which I had noted emotions, however, it is impossible to tell from this historical record what I actually felt about specific things at various points in the course. Even if I had the opportunity to interview course tutors and fellow students and they remembered me and what I said or did, the evidence would be insufficient to address the issue of what I felt. This is because it would only be a recollection of what I had, consciously or otherwise, chosen to show them, the public face as it were. The private face remains private no matter how public the record might be and it may often be in the private face that . . . truth may be said to reside.

[. . .]

In conclusion, the general issue about autobiography which has emerged from the foregoing discussion and my own research into professional auto-biographical memory is what we may term the fictive. Put simply, by the term 'the fictive', I mean what we believe to be true memories which may in fact be false or recreated purely through our own perspectives or inter-pretation of them after time (and with the deployment of hindsight). By this, I do not mean that memory is fiction in the sense, say, that Christopher Isherwood creates a fiction out of his memories of pre-war Berlin or Dickens in *David Copperfield,* but rather that memory re-creation is such a complex phenomenon that exact re-creation in the sense, say, that we can call up a piece of work stored in a computer and it will always be exactly as we last left it is impossible. For many reasons, such as, for example, the operation of self-schema in memory (Barclay, 1986, pp. 82–100), we remember events as we would like them to be remembered, perhaps showing ourselves in the best light, perhaps making more of our contribution, perhaps altering the record to enhance our own role or, in the words of Bartlett, 'the past is being continually remade, reconstructed in the interests of the present' (quoted in Neimayer and Matzler, 1994, p. 128).

The recognition that the teacher's voice should be heard is widely held. In education, researchers use personal narrative and assisted autobiographical enquiry because they believe that we must understand the lives and experiences of students, teachers and administrators if we are to understand the classrooms, schools and communities they create (Larson, 1997, p. 455). Teachers are often the one constant feature in the changing map of educational provision; 'In that unique position they witnessed continuity and change in school policies, pedagogical theories and practices, student attitudes and culture and family roles, values and structures' (Altenbaugh, 1997, p. 315). However, it is important to offer a critical process through which teachers can remember their practice over time with cohesion, structure and confidence as to veridicality. Without this, memories can be jumbled, unstructured, value-laden and uncritically offered from the perspective of the present. The concept of the fictive is offered here as worthy of further research to address these concerns. Critique of one's autobiographical memory deploying analysis of language and narrative besides extant evidence to arrive at the self-schema and values implicit in the way the event has been remembered will help re-create the truth of one's professional autobiographical past, enabling one to assess how one's professional practice has changed or endured over time.

References

Abbs, P. (1974) *Autobiography in Education.* London: HEB.

Altenbaugh, R. (1997) Past lives and present concerns, *Cambridge Journal of Education,* Vol. 27, pp. 313–29.

Brewer, W. F. (1986) What is autobiographical memory, in D. C. Rubin (ed.) *Autobiograhical Memory.* New York: Cambridge University Press.

Butt, R., Raymond, D. and Yamagushi, L. (1988) Autobiographical praxis: studying the formation of teachers' knowledge, *Journal of Curriculum Theorising,* 7(4), pp. 87–164.

Catterell, P. (1994) Oral history, in P. Catterell and H. Jones (eds) *Understanding Documents and Sources.* London: Heinemann.

Cole, M. (1985) The tender trap, in S. J. Ball and I. Goodson (eds) *Teachers' Lives and Careers*, pp. 89–104. London: Falmer Press.

Conway, M. (1990) *Autobiographical Memory*. Milton Keynes: Open University Press.

Conway, M. (1995) *Flashbulb Memories*. New Jersey: Lawrence Erlbaum Associates.

Fullan, M. (1991) *The New Meaning of Educational Change*. London: Cassell.

Goodson, I. (1992) *Studying Teachers' Lives*. London: Routledge.

Groeger, J. (1997) *Memory and Remembering*. New York: Addison-Wesley, Longman.

Grumet, M. R. (1980) Autobiography and reconceptualisation, *Journal of Curriculum Theorising*, Vol. 2, pp. 155–8.

Grumet, M. R. (1990) Retrospective; autobiography and analysis of educational experience, *Cambridge Journal of Education*, Vol. 20, pp. 321–5.

Hargreaves, A. (1993) Introduction, in M. Huberman (ed.) *The Lives of Teachers*. London: Cassell.

Hexter, J. D. (1972) *The History Primer*. London: Allen Lane.

Huberman, M. (ed.) (1993) *The Lives of Teachers*. London: Cassell.

Krall, F. R. (1988) From the inside out – personal history as educational research, *Educational Theory*, Vol. 38, pp. 467–79.

Larson, C. (1997) Re-presenting the subject: problems in personal narrative inquiry, *Qualitative Studies in Education*, Vol. 10, pp. 455–70.

Lortie, D. (1975) *Schoolteacher*. Chicago: University of Chicago Press.

Neimayer, G. J. and Metzler, A. E. (1994) Personal identity and autobiographical recall, in U. Neisser and R. Fivush (eds) *The Remembering Self*. New York: Cambridge University Press.

Pinar, W. (1980) Life history and educational experience, *Journal of Curriculum Theorising*, Vol. 2, pp. 159–213.

Pinar, W. (1981) Life history and educational experience, *Journal of Curriculum Theorising*, Vol. 3, pp. 259–86.

Searlemann, A. and Herrmann, D. (1994) *Memory from a Broader Perspective*. New York: McGraw Hill.

Sikes, P., Measor, L. and Woods, P. (1985) *Teachers' Careers, Crises and Continuities*. London: Falmer Press.

Stenhouse, L. (1979) *Case Study and Case Records: towards a contemporary history of education* (mimeo) (Norwich, CARE, UEA).

13

Arguing for Your Self: Identity as an Organising Principle in Teachers' Jobs and Lives

Maggie MacLure

Introduction: Adopting the Biographical Attitude

There is a lot of interest these days in the personal dimensions of teachers' lives – in knowing what teachers are like and what makes them tick. Researchers, managers, practitioners and policy-makers are suddenly (or so it seems) examining teachers' self-concepts, their value systems and the circumstances of their daily lives, past and present. As a result, informal, person-oriented genres such as biography, autobiography, life history, narrative and anecdote have become quite widely accepted within educational research and professional development (see Connelly and Clandinin, 1990). We might coin the term '*biographical attitude*' to describe this generalised concern with the teacher-as-person. It describes a 'slant' or posture towards issues of research, policy or development which places the biographical subject and her or his lived experience at the centre of the analytic frame.

So why has it become fashionable to adopt a biographical attitude? There are a number of possible explanations. It fits well, for a start, with the ideologies of holism which have become popular in professional education, where the definition of 'development' has been stretched to include people's personal qualities and values, as well as their professional expertise (see MacLure and Stronach, 1989). Professional development, in this view, involves a reflexive search for self-knowledge and self-improvement (e.g. Schon, 1983; Aspinwall, 1986). Related to this, the biographical attitude provides a rationale for 'user-friendly' reform: change will be better accommodated, the argument goes, if it resonates with the hopes, fears and circumstances of the individuals involved. Managers and policy-makers can therefore claim both administrative and humanitarian grounds for taking an interest in the personal dimensions of workers' lives. Whether these claims are couched in the soft vocabulary of 'ownership' of innovation, or the harder, objectifying language of 'human resource development', they are used to support the idea of a kind of niche-marketing of reform, tailored to the perceived identities and needs of the clientele (MacLure, 1989).

But if biography has its adherents amongst the decision-makers, it also has an appeal for those who feel themselves marginalised or silenced by those decisions. Borrowing from feminist praxis, and other critical/ emancipatory approaches, teachers and teacher educators are using personal testimony and life history as oppositional strategies for combating the punitive abstractions and reductions of dominant discourses – whether of bureaucrats, researchers, bosses or partners (e.g. Norquay, 1990). By insisting on the unheroic smallness and interiority of the personal 'voice', this particular form of the biographical attitude amounts to an insubordinate refusal, by those on the margins, to play the generalising games of the powerful (see, for example, Grumet, 1990).

Finally, biography holds its attractions – methodological and theoretical – for qualitative researchers. It promises greater explanatory power, by 'opening up for study the scaled boxes within which teachers work and survive' (Ball and Goodson, 1985 p. 13), and thereby offering better theoretical linkages between individual agency and social structures. At the same time, it lends virtue and validity to the research enterprise. By striving to remain faithful to subjects' own values and experiences, or letting them speak in their 'own' voices, researchers can appeal against the charge of interpretive 'theft' of other people's subjectivity.

The biographical attitude may be adopted for a number of different purposes therefore, which we might label *'self-revelatory'*, *'administrative'*, *'emancipatory'* and *'methodological'* respectively. This should be enough to convince us that virtue does not reside in the attitude *per se*: clearly, it can serve different ideological and practical ends. The remainder of this chapter explores further the implications – positive and negative – of adopting a biographical attitude, via an empirical study of the notion of identity amongst a group of teachers in England. The study suggests that identity is a continuing site of struggle for teachers, as no doubt it is for us all. It argues that identity should not be seen as a stable entity – something that people *have* – but as something that they use, to justify, explain and make sense of themselves in relation to other people, and to the contexts in which they operate. In other words, identity is a form of argument. As such, it is both practical and theoretical. It is also inescapably moral: identity claims are inevitably bound up with justifications of conduct and belief.

The Study: Teachers' Jobs and Lives

'Teachers' Jobs and Lives' was a research project which was supported by the Economic and Social Research Council (ESRC), from 1987 to 1990. At that time – as now – the teaching profession was in an embattled state, as teachers reacted to the structural changes that were starting to take place at all levels of the system. New contracts and conditions of service had been imposed by the government, following long months of industrial action. A batch of innovations such as the General Certificate of Secondary Education (GCSE), the Technical and Vocational Education Initiative (TVEI) and Records of Achievement had been introduced. In-service training was being restructured, and pilot schemes of appraisal were in prospect. By the end of the study, in 1990, details of the Education Reform Bill had emerged and subsequently become law, adding a new array of issues – the National Curriculum, assessment and local management of schools – to teachers' agendas of concern.

The project was interested in the effects of all these policy changes on teachers' work, career aspirations and morale. Hints at the effects had begun to filter through in media reports and professional journals, often in new coinages – 'burn-out', 'innovation over-load', 'deprofessionalisation'. Even so, there was relatively little specific understanding of the range and extent of the new tasks that teachers were carrying out, nor of the differential impact of the changes according to the local contexts and circumstances of individual teachers. The project proposed to adopt, in other words, a biographical attitude: it was interested, as the final report notes, in 'the links between the professional and the personal dimensions of teachers' lives as factors shaping their response to change' (MacLure *et al.*, 1990, p. 1). As already intimated, we found those links to be more complicated than we at first suspected.

The study involved a main sample of 69 teachers from three local education authorities (LEAs), chosen for their contrasting characteristics – demographic, geographical and political – in the industrial north of England, outer London, and rural East Anglia respectively. Within each LEA the research was based in a single site, and focused on a secondary school and two of its associated primaries. All of the project teachers volunteered to take part. The sample included teachers across all levels of the promotional structure and represented a broad spectrum of professional and biographical profiles in terms of age, experience, personal history and domestic arrangements. Teachers spoke of their present and past lives, and gave their views of their current and future prospects, in informal biographical interviews, each teacher being interviewed at least twice.

The interviews were open-ended and informal, and were carried out in venues congenial to the teachers. As interviewers, we tried to break down the usual 'asymmetry' between interviewer and subject, by talking about our own lives and work where it seemed appropriate; and we encouraged teachers to range as widely as they liked over their past, present and anticipated future lives. We made it clear, too, that we were as interested in anecdote as in measured self-analysis. In their informality and interpersonal ease, the interviews resembled those described by Woods as research 'conversations'; but unlike Woods we make no claims that we thereby managed to get the teachers to 'be themselves' (Woods, 1985, p. 14), liberated from the supposed 'distortions' of bias or impression management. Indeed the project methodology was critical of the idea of an essential or 'substantial' self (e.g. Ball, 1972), preferring the notion of identity as a set of discursive practices. Instead of trying to locate teachers' 'core' or trans-situational selves, or to find out what was common to the 'self' of all or most of the project teachers, we looked at how identity was claimed, talked about and otherwise *used* by the teachers for particular discursive purposes. In this we followed Shotter's prescription:

> to understand ourselves we must examine how currently we account for ourselves in our everyday self-talk, the procedures and practices we routinely use in making sense of our activities to one another.
>
> (1985, p. 172)

Consequently, the analytic framework applied to the interview data derives from work in the analysis of discourse,[1] and resists the construction of categories which abstract talk from its conversational context. To give an example: rather than collecting all expressions of, say, 'commitment' or 'idealism' in the interviews, and then trying to identify the common meanings in these categories, across all the teachers (as Nias, 1989, does, for instance), a discourse-based approach would ask how such notions as commitment and idealism are used by different teachers to make particular points, to defend particular views or actions, to claim particular moral stances. The method is exemplified below, in the discussion of teachers' use of the notion of 'community' in relation to identity claims (see also Mac-Lure, 1992).

Constructing 'the Context': Identity as an Organising Device

We found some general trends – most of them depressing – in the cumulative impact upon teachers of the educational reforms (see MacLure *et al.*, 1990, pp. 2–5). We also found variation in teachers' reactions to the reforms according to their contexts and circumstances. Contextual factors such as the LEA's political coloration, its spending priorities and its in-service education and training (INSET) record held real implications, both for the material conditions of teachers' work, and for their views of their individual prospects and predicaments. Other factors – regional and local – which affected jobs and lives included alternative employment prospects, housing costs, leisure facilities and the reputation of the school.

However, the impact of context upon teacher was by no means one-way. While the context certainly made a difference to the teachers' lives and work, each teacher also partially constructed that context according to her or his *biographical project*: that is, the network of personal concerns, values and aspirations against which events are judged and decisions made. So, although such gross characteristics of context provided boundaries and constraints, they were not predictive in any simple way of individual teachers' attitudes, expectations or practice. It did not prove possible to delineate the characteristics (far less the 'character') of the 'rural teacher' *vis-à-vis* the 'Northerner' or the 'suburbanite'. Nor did we find persuasive instances of other 'categorical identities' which would capture generalised predispositions or allegiances amongst subgroups of teachers – whether of age, seniority, primary/secondary, arts/science, etc. Features of context, or 'stratifying' factors such as age, subject affiliation or seniority, took on different meanings for each teacher. Take, for instance, the notion of the *community* as a central aspect of the context within which teachers work.

The meanings of 'community'

In an objective sense, each of the three sites is embedded in a particular, and distinctive community. The northern site is in an ethnically diverse inner-city area, where families of Bangladeshi origin form one of the largest non-white ethnic groups. The southern schools draw their pupils from an affluent suburb with large Greek and Turkish Cypriot communities. The East Anglian schools are located in a fairly large village with an all-white population, with a social mix of families who have lived in the area for many years, and 'newcomers' who commute to work in the nearby large towns. Each of these areas has its distinctive local conditions which influenced the project teachers' work and their relations to the community. For instance, many of the teachers in the southern site lived a long way from their schools, since they could not afford to buy houses in the area. By contrast, the teachers in the northern and eastern sites had more choice, since houses were, relatively speaking, less expensive. They had a more diverse set of reasons, therefore, for opting to live 'in' or 'out' of the community, as is shown below.

As one would expect, reference to the community was widespread in the data, and in the northern and southern sites this sometimes revolved around disparaging and reductive racial/cultural stereotypes: for instance, some (though by no means all) of the southern teachers characterised Greek families as materialistic and uninterested in education. However, over the sample as a whole, the term 'community' had quite different meanings for different people, and it was inevitably linked discursively with *other* categories – class, race, religion, etc. The following sketches indicate something of the complexity of the concept.[2]

- For Don, community was linked to *class*. As a local lad teaching in the rural area in which he grew up, the community consisted of the working-class families he had known all his life, his drinking partners in the local pub.
- Jack, head of the village first school, also linked community with class, but his main links were with the local middle-class fathers – businessmen and professionals with whom he socialised, and who supported the school in various ways. So *gender* also formed a tacit dimension of the meaning of community for Jack.

- For Eric, head of humanities at the village high school, community was linked both with *class* and with *religion*. Born in the locality, he described ironically two opposing communities: the workers/labourers who congregated in the pub on Sunday lunchtimes, and the middle classes (including many of his colleagues) who gathered in the (Church of England) church. Eric frequented the pub.

- Ted was head of the rural high school. Community had not only been central to his *pedagogy*, it had also been central to his *career*. He had worked hard to create a community school, for which he had gained national awards.

- Karen distanced herself from the village community, associating it with *age*: it was the older teachers, according to Karen, who lived in the villages and immersed themselves 'in the community', while the younger teachers lived in the town (though in fact this was not uniformly the case).

- Andy, a teacher in the northern junior school, linked community with *class* and with *politics*. Laughingly describing himself as a 'stripped pine socialist', he chose to live in the locality and identified strongly with the multicultural ethos of the school.

- For Laura, the new head of the northern nursery/infant school, the community represented *career*: trained as one of the LEA's specialist language teachers, she had become head of this show-piece school with a reputation for exemplary policies on multicultural education.

- In Edith's account, the links were between *race*, *culture* and *gender*, and indirectly with her own *career*. Teaching in the southern site, she described the Greek boys as sexist, and therefore a threat to her classroom competence, and also attributed her lack of career progression to sexism on the part of senior management.

Each teacher constructs a different relationship, then, to 'the community', according to her/his current and anticipated projects. The same may be observed of such 'stratifying' characteristics as age or primary/secondary.

A simple example relating to age. Averil felt her youth to be a problem. Conscious of being young enough to be the head's daughter, she thought he did not give her enough responsibility. Shelley, on the other hand, felt too old: stuck in the same job since she qualified, she had given up the idea of promotion, and felt jaded and lacking in the energy she had when she was younger. Both Shelley and Averil were 27.

On being a 'primary teacher'. Jack and Jill were both primary teachers in the rural first school, but they expressed quite different views on pedagogy and the rewards of teaching. Jill was really only interested in teaching reception classes. In her view, this was the age group that offered the most exacting intellectual challenge and the most exciting developmental potential. Jack insisted on teaching only the top class of 8-year-olds. Teaching the youngest seemed to him more like babysitting; they did not offer much of an intellectual challenge.

The meaning of 'age', or the identity of the 'primary teacher' is likely to vary, then, with the circumstances of each individual teacher. It may also vary within the accounts of any single person, according to the concerns of the moment. Age, for instance, may be an irrelevance for some of our activities; an impediment to others. We may feel differently about it at different times. 'Life-cycle' analyses of teachers' identities (e.g. Sikes, Measor and Woods, 1985) often fail to capture the shifting nature of age-related attitudes, depending upon the *discourse* into which age enters, on the part of the teacher concerned. The same can be said of those other contextual or stratifying concepts which have been used in some life history research to characterise (in a quite literal sense) different groups of teachers (e.g. chapters in Ball and Goodson, 1985). Rather than trying to 'explain' teachers in terms of sociological, contextual, subject or occupational categories, the project described here looked at the categories which people chose in order to explain *themselves,* and how these categories were used in the construction of identities. In the words of Potter and Wetherell, 'the question becomes not what is the true nature of the self, but how is the self talked about, how is it theorized in discourse' (1987, p. 102).

Argumentative Identities

As the examples above suggest, identity claims can be seen as a form of *argument* – as devices for justifying, explaining and making sense of one's conduct, career, values and circumstances. One way of making such claims is to assemble a list of categories that exemplify what one is *not,* in order to define oneself oppositionally, as the (virtuous) mirror image. As Potter and Wetherell note, the most obvious form of this kind of identity claim is the explicit disclaimer (e.g. 'I'm no sexist but . . .'), where the aim is to 'prevent the listener interpreting the talk in terms of this noxious identity by acknowledging the possible interpretation and then denying it' (1987, p. 77); but there are other, more subtle ways of making such disclaimers. Many of the project teachers described themselves in this oppositional way, often building up complex profiles of the sorts of teachers they were 'not'.

- Yvonne defined herself (and her colleagues in the home economics department) in opposition to those whom she called the 'trendies', and whom she characterised as: careerist, left-wing, scruffily dressed, committed to 'progressive' teaching methods, over-sympathetic to the less able, and living in the inner city. In assembling this – perhaps surprisingly diverse – array of characteristics, she defined herself oppositionally as: vocationalist; unpolitical (or apolitical); well-dressed; committed to 'traditional' methods; opposed to mixed ability teaching; and living in the suburbs.

Yvonne *simultaneously* delineates a professional/moral identity and elaborates a justification of her practice, pedagogy and lifestyle. Similar processes are at work in Karen's account (see further MacLure, 1992):

• Karen taught the upper years in the rural 8–12 middle school. She defined herself in opposition to her colleagues who refused to strike during
  the action; who lived in the villages rather than the town, were older
  members of staff; favoured 'traditional' methods, and were reputedly
  still hostile to the 'ethos' of middle schooling, since in her view they
  retained their commitment to the small village primaries from which
  they were redeployed.

In fashioning these oppositional identities, Karen and Yvonne draw together a wide range of disparate concerns within a single argumentative
structure. This is a feature of all identity claims: seemingly abstract, educational issues relating to curriculum, pedagogy and professionalism are
woven together with local and idiosyncratic concerns such as lifestyle and
politics.

'This Noxious Identity': Teacherhood in Crisis?

Although the identities claimed by the project teachers were diverse, there
were indications that many found teacherhood problematic. While some
were still able to fashion 'convergent' identities which expressed a strong
allegiance to the teacher role, many seemed to testify to 'spoiled' or 'subversive' identities.

Spoiled identities

Many teachers reported a deep sense of alienation from the values and
practices of their institution, or the LEA, or central government. The most
troubled of these were the teachers who were no longer able to reconcile
their identities with the job in any sense, and had taken early retirement,
tendered their resignations (in one case with no new job in prospect) or
experienced long periods of illnesses diagnosed as stress related.

Many others claimed they would like to get out, or that they felt trapped
and alienated. Often expressed in the telling phrase 'my face doesn't fit',
these teachers reported a pervasive sense of bewilderment and frustration
at a system which did not, as they saw it, recognise their virtues or reward
their efforts. While any occupation will embrace a number of people who
feel alienated, their prevalence here was noticeable.

• Anna reported feelings of deep frustration in her job as a home economics teacher in the southern secondary school, saying repeatedly that

her face 'didn't fit'. She worked very hard, and put in a lot of time organising the catering for staff and public events. But she felt under-valued and personally slighted by the senior management, and thought her contributions were overlooked in favour of those of her husband, who also taught at the school.

Like others in the study, Anna suspected there was a credibility gap be-tween the 'official' rhetoric of the school and the LEA on the one hand, which encouraged hard work and creativity, and what she saw as the covert agendas of her superiors. She suspected that rewards and esteem were in fact being distributed on quite different grounds, but was not even sure exactly what these grounds were.

Other teachers conveyed their sense of spoiled identity in 'golden age' accounts that compared the dissatisfactions of the present with the satisfac-tions of a lost past. These were stories of a profession which had changed for the worse; of schools and colleagues who were not as they had once been; of ambitions and ideals which had been abandoned.

- Betty followed her father (a headteacher) into the profession. In those days, she said, teachers were respected members of the community and children came to school expecting to learn. She attended INSET courses and tried hard to keep abreast of her LEA's policies on anti-racism and anti-sexism. But she still felt a sense of disappointment and disorienta-tion in the job these days.

Betty's regret for the passing of a perceived 'golden age' of respect and traditional values is not an unfamiliar story. Nor is Roger's, yet *his* golden age, which covers roughly the same chronological period as Betty's, is one of innovation, challenge and risk-taking:

- Roger had been in at the start of the middle school movement, and had taken part as a young teacher-researcher in a prestigious national curric-ulum research project in the 1970s. But Roger had now been in the same rural middle school since it opened 12 years ago. The profession, he said, no longer offered him the chance to realise those personal values and ideals with which he started out.

If middle school reorganisation was the start of a golden age for Roger, for Jack it spelled the end of ambition:[3]

- Jack had been head of a village primary school in the 1970s. On reorgan-isation into a first/middle school system, he got the headship of the first school, though he would have preferred the middle school. Jack la-mented the passing of the small rural primaries, and particularly missed the chance to teach older children (see above).

Betty, Roger and Jack all looked back to a time when the profession was other (and more propitious) than it is now. But in important ways each was remembering a *different* profession, and claiming a different teacher identity.

Subversive identities

A surprisingly high proportion of teachers (more than half) wanted to deny at least part of the identity of 'teacher' – a phenomenon which has been noted by other researchers (e.g. Nias, 1984, 1989), although not to the extent that we found in this study. One manifestation of the subversive identity is the denial of *social* contact with other teachers. Many project teachers were at pains to emphasise that they did not socialise with teachers out of school, claiming a disdain for talking 'shop', and characterising teachers as a group as boring.

- Di was the breadwinner while her husband studied for a PhD. She put a lot of effort into her job, and enjoyed it immensely. She was selected to take part in her LEA curriculum development programme and was following a part-time MA course. But she 'wouldn't be seen dead' socialising with other teachers in the pub in the evenings.

Many other teachers expressed similar sentiments, suggesting that the identity of 'teacher' is associated with negative qualities such as dullness. These teachers seemed happy to embrace the *role* of teacher, but wanted to shrug off the identity. This is borne out by the frequency with which project teachers recounted subversive stories of the past: youthful misdeeds; extravagances and indiscretions; college escapades; interesting or exotic vacation jobs; dramatically disastrous first teaching posts. Although (and perhaps because) safely consigned to the past, such anecdotes could be read as claims to having had an 'interesting life', and therefore as attempts to go beyond the perceived limitations of the teacher identity. Further examples of subversive identities came in 'only-here-for-the-beer' denials of vocation, or in the insistence by some teachers that their 'real' lives and identities lay elsewhere: in their leisure pursuits; in their families; in their religious beliefs and activities; in their community works or political affiliations.

It is difficult to interpret the data on identity, partly because of the scarcity of comparable data. It may be, for instance, that the claiming of a mischievous past and a subversive identity is a widespread phenomenon in autobiographical reflections. Since (auto)biography tends to be a narrative genre, we may feel constrained to make the life plot 'interesting', according to some quasi-literary criteria. Alternatively, diversity and scepticism may be no new thing in teachers' identities: research may simply have failed to illuminate them. Or it may be that the old iconographies of teacherhood, with their virtues of vocation, care, dedication and self-investment, are being eroded under the pressures and interventions of the late twentieth century, while the new identities of 'professionalism' which are being offered by employers and policy-makers are becoming ever more difficult to believe in. The next section explores this possibility in relation to the notion of 'career'.

The Story of Career

career *n*. a path through life or history.

(*Collins Concise English Dictionary*)

One way of looking at the notion of career is as a special genre of life stories that we tell to make sense of what we have done, are doing, and might do in our jobs. As the dictionary definition implies, career stories are typically told as journeys through time, so they must be assembled to fit discrete events into a plausible trajectory. One possible interpretation of the data in this study is that the career story is becoming more difficult to tell. Certainly, teachers at all levels reported a fast-diminishing sense of agency or control, as their responsibilities multiplied without increase in the power to choose or decide. And for those at the foot of a promotion ladder which had lost several rungs over the period of the study, policy decisions which affected their prospects – such as who got the merit allowances, how INSET was apportioned, which activities were noticed and approved – seemed pragmatic at best and capricious at worst. Nor should we imagine that the career story has become any easier to tell over the intervening couple of years, as the full implications of local financial management and the National Curriculum have begun to be felt. Indeed, the very notion of teaching as a full-time, permanent and lifelong career for most teachers may be disintegrating, with the rapid spread of short-term, part-time contracts. One pessimistic future scenario for the structure of the profession would be a work force split between a large, transient, de-skilled 'underclass' and a small, full-time professional élite (see MacLure *et al.*, 1990).

The story of career as a *strategic* path through life or history, and one which progresses rather than regresses, may therefore be harder to tell these days; and part of that difficulty may lie in the disintegration of the old exemplars of the teacher-protagonist, under the kinds of contemporary pressures mentioned above. The virtues of vocation, dedication, care are no longer felt to lead (whether or not they ever really did) to career advancement or institutional recognition, though there is still a rhetoric of rewards for good classroom practice. Instead, teachers are being offered new professional identities which emphasise deeds and conduct outside as well as inside the classroom: the reflective practitioner; the self-actualising professional; the extended professional. But the teachers' accounts suggest that these new identities are equally problematic, and not only for those who are reluctant to relinquish the old ones.

The teachers in this study sound very different from those primary teachers studied by Nias, whose 'self-defining characteristics' included idealism, conscientiousness, tenacity, intellectual curiosity and individualism, even if only as unattainable ideals (1989, p. 37); and who defined 'feeling like a teacher' as being whole, being yourself, and being natural (p. 182). According to Nias, most of the 50 mid-career primary teachers she interviewed 'had incorporated their professional identity into their self-image (i.e. "they felt like teachers")' (p. 181). As already noted, the teachers in our study seemed much more unruly and varied in their sense of their selves, much less secure in their identity as teachers, and much less securely anchored in a notion of teaching as a career. Some of them sounded like Nias's teachers, but a lot of them did not.

Whether this seeming crisis of identity and career is really a new phenomenon amongst teachers is, however, difficult to resolve. The pervasive preoccupation with the nature and adequacy of the self may also be a reflection of teaching's continuing status as a 'semi-profession', whose claims to professional status revolve around investment of the self in the occupational sphere. What is clear is that there is considerable unease amongst teachers about the restricted range of culturally endorsed professional identities available to them, and widespread resistance to the old iconographies of the dedicated carer. This suggests that if working conditions and professional development were really to accommodate the needs of individual teachers, policy-makers and researchers would have to contemplate a much more diverse range of needs, interests and identities than they are doing at present.

Conclusion

The research reported here has begun to indicate how teachers' identities may be less stable, less convergent and less coherent than is often implied in the research literature, and points to a cultural or occupational unease connected with the notion of the teacher identity. It has also begun to show how autobiographical accounts knit together the disparate dimensions of teachers' lives – curriculum, career, home life, pedagogy – in ways that are always bound up with values and with action. To lay claim to an identity, then, is to engage in a form of argument rather than description; and biographical accounts are inescapably explanatory, moral and justificatory. People use them to *make sense* of themselves and their actions – to find order and consistency in the journey from past to present; to work out where they 'stand' in relation to others; to defend their attitudes and conduct.

This view of identity and biography makes it difficult to answer some of the questions that most interest those who adopt the 'biographical attitude' sketched at the beginning of this chapter. It undercuts the search for a 'core' or 'essential' self as the well-spring of the individual's actions and choices; and it renders very problematic notions of the ways in which the past influences the present, or the child the adult. But it is helpful in pointing to the ways in which teachers may (or may not) feel constrained by the culturally available iconographies of teacherhood; and in delineating the links between identity, agency and practice, as these are elaborated by the people concerned.

There are also developmental and ideological implications. As noted in the introduction, one dominant ideology directing current work in biography is that of holism, in which teachers' lives become a topic of concern for what they are *not*; where identity is always incomplete, alienated or inaccessible; and where the aim is to remedy these shortcomings of the self. The notion of development comes to be applied, not only to professional practice or public conduct, but to identity itself, which is held to be in a state of suspension – waiting to be recovered, restored, reintegrated or emancipated. This holistic seizure of identity and agency is not, of course, confined to education. but is prominent in management science, social work, psychotherapy, police training (see Denzin, 1989; MacLure and Stronach, 1989). This study suggests that the holistic ideology of self-discovery or self-improvement may actually mask a narrowing down of the range of options as to what a person may be or become, into a small set of coercive identities.

Acknowledgements

Teachers' Jobs and Lives was supported by the Economic and Social Research Council, award nos. COO232405 and ROOO231257. The other members of the research team were John Elliott, Ian Stronach and Alan Marr, whose contributions to that research are reflected throughout this article.

Notes

1.   Terms such as discourse analysis, conversation analysis and ethnomethodology encompass several different approaches, each with their distinct characteristics. But they share a view that language constructs reality, rather than simply reflecting it: qualities such as truth, fact, authenticity, validity and identity are held to be interactional accomplishments – matters to be claimed and defended in discourse – rather than properties that reside 'in' people or data. See, for example, Potter and Wetherell, 1987; Mulkay, 1985; Garfinkel, 1967; Coulter, 1979; Smith, 1978.

2.   For reasons of space and inclusiveness, I have not included 'illustrative' quotations from the teacher interviews. This has its disadvantages, especially in a paper that draws on discourse analysis. It makes it hard for readers to judge the validity of my interpretations, and fails to show how the teachers themselves put together their various identity claims. It may make the teachers seem rather remote too – though the idea that copious quotation allows us to hear teachers' 'own voices' is a misapprehension. There is no such thing as an unmediated text (see MacLure, 1992, for a discussion of this issue).

3.   Jack's life story is the subject of an in-depth study – MacLure and Stronach (1992).

References

Aspinwall, K. (1986) Teacher biography: the in-service potential, *Cambridge Journal of Education*, 16(3), pp. 210–15.

Ball, S. (1972) Self and identity in the context of deviance: the case of criminal abortion, in R. Scott and J. Douglas (eds) *Theoretical Perspectives on Deviance*. New York: Basic Books.

Ball, S. and Goodson I. (eds) (1985) *Teachers' Lives and Careers*. Lewes: Falmer Press.

Connelly, F. M. and Clandinin, J. (1990) Stories of experience and narrative inquiry *Educational Researcher*, 19(5), pp. 2–14.

Coulter, G. (1979) *The Social Construction of Mind*. London: Macmillan.

Denzin, N. (1989) *Interpretive Biography*. London: Sage.

Garfinkel, H. (1967) *Studies in Ethnomethodology*. Englewood Cliffs, NJ: Prentice-Hall.

Grumet, M. (1990) Voice: the search for a feminist rhetoric for educational studies, *Cambridge Journal of Education* (Special Issue on Biography and Life History in Education, edited by M. L. Holly and M. MacLure), 20(3), pp. 277–82.

MacLure, M. (1989) Anyone for INSET? Needs identification and personal/ professional development, in R. M. McBride (ed.) *The In-service Training of Teachers*. Lewes: Falmer Press.

MacLure, M. (1992) Mundane autobiography: some thoughts on self-talk in research contexts. Centre for Applied Research in Education, mimeo. Also in *British Journal of Sociology of Education*, 14(4), 1993.

MacLure, M. and Stronach, I. (1989) Seeing through the self: contemporary biography and some implications for educational research. Paper presented to the Annual Meeting of the American Educational Research Association, San Francisco, March–April 1989.

MacLure, M. and Stronach, I. (1992) Jack in two boxes: a postmodern perspective on the transformation of persons into portraits. Paper presented to the Annual Meeting of the American Educational Research Association, San Francisco, April 1992.

MacLure, M., Elliott, J., Marr, and Stronach, I. (1990) *Teachers' Jobs and Lives (Phase 2)*, End of Award Report to the ESRC, mimeo.

Mulkay, M. (1985) *The Word and the World*. London: Allen & Unwin.

Nias, J. (1984) The definition and maintenance of self in primary teaching, *British In-service Education*, 13(3), pp. 267–80.

Nias, J. (1989) *Primary Teachers Talking: a Study of Teaching as Work*. London: Routledge.

Norquay, N. (1990) Life history research: memory, schooling and social difference, *Cambridge Journal of Education*, 20(3), pp. 291–300.

Potter, J. and Wetherell, M. (1987) *Discourse and Social Psychology*. London: Sage.

Schon, D. (1983) *The Reflective Practitioner: How Professionals Think in Action*. London: Temple Smith.

Shotter, J. (1985) Social accountability and self-specification, in K. J. Gergen and K. E. Davis (eds) *The Social Construction of the Person*. New York: Springer-Verlag.

Sikes, P. J., Measor, L. and Woods, P. (1985) *Teacher Careers: Crises and Continuities*. Lewes: Falmer Press.

Smith, D. (1978) K is mentally ill: an anatomy of a factual account, *Sociology*, 12(1), pp. 23–53.

Woods, P. (1985) Conversations with teachers: some aspects of life history method, *British Educational Research Journal*, 11(1), pp. 13–26.

Index